The Political Economy of Employment Relations

Employment has changed dramatically in the last few decades with the onset of neoliberal globalization. This change has been examined from a variety of different disciplinary perspectives, with scholars from such fields as development studies, labor economics, and industrial relations focusing on a number of different units of analysis.

The Political Economy of Employment Relations provides an exceptional contribution to the existing literature by presenting alternative theory and practice on employment relations. It is within this critical intervention that the solidarity economy emerges as a unique theoretical construct and unit of analysis that exposes the alternative paths that employment relations may take when faced with the contemporary challenges of neoliberal globalization. This book analyzes globalization, global economic crisis, and issues of work and labor from the point of view of the developing world, presenting local case studies from various countries including the United States, India, Spain, Greece, and Turkey, and outlining alternative approaches to global employment challenges.

This volume is relevant for those with an interest in industrial relations, the sociology of work and occupations, labor economics, and development studies.

Aslihan Aykac is Associate Professor in the Department of International Relations at Ege University in Izmir, Turkey.

Routledge studies in labour economics

1. Youth and the Crisis
Unemployment, education and health in Europe
Edited by Gianluigi Coppola and Niall O'Higgins

2. Workers and the Global Informal Economy
Interdisciplinary perspectives
Edited by Supriya Routh and Vando Borghi

3. The Political Economy of Employment Relations
Alternative theory and practice
Aslihan Aykac

The Political Economy of Employment Relations

Alternative theory and practice

Aslihan Aykac

Routledge
Taylor & Francis Group
LONDON AND NEW YORK

First published 2017 by Routledge

2 Park Square, Milton Park, Abingdon, Oxfordshire OX14 4RN
52 Vanderbilt Avenue, New York, NY 10017

Routledge is an imprint of the Taylor & Francis Group, an informa business

First issued in paperback 2020

British Library Cataloguing in Publication Data
A catalogue record for this book is available from the British Library

Library of Congress Cataloging in Publication Data
Names: Aykac, Aslihan, author.
Title: The political economy of employment relations : alternative theory and practice / Aslihan Aykac.
Description: Abingdon, Oxon ; New York, NY : Routledge, 2017.
Identifiers: LCCN 2016009914| ISBN 9781138647480 (hardback) | ISBN 9781315627021 (ebook)
Subjects: LCSH: Industrial relations. | Labor. | Personnel management.
Classification: LCC HD6971 .A95 2017 | DDC 331–dc23
LC record available at https://lccn.loc.gov/2016009914

ISBN: 978-1-138-64748-0 (hbk)
ISBN: 978-0-367-66817-4 (pbk)

Typeset in Times New Roman
by Taylor & Francis Books

To Denizhan

Contents

Tables

Preface

The globalization of the capitalist mode of production has been one of the main issues studied by social scientists in the last three decades. The amount of literature accumulating on the topic from innumerable disciplinary and interdisciplinary perspectives is colossal. As a student of the social sciences since the early 1990s, I have found that this research is not leading toward a new perspective on or a new concept or interpretation of global transformations, but toward a new realm that may exist outside the global. It is compelled by the legacy of "There is no alternative."

The search for an alternative to the global may be fanciful. After all, the long-term historical analysis of the capitalist world economy shows the potential of the system to renew itself. Yet the very same authors who have underlined this potential for renewal have also suggested that there are uncertainties that await the capitalist system and the civilization that depends on it (Hopkins and Wallerstein 1996; Arrighi 2009; Hobsbawm 1994). These uncertainties are partly due to the planetary expansion of the capitalist mode of production, the environmental destruction caused by this expansion, and the accompanying social consequences of these challenges. However, the disillusionment with alternatives to the capitalist world economy has managed to blur visions of an uncertain future. Yet the research presented here is not about a future alternative. It covers present-day alternatives as prototypical variations. This book does not offer predictions about the uncertainties humanity is about to face.

The post-global alternative is not only a temporal expression, it is a spatial one as well. The works of Unger (2009), Santos (2006), Munck (2007) and others refer to alternative economic relations in less developed parts of the world and focus predominantly on Latin America. Others write on India (Dreze and Sen 2015), and still others focus on alternative economic relations for a crisis-ridden Europe (Varoufakis 2015; Amin 2009). These alternative economic relations are neither interrelated enough to provide a structural alternative, nor spatially dispersed enough to represent a general pattern. The post-global does not stand as a homogeneous spatial construct, and it does not imply an expansionist model that seeks to override the existing capitalist system. It prioritizes, according to social-scientific research, the local as a moment of origin, which represents local practices, resources, and relations. This origin relies heavily on grassroots mobilization and precludes any possibility of models being imposed from above.

Social, economic, and cultural differences in the global village preclude the possibility of an overthrow of the current economic system or the occurrence of a world revolution. The historical experiences and existing social dynamics require a readjustment of our understanding of what a revolutionary process is. Instead of seeking a radical transformation through abrupt social change, one may search for the germination of systemic change through smaller motivations. These local alternatives may not have the discursive power of a world revolution and may not unite under a single progressive pattern, but they follow their own paths and generate their own pace of progress. They may not be universally representative and cohesive, yet the way they take root in individual idiosyncrasies may be the source of a revolutionary catalyst.

Acknowledgments

This book is the result of research conducted during my sabbatical leave for the 2014–2015 academic year, for which several support circles deserve acknowledgment and gratitude. My sabbatical leave was funded by the Fulbright Visiting Scholar Program. I would like to thank the Council for International Exchange of Scholars in the United States and the Fulbright Commission in Turkey for their institutional support for facilitating my research and my stay in the United States.

I spent my sabbatical leave conducting research at Rutgers University's School of Management and Labor Relations. I would like to thank Dean Susan Schurman for her institutional and academic support during my stay at Rutgers, which was the primary source of my motivation while researching and writing. During my stay at Rutgers, I had the benefit of meeting with and receiving feedback from several distinguished scholars at the School of Management and Labor Relations. I would like to thank Dorothy Sue Cobble for her hospitality and generosity in academic exchange. I would also like to thank Janice Fine, Tobias Schulze-Cleven, and David Bensman for their time and concern.

Finally, I would like to thank my family and friends for their support and patience during the completion of this highly motivating yet arduous task. As I was writing this book, my six-year-old son began first grade in the United States without knowing a single word of English. This book is dedicated to him for his hard work and comradeship.

Izmir, 2015

Introduction

We have not reached the end of history after all. The historical moment that globalization has reached requires a deeper analysis of the contradictory movements embedded in global processes. The global integration of markets and the global expansion of the division of labor may look efficient in managerial terms, but the mushrooming of a severe economic crisis has challenged this rather crude picture of efficiency. In addition to the crisis itself, the inconsistencies of political responses to it – bailing out corporations on the one hand and enforcing austerity measures on the other – is another contradiction of the existing capitalist economic system. The Polanyi problem, or Karl Polanyi's theory of the double movement, proves to be highly explanatory in this regard: the self-regulating market running on the fictitious commodities of land, labor and capital will eventually lead to social problems and economic instability, which in turn will only be able to be resolved by regulating the market. This leads to the vicious circle of deregulation and regulation, or, put differently, the inherent contradictions of capitalism.

The shattering images of globalization, the age of uncertainty, namely, the immigrant bodies lying on the seabed of the Mediterranean, the peoples of South America making another world possible, and the resistance movements of various sizes and scopes appearing all around the world are an indication that change is on the horizon. The capitalist world economy and the nation-state will not be the premises of the next generation of political and economic organization. It is not possible to aggregate demand in broad categories of economic development, equality, political representation, and democracy. The interests that culminate in the new social movements are much more diverse and intersectional, and they can hardly be resolved into purely rational choices toward progress, efficiency, and optimality.

The solidarity alternative constructed in this book seeks to present a new way of thinking about political and economic organization that prioritizes social issues over economic ones. The market in an alternative economy is regarded as no more than a domain of exchange. The rules of the capitalist market, namely, supply and demand and perfect competition, among others, become secondary to supplying the needs of a larger constituency, cooperating in the production process, and maintaining an environmentally sound, fair production system. The solidarity alternative does not presuppose the existence or the support of the state. In fact, the alliance of the state with the capitalist market shows historical resilience.[1] The state has been the sole administrator of the social problems generated by capitalism, and has been the sole party responsible for the control and management of the so-called "dangerous classes"[2] and the task of redistribution (but not redistributive justice). The state in general and the welfare state in particular redistributed enough to maintain the dangerous classes and yet keep the capitalist gears rolling. The solidarity alternative integrates production and redistribution within the same institutional and social contexts in order to overcome the clash of interests between different segments of society. In a system where the material bases of social organization are unified under one roof, conflict resolution requires greater room for participation and the individualization of democratic practices. Representative democracy provides limited opportunities to embrace this kind of diversity. Workplace democracy as a vertically integrated local system of representation is better able to address immediate issues on site, overriding bureaucratic processes and party interests. This form of democracy is not only a procedural challenge, but an issue-based enhancement as well, since issues pertaining to the spheres of work and non-work often overlap in communities. Finally, unions are a necessary yet insufficient means for worker organization. The recent growth of alternative organization models is also indicative of the transformations taking place, albeit sporadically, across the world. New labor internationalism seeks to break the traditional bond between labor and unions in order to build a new bond between labor and a diverse set of organizations that includes worker centers, community groups, and worker associations. The four tasks and organizational dimensions of the solidarity alternative – reorganization of production, redistribution, workplace democracy, and new labor solidarity – unite at the local level. The local as the epicenter of these multiple constituencies provides the grounds on which solidarity can operate. This is neither a revolutionary overthrow of, nor a replacement of, the now *ancien régime* of the capitalist state. This is an alternative for those hoping to opt out of a system that they are only peripherally attached to.

The solidarity alternative does not come in a single form, a standard institutional context, based on a typical economic domain. It comes in many forms and shapes derived from the multiplicity of human and natural resources in a specific locus. It is unique in the way it responds to the social and economic issues of that locus. The Zapatista Army of National Liberation (EZLN) in Chiapas, Mexico, has been active in organizing an autonomous community movement under indigenous leadership since 1994. The movement struggles against the Mexican government and its neoliberal commitments, as well as against the North American Free Trade Agreement (NAFTA). The movement is locally autonomous in terms of health, education and agrarian production. In South America, Brazil's Landless Workers Movement, *Movimento dos Trabalhadores Rurais Sem Terra* (MST), in which the landless rural workers occupied large estates of land for agrarian production, became a national movement in 1984. It is a grassroots movement that seeks to overcome the social and economic problems of the rural population by acquiring land necessary to sustain agrarian production. Education and agrarian production are the main issues in the movement, which now has about two million members and a national network. However, these alternative movements do not necessarily emerge in agrarian contexts. In Argentina, bankrupt or abandoned factories have been taken over by unemployed workers and converted into cooperatives. La Base Fund in Argentina provides microcredit to unemployed workers to start their own economic activity and evolve into cooperatives. Although most of these alternative economic models come from Latin America, there are emerging movements elsewhere, as the struggle to find a way out of the global economic crisis is also a global one. Factory takeovers have also taken place in France, Spain, Greece, and Turkey, although not as often as in Argentina. Solidarity does not necessarily emerge as a result of economic motivation; it also emerges as a result of the empowerment and emancipation of indigenous peoples and/or local communities. A more recent local struggle has emerged out of war-torn Syria, where the Kurdish population is not only defending their territory against the brutal Islamic State, but is also pushing for women's empowerment, democratic participation and autonomous governance.

A very loose, unstructured and fluid revolution is in the making. It is geographically dispersed, and its pace of progress is varied. The scope, outreach and constituents of each movement are different. The tasks that are undertaken and the goals that are set are unique to the local setting. But it is the very culmination of a non-state, non-market[3] mode of social organization that defines social well-being beyond material well-being. The efforts to recover the community and local organization will intensify as the malfunctions of the capitalist world economy worsen. The next task is to make sense out of this rather amorphous transformation.

On development

For quite some time now, scholarly interest, when it comes to the topic of development, has focused on the "why" and neglected the "how." The history of development economics is filled with innumerable varieties of developmental models designed to overcome the social and economic backwardness of various societies. Generations of scholars, from the advent of mercantilism to the times in which Rostow (1960) and Acemoglu (2009) wrote their books, aimed to unravel the intricacies of underdevelopment and provide insight with regard to the issue of development by generating policy alternatives. Various models were used by governments to take their respective countries to a desirable level of development. Yet the developmental inequalities among nations remain the same, if they are not significantly worse.

Developmentalism, irrespective of the model that is adopted, has not overcome the structural inequalities generated by the capitalist mode of production. In its most essential premise, the capitalist world economy runs on the developmental gap between societies in order to maintain surplus generation and ceaseless accumulation of capital. Limiting the historical flashback to the postwar era, Rostow's modernization approach to external borrowing – that is, national industrialization to cater to domestic markets and the maturing of a consumer society – was applied in the form of Import Substitution Industrialization (ISI). The end result for most countries was a heavier dependence on developed economies and greater indebtedness. The alternative export-oriented industrialization widely adopted by less developed countries since the 1980s has only led to greater social and economic degradation.

An in-depth critique of developmentalism requires a review of its basic assumptions. The first is the inevitable necessity of development. The universal imposition of a linear and united path toward the modern and industrious society is an illusion. The modern society, with its social and environmental problems and its economic limitations, is nowhere near an ideal type. Second, economic growth is assumed to be the primary indicator of development. Economic growth does not represent development unless it is supported by a redistribution system to develop the social and cultural basis prevalent in a given setting. The major critique of China's recent growth was based on its disregard for social development. The collapse of the Soviet Union is another example of the disillusionment that came with excessive focus on economic growth at the expense of social development and well-being. Third, development, falsely regarded as synonymous with economic growth, is best achieved by extensive industrialization. Industrialization does generate growth in a sustained manner; however, it is also confined to the margins of demand. Industrial production, whether it is Fordist or flexible, high technology or labor-intensive, produces at a rate beyond human need. Falling demand is artificially enhanced by a consumerist ideology and the pre-defined economic lifecycle of goods and product diversity. The relationship between need and production is altered in such a way that need is created to maintain the industrial production. This reversal of the relationship between social need and industrial production results in massive economic and environmental waste, which in turn generates social turmoil. The growing rate of consumer debt is the result of maintaining industrial production at a rate that sustains economic growth. Beyond economic concerns, there is the environmental concern, where waste collection has become an industry in and of itself. Finally, local factors, such as social or cultural issues, are considered auxiliary in the making of a developmental pattern. The history of the capitalist world economy is filled with examples of externally imposed development plans and the dire consequences that they lead to. This was true in the case of colonialism and in the period of Third World developmentalism, and it is true now with neoliberalism. It is the false universalisms of the development discourse that have led to a world of global inequality.

Development studies have been an integral part of the literature analyzing work and labor relations. Analytically, development has long been regarded as the remedy to problems of unemployment, underemployment, lack of productivity, and labor market segmentation. For countries that rely heavily on traditional economic sectors, and hence depend on low-skill, low-income jobs, the way forward is supposed to be industrialization followed by an integration with the capitalist world economy, industrial upgrading, and moving to more productive, high-technology areas that would gradually bring social progress in the form of modernization, urbanization and the making of a skilled workforce. There is not a single example in the developing world of an economy that grew according to such a flawless pattern. However, before prescribing development strategies in an abstract manner, it may be instructive to first study the economic relations now prevalent across the globe.

Institutional approach

The institutional approach to economic relations can hardly be associated with a single discipline: political science, economics, and sociology have all contributed to this line of analysis, which cannot be reduced to a simple methodological preference. More than a disciplinary or methodological concern, the institutional approach frames institutions as authoritative agents that represent different interests and regulate the economic system. Institutions are regarded as representative actors embedded in social relations irrespective of their *sui generis* motivations for existence and the possibility that there might be parties or interests excluded from institutional representation.

The institutional approach toward the analysis of work and labor relations has focused on the impact of institutions, the legal and organizational frameworks they pursue and the relationships between these elements. One of the main reasons for the persistence of the institutional approach is its emphasis on structural analysis and the operationalization of institutions as units of inquiry on structural dynamics. The concepts of structure and institution are used almost interchangeably, overriding and undermining alternative operationalizations and measurements regarding work and labor relations. The most obvious example of this is the emphasis on national labor regimes built on employer organizations, unions and the nation-state. Although there have been noteworthy developments that fall outside of this tripartite system, the institutional analysis of the national context still dominates the scholarly interest on work and labor relations. An international parallel to this is the system implemented by the International Labour Organization (ILO), which relies primarily on a tripartite means of representation and social dialogue: "The ILO encourages this tripartism within its constituents and member States by promoting a social dialogue between trade unions and employers in formulating, and where appropriate, implementing national policy on social, economic, and many other issues."[4] The structure of the ILO itself resembles that of a government, with the International Labour Conference, the Governing Body, and the Office ensuring the recognition of a formal framework based on the ILO's constitution, conventions and declarations.

Methodologically, the institutional approach provides several advantages, including the access to aggregate data that is easily compiled in a multivariate, longitudinal manner. This data, whether received directly from national offices or international institutions, is aggregated by governments and in many cases is altered to support government objectives. For example, economic indicators such as unemployment, informal employment, inflation and minimum wage are not always represented accurately. The issues of child labor and informal employment are areas in which measurement problems persist.

The main limitation of institutional analysis is that it does not have enough room for parties, interests, movements and organizations that fall outside of the realm of these institutions. In many cases, the analysis remains confined to formal issues, official expositions and mainstream resolutions. In a context where a significant portion of the world's labor force is informal, unregistered and unorganized in the traditional sense, institutional analysis has a limited analytical capacity to encompass broader labor issues. As for governments, their sovereignty is significantly reduced both nationally and internationally, as their political and economic survival are tied more and more to the smooth functioning of the global market. More often than not, we see the ratification of ILO conventions by governments and the making of official statements of commitment to core labor standards, and yet violations of labor rights are as intense as ever, in many cases not even being officially recognized or recorded. Lastly, the widening gaps of inequality between capital and labor, socially, structurally and institutionally, in the distribution of wealth, in the accession of rights and benefits, and in the delegation of power require a wider scope of analysis than the institutional approach can provide. Many of the examples referred to under the rubric of alternative economic relations do not fit into an institutional framework. In many cases, they evolve in a rather unstructured manner. Their potential for success depends very much on the capabilities of their constituents, which develop on the field. Formal means of education, training and information dissemination do help with the learning process, yet only if they are accessible.

Permeable boundaries of work and industrial relations sociology

The bifurcation in sociology of work and industrial relations is addressed at several instances throughout this book. This bifurcation is observed at different levels of abstraction. The conceptual distinction between work and labor, employment, occupation, and job demarcate the analytical boundaries of the processes and relations observed in production. The spatial distinction between the workplace and the household, between the industrial setting and the social setting, is another dimension of this bifurcation which reflects upon the institutions and the relations in the vicinity of the core concept of work. A parallel distinction is prevalent in the analysis of institutions, where the sociology of work focuses on the workplace and the labor markets, and industrial relations focuses on labor unions and collective bargaining mechanisms. Methodologically, a heavy reliance on empiricism and quantitative analysis is a common to both disciplinary approaches, and this leads to a shared limitation when it comes to theory-making.

How essential or useful is this distinction within the work and labor relations literature? How can the domain of work and labor be separated in an empirically efficient manner? To what extent is this distinction discursive or empirical? The sociology of work and industrial relations operate in a complementary relationship. As two sides of the same coin, they look at a single system of production from different angles. The causal relationship between their variables, namely the labor market and labor unions, workplace dynamics and collective bargaining, and production process and union demands, are components of an integral whole. The boundaries of the two sets of literature are more permeable than sectarian. Especially in the unique historical conjuncture of post-global capitalism, where the workplace has crumbled and work has ceased to be a monotypic category, unions are increasingly being joined by alternative agents, and collective bargaining systems are giving way to alternative domains and strategies of struggle: the old lines of division are no longer effective determinants of discursive or methodological categories. The major criticism of the existing literature is neither methodological nor categorical; instead, it is an effort to enhance the range of analysis and synthesis in order to achieve a deeper understanding of a broader domain. If the concepts and the variables are changing, then the analytical boundaries need to give way to methodological, and hence theoretical, novelties.

Divergence in the footsteps of Marx

The study of the production process and the social and economic relations that surround it can be most comprehensively analyzed through a Marxist lens. The strength of Marxist analysis depends on a number of components. The structural analysis of the capitalist system as a whole and the historical materialist interpretation of the aforementioned social and economic relations is the most general component. More particularly, the extrication of the production process through different levels of abstraction unravels the inherent contradictions of the system, most notably the appropriation of surplus value. Class as a social category exposes the immediate consequences of the capitalist mode of production and the ideologies constructed for the sustenance of the capitalist mode of production.

The weaknesses and limitations of the Marxist analysis of capitalism are as important as its strengths in challenging the capitalist mode of production and the existing literature, whether Marxist or not, on the capitalist world economy. First, there are new issues that do not fit into the conventional Marxist framework, which looks at the systemic contradictions of capitalism and the nature of the class struggle and which espouses the need for structural analysis. The material transformations of the capitalist world economy reflect upon the social organization in a diverse set of ways. Munck's collection of essays at the turn of the millennium presents how Marxist thought addresses key issues of the new millennium such as gender, environment and culture (Munck 2000). Second, as much as the material conditions that change and therefore require novel interventions, the epistemological flourishing from different social settings have challenged Marxist analysis on multiple fronts. The growing body of literature from the South underlining the importance of non-Western epistemologies (Santos 2008), non-Western ways of knowing, is one challenge that contemporary Marxist analysis needs to come to terms with (Connell 2007; Mignolo 2012). Third, the epistemological challenges to Marxism are also supported by social challenges coming from praxis. The mobilization of the proletariat for a revolutionary overthrow of the bourgeoisie has not materialized. In a time when the proletariat has given way to the precariat, the state ceased to be the ultimate political objective: the constituents, strategies and objectives of a Marxist struggle may no longer be unilateral. Unger's *Left Alternative* provides an elaborate discussion of a new understanding of solidarity, the need for new alliances between classes, and the task of downgrading the utopia of a communist society (Unger 2009).

Framework for an alternative economy

A redefinition of ownership and property relations is crucial to understanding the emerging alternatives to existing economic relations in both production and consumption, as these concepts are continuously broken down and reformulated in contemporary social relations. Several examples may be illustrative of this state of flux. The emergence of the rental economy is one such challenge. The variety of goods and services that can be rented, thanks to the expansion of the Internet's marketing capacity, is immense. The rental of textbooks, designer bags, rooms, or cars (on a short-term basis) have become commonplace experiences for increasingly mobile individuals and especially for urbanites confined to ever-smaller residential options. Conceptualized as the rental economy, this trend may add a new twist to the social connotation of ownership and as a result may challenge the promotion of consumerism with special days, discounts and commercials (Miller 2014).

It may be somewhat more appropriate, however, to think of this economic expansion as the sharing economy rather than the rental economy. Most importantly, as much as people rent from companies or other individuals, they also increasingly rent to others in the form of both goods and services. The most popular examples are airbnb.com, the room rental service where homeowners rent their guest rooms to individuals, and uber.com, where individuals provide taxi services with their own cars. The transportation and accommodation services provided by individuals has been a serious challenge to the travel and tourism industry, leading to protests and demonstrations by taxi drivers in several European countries and the United States (Burns 2015; Fleisher 2014).

In fact, neither the rent relationship nor the commodification of individualized or personalized services is new. What is new is the expansion of these rent relationships thanks to increasing information flows through the Internet. "The big change is the availability of more data about people and things, which allows physical assets to be disaggregated and consumed as services. Before the internet, renting a surfboard, a power tool or a parking space from someone else was feasible, but was usually more trouble than it was worth" (The Rise of the Sharing Economy 2013). The second novelty is that more and more people see the need to resort to providing such services as income levels continue to fall in the formal economy.

To stick with examples from Europe and North America would both trivialize the issue and only provide a parochial perspective. Both rental relationships and the share economy existed before the technological advances of the Internet, albeit in a more provincial manner and in more primitive forms. In the earlier stages of tourism development, it was common for locals to rent their spare rooms or take hitchhikers in their cars. In agrarian societies, tractors and other equipment would be used collectively. Similar experiences continue to exist in the non-Western world, even if they do not draw as much attention. The solidarity economy or the social economy is not limited to areas of production and employment, but also includes activities that enhance the quality of life at the local level.

The recent collection edited by Matsui and Ikemoto includes models based on microcredit and the well-known Grameen model that cater to small-scale production schemes, but it also focuses on such issues as renewable energy, nutrition, access to clean water, and the development of organic agriculture (Matsui and Ikemoto 2015). As the economy is not limited to production and consumption, the redistribution of resources in their crudest form also implies an economic contribution to the welfare of individuals. A very good example of this is access to clean water. While water privatization in countries like Bolivia and Honduras has led to a huge debate, the establishment of a water supply business based on the social business model in Bangladesh has generated a social enhancement in the communities of that nation, where 90% of the water supply is contaminated with arsenic due to various geographical factors (Tsuboi 2015). The task of building clean water access requires not only investment in infrastructure but dissemination of information and the creation of awareness. The examples of Bolivia and Honduras represent the market perspective, while that of Bangladesh represents a solidaristic alternative.

Writing on the building of community economies, Gibson-Graham provide an interesting poststructuralist analysis on capitalism and the counter-hegemonic alternatives emerging from different parts of the world. Their objective is to develop a political discourse of the community economy that underlines economic interdependence. Through this objective, the authors "offer potential coordinates for counter-hegemonic projects of constructing 'other' economies" (Gibson-Graham 2006: 79). By defining the economy as a site of decision and ethical praxis, the authors aim to overcome the conception of economics as an ultimate end in the material world. The focus on the community economy underlines the social and interconnected nature of economic relations. In the construction of community economies, the authors focus on four major concerns:

- what is necessary to personal and social survival;
- how social surplus is appropriated and distributed;
- whether and how social surplus is to be produced and consumed; and
- how a commons is produced and sustained.

(Gibson-Graham 2006)

There are several examples emerging in different parts of the world that rely at least partially on these concerns. The Zapatista movement in Mexico is important in the way it exercises autonomy not only politically but also economically, where production and redistribution is organized on a local basis. Community development in Kerala, India, has resulted in significant improvements in human development indicators. Gibson-Graham also refer to less popular examples such as the Migrant Savings for Alternative Investment (MSAI) and Shack / Slum Dwellers International (SDI).

Considering the long-term history and the geographical diversity of such experiences, there is the need for a broader conceptualization that will help us analyze the Western and the non-Western examples at the same time. This is where the solidarity economy will be the central axis of understanding the world's changing economic organization and employment relations. Santos defines the solidary economy as an alternative to the development approach dominant in the capitalist world economy (Santos 2006). [5] Top-down decision-making without the input of local communities is one limitation of the capitalist approach. The second limitation is the way in which economic growth through industrialization is seen as a generator of development. In fact, existing evidence of global inequality shows us that economic growth and development are not necessarily corollaries. Instead of this conventional understanding of the economy, Santos promotes economic alternatives from the South, such as cooperativism, alternative development that is local, ecologically sound, and democratic.

According to Quijano, there are three major structural challenges posed by the solidary economy. First, the solidary economy challenges the capitalist mode of production, for reasons that should be obvious by now, surplus appropriation, unequal exchange and ceaseless accumulation of capital. Second, the new alternative also challenges the state, which operates within the capitalist system, where political actors are more and more intertwined with economic actors. For Quijano, "the state continues to be, within capitalism, not only a tool wielded by those who dominate and exploit, but also the arena where social battles are fought over the limits, conditions and modalities of domination and exploitation" (Quijano 2006: 421). Third, the solidary economy challenges the relationships of private property, exploitation and domination that the capitalist economy is erected upon. The lack of a political and ideological agenda in the popular economy compels the marginalized, the underclass and the outcasts to seek out alternatives. As empirical evidence shows, these alternatives emerge from the community, where new social movements seek new survival strategies on a grassroots level.

Despite its left-oriented Marxist approach, the solidary economy can be distinguished from classical Marxist approaches in two respects. First, although the solidary economy is highly critical of the capitalist mode of production, it is more geared toward immediate economic relations than it is toward the ultimate objective of the overthrow of capitalism. Therefore, the first distinction has to do with the former's objective and motivation, namely, the reorganization of economic relations. Second, although the idea and the principles of the solidary economy are revolutionary, the strategy or the course of action toward the aforementioned objective is more transformative than it is revolutionary. The solidary economy is based on the alliances of a variety of social movements rather than the unified interests of the masses. The primary motivation is gradual social transformation rather than abrupt social change.

In contradistinction to the concept of the solidary economy, which is more leftist and sees alternative economic activities and relations as completely outside of the realms of the market and the state, the concept of social economy aims to encompass a diverse set of economic activities that operate along the margins of the mainstream economy. Matsui and Ikemoto have a relatively more liberal interpretation of the solidarity economy, starting off with the premise that the market economy is indispensable. Therefore, their notion of solidarity aims not to replace the market economy or to create an alternative to it; rather, it seeks to support the market in problem areas: "The concept of solidarity is being proposed in this book as a unifying idea to seriously supplement the workings of the market" (Matsui and Ikemoto 2015) In terms of the forms and methods embraced by the solidarity economy, Matsui and Ikemoto focus on the social business model, which they see as operating in parallel with the conventional business models of the market economy: "By utilizing managerial skills and work incentive, social business tries to earn extra profit as much as possible" (Ikemoto and Matsui 2015). While the adoption of managerial techniques or business models may be relevant to maintain efficiency, they override the principles of autonomy and democratic participation, as well as the common good. These techniques and models may be symbolic gestures rather than structural transformations if they don't put an emphasis on collective benefits and redistribution.

For Amin, the social economy was regarded as a temporary solution to economic problems of unemployment, inequality and redistribution at the turn of the millennium; however, the sustained success of examples and the growing need for an alternative to the chronic crises of capitalism, rendered the social economy "a post-capitalist possibility based on social participation and an explicit ethic of care" (Amin 2009). There are three major points that are noteworthy in establishing a framework for the analysis of alternative economic structures. The first is the relationship of the alternative economy to the market and the state. Whether the alternative economy operates alongside the market economy or forms an alternative to it will provide insight about the forms of economic activity, the role and the commitment of its constituents, access to resources and overall feasibility. Compared to the state, the social economy is by no means synonymous with the public sector. There is an understanding of the common good and shared interests, but the emphasis on autonomy, collective management, greater room for participation and an improved understanding of redistribution is not as diluted or abused as it is in the case of the state. There is greater room for direct and immediate impact on the social economy, as it is more local and less hierarchical. The social economy stands as a third alternative system in the overall economy. Its primary objective is to realize certain benefits at the community level and organize economic activity in a way that is beneficial to people and to the planet, locally and globally (Pearce 2009). Whether the social economy functions with the market and the state in such a way as to fill in the gaps emerging from their deficiency, or whether it represents an alternative to the market and the state makes a difference, for it will change the outcome: "How the social economy is conceptualized in relation to the rest of the economy has a direct bearing on what is expected from it" (Amin 2009). Given the heterogeneity of forms, functions and structures observed in the social economy, it may be more appropriate to refer to a typology of social economies rather than to the social economy as a single, homogeneous entity.

It is this heterogeneity that is addressed in Amin's second point. The particular forms, functions and structures observed in the social economy are directly shaped by the local context: "What the social economy can deliver ultimately depends on the economic, cultural and institutional context in which it develops" (Amin 2009). In the presence of a successful market economy, but a weak welfare system, the social economy may be a complementary system that functions alongside the market. In the case of market failure, as in the current case of Greece or several Latin American countries, the social economy becomes an alternative to the market. In relation to the state, authoritarian systems with limited room for democratic participation or collective mobilization, the social economy would emerge as an alternative to the existing system. Democratic consolidation would promote the development of a social economy and would even benefit from it with increasing participation and social awareness. The relationship between the state and the social economy can be analyzed by way of social safety nets and welfare regimes. In weaker welfare regimes, the social economy will emerge as an alternative, and in stronger welfare regimes the social economy will perform a complementary function. Local factors are not limited to the structure of the market or the nature of the political system. Social and cultural factors are directly influential in the making of the social economy. In Latin America, the social economy develops completely outside of the market and the state, whereas in Bangladesh the social economy relies on fund transfers from the market. Social movements like the Zapatistas or the Landless Workers Movement (MST) in Latin America are much more radical than their counterparts elsewhere in the world. Consequently, the immediate circumstances in which the social economy is established are just as important as such factors as institutional structure, economic setting, and political or civic culture.

The diversity of the local context brings forth the third point that Amin underlines about the building of the social economy. How can the goals of the social economy match the local context? There has to be an equilibrium point where the goals and the local circumstances can be balanced. In the search for reconciliation between market goals and the provision of welfare, the need for state legal, institutional and/or material support leads to various policy expectations. These policy expectations fall on a spectrum of political intervention that ranges from minimal support to a full recognition of the social economy "as a site of transformation towards a needs-based and solidarity-enhancing society" (Amin 2009).

The solidarity economy refers to economic activities of various sizes and scope that fall outside of the domain of the state and the capitalist market. As such, it may or may not be formal, structured and organized. It does not depend on the state in terms of resources and is not governed by the parameters of the capitalist market. Solidarity economies operate locally, make use of locally available resources and economic inputs, and cater to the economic needs of local inhabitants. The solidarity economy is defined on the basis of four major pillars: production, redistribution, workplace democracy, and labor solidarity. This book will trace the development and operation of these pillars to construct an analytical framework for solidarity economies.

Organization of the book

This book is organized into six chapters and a conclusion. The first four chapters will provide a theoretical overview of global dynamics that lead to the search for alternative theory and practice. The fifth chapter provides case studies that are representative of the theoretical challenges that can be encountered in such a search. The sixth chapter and the conclusion engage in an analytical effort to integrate the research undertaken here into a larger body of literature, something that requires the simultaneous use of different levels of abstraction.

The first chapter focuses on possible alternatives to the global organization of production. The first section critically analyzes the global organization of production, beginning with the flexible mode of production as the contemporary *modus operandi* and then looking at multinational corporations as major actors in the production process. The second section shows how global value chains expose the geographic expansion, organization and operation of the global division of labor. The third and final section looks at the global economic crisis and exposes the structural limitations of this organizational model. The main contribution of this chapter is the discussion on the solidarity alternatives to production and a reflection on the limitations of the global organization of production. Cooperatives, employee ownership and self-employment are evaluated as possible alternatives. The most important aspect of these alternatives is that they serve as non-market outlets for those marginalized by existing global structures.

The second chapter focuses on the theme of redistribution. The first section presents the decline of redistributive justice during the process of neoliberal globalization and the rise in global inequality. The second section shows how the privatization of public services and welfare systems expose the transformation of mainstream institutional responses to social inequality. The third section examines austerity measures as the nadir of welfare retrenchment in its current state. The fourth and final section exposes the solidarity alternatives of redistribution, such as pension plans, healthcare, education, economic support and childcare. These are non-state mechanisms of redistribution established by unions, cooperatives and civil society organizations. They mostly operate on a voluntary basis and are locally organized.

The third chapter focuses on the issue of democracy. The first section begins with a critical analysis of democratic practice under neoliberal globalization. The weakening of the nation-state alters the efficiency of mainstream democratic practices associated with the nation-state, including voting, party politics and representative democracy. The second section looks at the rise of global social movements, particularly global justice movements, and identity politics, and reflects upon the limitations of conventional politics. The third and final section conceptualizes workplace democracy as a solidarity alternative. Democracy organized at the local level as opposed to national or global levels provides greater room for participation and resolution of immediate problems pertaining to communities. Participation may include more mainstream practices such as voting, but it also extends to direct participation as organization is more local. Workplace democracy may use different strategies in order to attract a larger number of constituents and address a diverse set of issues.

The fourth chapter takes a look at employment relations. The most detrimental impact of neoliberal globalization has been on global labor. This impact can be observed in both advanced capitalist countries and developing countries. The global challenges facing labor necessitate a conceptual analysis of work and occupations, employment, and labor relations. The first section presents these challenges, while the last section discusses questions regarding the future of organized labor. The chapter as a whole elaborates on new labor solidarity as an alternative that joins traditional labor organizations with newer organizational forms. A comparative analysis of these organizations exposes the new issues that need to be addressed, new constituents to be recruited and new strategies to be employed by these different organizational bodies.

The fifth chapter materializes the thematic discussions of the previous chapters in case studies. These case studies are chosen from different parts of the world; they have different historical backgrounds; and they also differ in size and scope. The objective here is to expose the diversity of alternatives rather than to classify them. Each one will be analyzed on the basis of themes discussed in the previous chapters; however, each case will not be representative of all the themes discussed in the book.

The sixth chapter aims to integrate the empirical evidence from the case studies with the previous theoretical discussions. This will be done at different levels of abstraction organized into four sections. The first will discuss the local responses and their effectiveness against global pressures, especially in relation to the global economic crisis; the second will focus on the institutional and organizational aspects of solidarity alternatives; the third will specifically deal with the theoretical intervention that the research presented in this book makes in fields of the sociology of work and industrial relations – this is the section where research findings are linked to the existing literature – and the fourth will underline the need for relinking empirical research with theoretical analysis. The critical engagement with the existing research will expose theoretical gaps which future research can address.

Notes

1 The Poulantzas–Miliband debate could be a fruitful starting point for tracing the historical transformations of the state's alliance with the capitalist class.
2 To use the well-known term from Charles Loring Brace's The Dangerous Classes of New York and Twenty Years' Work among Them (1872).
3 The "non-market" challenges the capitalist definition of the market and the relations emanating from it, and it aims to redefine the market as a simple domain of exchange instead.
4 From the ILO website: http://www.ilo.org/global/about-the-ilo/how-the-ilo-works/lang–en/index.htm. F
5 Santos and co-authors use the term "solidary economy". The book will define and use "solidarity economy" to encompass solidary economy, other definitions such as social economy or alternative economy, and the analytical dimensions of production, redistribution, participation and representation.

1 Reorganizing production

Analyzing a network of temporally and spatially dispersed production processes requires an extended conceptual framework. Such a framework can help expose the range of the division of labor, the dominant mode of production that characterizes the capitalist system, the major actors and the tasks they undertake, and the network relations that facilitate these production processes on a global scale. The global organization of production is based on flexible specialization, which is the dominant mode of production facilitated by multinational corporations. Globally dispersed production processes are interlinked in global value chains. Despite all its technical sophistication, the globalization of production is inefficient when it comes to avoiding yet another global economic crisis. This raises the following question: is there another way to produce, that is, to organize and facilitate production processes that may avoid the inescapable limitations of the capitalist system? This chapter tries to answer this important question.

The global organization of production

The transition from the Fordist mode of production to flexible specialization was essentially an effort to overcome declining profit rates following the postwar reconstruction period. Flexibility emerged as a solution to a capital accumulation crisis, and it basically enhanced the limits of surplus acquisition from labor. According to Appay, "this kind of analysis is developed from a managerial point of view and, from that perspective, flexibility is the means by which employment is adjusted to market uncertainties, changes in products, technology, skills and volume of labour" (Appay 2010: 27). The physical infrastructure of flexibility was based upon immense technological developments in transportation and communication systems which enabled the flow of capital to favorable and profitable geographies and the further relocation of capital once better circumstances emerged in new areas. The competition among entrepreneurs in the market reflected a parallel competition among governments that sought to attract capital and integrate their respective economic systems into the global economy. Labor faced a double burden within this new, highly integrated, and flexibly organized production context because it lost the social protection of the state and it came to be heavily exploited by capital.

The principle of flexibility can be applied in several different ways. Olmsted and Smith introduce four major categories regarding flexibility. Numerical or operational flexibility refers to the number of workers employed to optimize the production process and maximize profit. Businesses make use of optimal combinations of full-time and part-time workers to establish operational flexibility. Functional flexibility refers to skills development and the reorganization of tasks included in the production process. Cross-training and job enlargement are certain strategies mentioned by Olmsted and Smith that contribute to functional flexibility. Financial flexibility refers to cost-cutting strategies that are combined with the two aforementioned categories of flexibility. These may include the relocation of production sites, outsourcing and subcontracting, and temporary lay-offs with respect to volatility of demand in the global economy. Finally, structural flexibility is a systematic response to the increasing diversity in work-time and work-space arrangements (Olmsted and Smith 1994: 3).

Evaluating the impact of flexible specialization from the actors' point of view, flexibility benefits capital while putting a heavy burden on labor. Flexibility brings a significant reduction in production costs for capital as less and less labor is employed and production schemes respond to demand changes in the market. Capital reduces risks, such as declining profit margins, falling demand, and market fluctuations through external flexibility, when businesses rely on outsourcing and subcontracting production tasks.

From a labor point of view, an increase in flexible work arrangements leads to the growth of the precariat (Standing 2009: 139). Appay underlines an important analytical distinction between flexibility and precarity, which differentiates the business perspective and the labor perspective toward globally organized production systems. Accordingly, "flexibility refers to the constraints of the markets, to management strategies of transferring risks to workers, whilst precarity refers to the resulting situation for the workers" (Appay 2010: 27). Workers in non-standard work arrangements have limited opportunities for skill formation in the workplace, and their chances of upward mobility diminish over time: "A few can even still look forward to having access to structured, more or less predictable opportunities for upward mobility, although in an era of flexible production networks, moving up, more often means changing jobs by moving from one company to another" (Harrison 1994: 197). Limited upward mobility generates a gendered impact, as feminization of the workforce accompanies flexibilization. Other structural aspects of the growing precariat include high turnover rates together with a gradual decline of full-time employment opportunities. The precariat face difficulty in maintaining their households due to the amount of work they get to perform – if not due to declining wages. Harrison stresses that the increasing flexibility of business networks in the global economy helps companies deal with the uncertainties of the market and competition among firms. Increasing vertical disintegration through outsourcing and subcontracting generates a polarization in the labor market between core workers who benefit from lifetime full employment and limited turnover rates, on the one hand, and a massive number of workers who are marginalized in non-standard forms of employment, on the other (Harrison 1994: 209–210).

From the state's point of view, the growth of the precariat leads to a decline in the contribution of workers' premiums to the welfare system. The lowering of taxes and non-wage labor costs to attract investment generates budgetary constraints, which then leads to governments having to cut unemployment benefits for those who are regarded as the free riders of the system: "The response by the state was to cut benefits by trying to cut the income replacement rate, to encourage the unemployed to take jobs. The trouble was that as the labour market was flexibilizing, fewer unemployed could expect to find jobs paying a wage as high as their former jobs" (Standing, 2009: 139). The lack of a decent job for those willing to work and the lack of sufficient welfare support for those not working resulted in what Standing calls the "unemployment trap," which over time worsens to such an extent that it cannot be resolved by government intervention. The more governments deregulate labor markets by cutting down on work-related welfare provisions, the more they are compelled to spend on poverty-related social issues. Hence, flexibility is a double-edged sword for governments, which try to attract capital investments by weakening labor standards and economic costs and which are then forced to spend more on social policy for the marginalized segments of the workforce.

On top of the intriguing challenges from the actors' point of view, the legal and the institutional mechanisms framing the flexible mode of production are insufficiently responsive to the socioeconomic consequences that it generates. Labor relations are consistently deteriorating due to weakening unionism, the disintegration of collective bargaining systems, declining welfare provisions and tightening austerity measures at the national level. Unions have been less adaptive to changing labor relations under flexible production systems, as their focus has remained on male blue-collar workers, whose main interests were working conditions, wages and other workplace issues. Social movement unionism, through the incorporation of non-work issues in union agendas and through alliances with other social movements, served to be an important venue of transformation in union organizations (Waterman 1993). The ILO has failed to respond to the flexibility debate, which began in the 1990s, at the international level (Standing 2009: 92). The changing definitions of work and labor relations rendered the ILO conventions useless or inapplicable, as they were initially formulated to cover full-time, regular employment patterns in the formal labor market. ILO Convention 177 on home-based work was criticized by many as being Western-oriented and neglecting the gender dimension of flexibility, as a major portion of home-based workers are women (Prugl 1999). ILO Convention 122 on employment policy is formulated in such a way that the issues of flexibility and competition in the global labor market are completely disregarded: it euphemistically supports policies toward "full, productive and freely chosen employment."[1] The ILO can further be criticized for the weakness of its tripartite system (i.e. employer organizations, unions and the nation-state) and a lack of monitoring and enforcement around the world, especially in less developed regions. Such criticism is not limited to the current context of work and labor relations.

One can trace two major lines of argument, the liberal and the Marxist, criticizing the concept of flexibility down through the years, and both lines of argument can be used to form a theoretical analysis of the issue at a higher level of abstraction. The liberal perspective argues for the inevitability of the flexible mode of production, given the overproduction bottleneck and declining profit margins under Fordism. The rigidity of the Fordist mode of production, caused by the automated system of standard goods production based on lifetime full employment, became too costly following the postwar economic boom. Flexibility emerged as an option to overcome this rigidity by implementing cost-cutting measures, the most notable of which being the cutting of labor costs. Flexibility in production enabled the mobility of capital to labor-abundant parts of the world, which served to be new and cheap sources of labor and new markets. The liberal discourse generated a number of arguments. First, trade liberalization would gradually level the wage differentials among different labor markets to the advantage of areas with abundant low-skill labor. Second, the system would generate employment opportunities for people who would otherwise be unemployed through the outsourcing and subcontracting of production activities to less developed parts of the world. Third, the global expansion of production systems would generate skill-formation among labor and technological spillover effects for local producers. Therefore, globalization in general and global production in particular would lead to more competition, where firms, small and large, would seek a greater share of the pie through industrial upgrading. While this argument may have looked inspiring in the 1990s, the current course of the global economic crisis suggests that liberal political economy has lost empirical ground both in capitalist and labor-related terms (Milberg 2004).

The Marxist perspective contains criticisms of flexibility that range from structural critiques (based on the fact of global economic inequality) to issue-based evaluations in terms of flexibility's labor, youth and gender implications, and its diverse impacts on less developed parts of the world. Coffey and Thornley go as far as to argue that the literature on post-Fordism in the 1970s and 1980s and (later) on lean production in the 1990s was in fact formulated by combining real developments with fiction to legitimize flexible production and precarious forms of employment. Therefore, "these conceptualizations and attendant derivations require careful evaluation for reasons of positive analysis both of production forms and of production ideologies, to inform collective responses to increasing precariousness of production and employment" (Coffey and Thornley 2010: 57).

Empirical studies on the flexible mode of production and non-standard employment expose in detail the repercussions of changing work and labor relations through micro-level analysis. Findings cluster around a number of issues. First, the time-space compression of the industrial era is radically altered with numerical and functional flexibility. Irregular working periods together with the growing services industry and home-based work blur the boundaries of work and non-work (Bianchi and Wight 2010). The distinction between time allocated to the production and time allocated to the reproduction of labor becomes redundant (Drago and Wooden 2010). The joint use of the household as workplace and living space further blurs the boundaries of work and non-work. Second, work and family issues intensify with the feminization of the global labor force and the replacement of the male breadwinner model with the dual-earner family (Moen and Huang 2010). Women remain the primary providers of domestic services in the household despite increasing rates of labor force participation and employment (Schneider 2011; Caprile and Krüger 2005). Several studies focus on the issue of multitasking and combining tasks in a gendered manner (Offer and Schneider 2010; Schneider 2011). The temporal and spatial challenges in work and labor relations that reflect upon non-work spheres are empirically analyzed in the work-life balance literature (Warhurst, Eikhof, and Haunschild 2008).

The third issue is the declining welfare benefits available for working families and their dependents. Non-standard employment patterns marginalize workers and their dependents, as welfare systems have traditionally catered to full-time workers in the formal labor market. Several countries have initiated social security reforms as a response to changing work and labor relations under the impact of globalization. Many of these reforms were geared toward overcoming the mismatch between flexible work systems and the social security systems of the previous era that were based on an understanding of lifetime full employment patterns. Usami's edited volume includes a number of case studies from newly industrializing countries where social security reforms seek an equilibrium point between neoliberal labor market conditions and the provision of social security benefits to working families and their dependents (Usami 2010).

This brings us to flexicurity, which deserves particular attention as a systemic means of reaching a compromise between changing employment patterns and social security systems that is used as part of the European Union's employment strategy. While flexible employment patterns continue to dominate the labor market, active labor market policies and lifelong learning programs aim to enhance employment rates; in addition, social security provision continues, albeit in a modified form. Barbieri draws attention to two major conclusions on the impact of flexible work schemes on the labor market (Barbieri 2009: 625). First, in most countries mid-career skilled male workers are not significantly affected by the spread of flexible work schemes, whereas newcomers, especially women, are more prone to precarity at work. Second, industrial unskilled workers and routine service workers are more affected by flexibility at work compared to service class workers, who have sustained job security. Flexibility at work results in the consolidation of existing inequalities, both economic and social. While there have been successful aspects to flexicurity, the global economic crisis and the resort to austerity measures in Europe suggest that it is far from being an optimal solution for labor reform.

Government responses to flexible employment are not limited to social security reforms. The Japanese context is unique in the way that flexibility intersects with demographic factors in light of an aging population and declining birth rates. The Japanese government intervenes by promoting less working hours, greater flexibility for women at work (to promote childbearing), and various legal, financial and educational measures that seek to mitigate the risks that come along with a declining population. Treating flexibility as a demographic policy rather than a profit-oriented economic policy is clearly a different take on the current practice of flexibility in the workplace (Iwao 2010). To what extent Japan will overcome its population crisis through flexibility policies remains to be seen. Two major conclusions can be drawn from the general discussion of government policies regarding flexibility. First, governments are compelled to generate effective policies to adjust social settings to flexible working conditions. Second, policies regarding flexibility have to take local factors into consideration in a longitudinal manner.

The consolidation of the flexible mode of production as the *modus operandi* of contemporary capitalism has brought about formal and institutional approaches toward unemployment, poverty and social exclusion in the form of workforce development programs targeting the flexible labor market. Active labor market policies implementing training programs, job placement programs, and self-employment support programs now help individuals get out of the unemployment trap (Bonoli 2010). Bonoli classifies active labor market policies with respect to investment in human capital and employment orientation toward the market, and comes up with four major policy categories: incentive reinforcement, occupation, employment assistance, and upskilling. Each category includes a number of different policies, and these policies are applied in different combinations depending on the local context, the nature of the labor market, and the industrial setting. As the historical evolution of labor policies indicates, flexible employment patterns have become a taken-for-granted aspect of labor relations to the extent that lifetime full employment patterns have ceased to exist.

Community-based approaches, in contradistinction to government programs, are geared toward counteracting the impact of flexible employment patterns that marginalize workers both economically and socially. Worker centers emerge in such marginalized segments of working class communities to fill in the gap left by declining unionism and weakening government regulation of the labor market (Fine 2006). Worker centers, whose structure differs from that of conventional unions, focus on work-related issues and various social issues ranging from immigration to inequality to political representation. Worker centers are organized in the community and are active in the workplace; they may qualify for Waterman's concept of social movement unionism (Waterman 1993). Other workforce development programs include online training programs for the working poor that are designed to help them acquire skills and improve their credentials so that they can apply for better jobs (Gatta 2005) and benefit from information dissemination by public employment agencies and labor offices.

However, several issues remain to be explored with regard to the future of flexibility and its accompanying social arrangements. Peper and his colleagues underline the need for further international comparative research in "finding ways to achieve a better integration between work and care, or more broadly between work and life" (Peper et al. 2005: 325). The ultimate objective remains the reconciliation of work and non-work areas of life for the majority of people, especially the more vulnerable social segments of society such as young parents. The authors, very much in line with the research question posed in this study, conclude by asking a central organizational question: "How should we organise the work in a way that enables different groups of employees (with and without children, men and women) to make optimal use of their human capital?" (Peper et al. 2005: 326). The means toward this ultimate end range from social policy to new workplace practices, or from organizational change to external dynamics such as labor market demand. Gender will remain an important research dimension due to the persistence of the gendered nature of work and domestic life.

The globalization of production is facilitated by the overarching domination of multinational corporations (MNCs). The MNC as a mode of economic organization is not unique to the contemporary world economy. Prototypes of MNCs have been observed as early as the sixteenth century with colonial expansion and long-distance trade. In principle, MNCs can be described as corporate structures that operate in more than two countries, under which several subsidiaries are interconnected by way of production and trade. There are various ways in which MNCs expand globally: 1) through mergers and acquisitions with domestic companies; 2) through franchise agreements; 3) through direct investment; 4) or through outsourcing or subcontracting, where parts of the product are contracted to various smaller-scale manufacturers. Two major methods of investment that MNCs engage in are foreign direct investment, where new production sites are established, and portfolio investment, where corporations invest merely for the sake of financial gain and not for the sake of production or control over assets (Ritzer 2011: 75). The diverse venues of expansion suggest that the experiences of MNCs can hardly be regarded in a monolithic manner. The majority of MNCs are from developed countries, and a major portion of their investments are located in developed nations rather than developing ones. One reason for this is that investments in the developing world, whether in the form of foreign direct investments (FDIs) or through outsourcing, are in labor-intensive segments that comprise only a small portion of MNCs' economic assets.

Several motivations lie behind the global expansion of business operations. The primary objective is profit maximization. International businesses seek low-cost economic inputs, whether in the form of natural resources or labor, in pursuit of this objective. Second, companies expand to new markets to increase demand, and in many cases corporation relocate as much for the new market as for the low-cost economic inputs. Third, corporations want to limit their liability and hedge their risks against fluctuations in demand or unexpected volatility in world markets. Operating in several national settings at the same time enables the transfer of risk and increases the opportunity for the movement or relocation of capital in times of economic risk.

MNCs take advantage of technological improvements in communication and transportation to organize their production chains in the most efficient manner possible. There are several factors behind the objective of efficiency. First, there is product efficiency, where the production process is optimized by minimizing costs and maximizing output in line with the very essence of neoclassical economics. Product efficiency is further enhanced by a political and institutional framework that further reduces costs and risks, such as the cost of natural resources or the taxes that may elevate production costs. Third, MNCs achieve what may be called "a marketing efficiency" by relocating their production facilities on the basis of their proximity to markets. To give an example from the apparel industry: while it may be more suitable to produce in Mexico for the North American market, Turkey or Poland would be a better option for the European market. In services production, efficiency is more advanced because the commodity is intangible and can be transferred easily by various technological means. The most cited example of this has been the relocation of information technology (IT) services such as call centers to India. In services production, the relocation of capital brings a spatial advantage and a temporal advantage. The incorporation of different time zones in the production process of services enhances the time-space compression aspect of globalization.

There has been much debate beyond the rather descriptive and conventional account of the organizational aspects of MNCs, and it has centered on the impact of MNCs on labor, especially in the context of a significant disparity in national development. The flight of capital from home country to areas with cheap labor and access to other resources has had detrimental effects on labor in the developed world and has commonly been associated with the emergence of the "rust belt town." The labor impact of MNCs in the developing world has generated much more controversy. Business interests have argued, with a rather inexplicable optimism, that through neoliberal globalization and trade liberalization labor in developing countries have had employment opportunities that it would otherwise not have because of limited capital investment. Trade liberalization would level out wage differentials among geographies of diverse developmental stages in the long-run and hence move toward a more egalitarian distribution. MNCs, as the primary agents of the liberalizing approach, are in fact playing a role in fulfilling the long-awaited dream of developmentalism. The critical eye toward the impact of MNCs in the developing world, however, has underlined the issue of the exploitation rather than the employment of labor. The massive literature on sweatshops and maquiladoras, the very popular Nike case in Pakistan, and the abusive labor practices in China are some examples of this critical perspective. To juxtapose the liberal and the Marxist analyses of MNCs and their labor practices under globalization may be trivializing and reductionist. There is need for a deeper analysis of the combination of factors that may lead to unique circumstances and labor relations, given the diverse sizes of MNCs, the countries they operate in, and the industrial variation in employment patterns and labor relations.

Table 1.1 compares the top 100 transnational corporations (TNCs) worldwide with the top 100 TNCs from developing and transition economies on the basis of assets, sales and employment (UNCTAD 2014).[2] The 100 largest TNCs worldwide maintain a major portion of their assets, sales and employment in foreign terms, which simply means that they produce and sell on foreign grounds by making use of foreign labor. The TNCs from developing and transition economies hold most of their corporate assets in domestic terms; their sales in domestic and foreign markets are proximate, with domestic sales slightly greater; and a major portion of their employment is domestic. Hence, the degree of transnationalization differs in developed economies and developing ones, which is an indication of the returns they receive from the global market.

Mosley provides a systematic analysis of the way multinational production is organized and of its impact on labor relations. The most important aspect of multinational production is the nature of its ownership in the host country: "The way in which multinational firms organize their overseas production affects labor rights outcomes. Directly owned production augurs positively for labor rights, while subcontracted, arm's-length production has negative consequences for workers' rights" (Mosley, 2011: 4) Mosley highlights major differences between MNC-owned production and MNC-subcontracted production in comparing different modes of entry in a multinational context. The primary concern of MNC-owned production is the application of best practices in foreign branches, where the provision and monitoring of core labor standards is important for the corporate image, especially as part of corporate social responsibility against transnational advocacy and consumer pressures. The primary concern of MNC-subcontracted production is cost efficiency; therefore, the cost of labor rights, wages, and non-wage benefits becomes more important than corporate image. The second mode of entry into the internationalization of production is more common in labor-intensive industries and takes place mostly in areas with limited or no government regulation such as export-processing zones (EPZs). The former is a horizontal integration model, where each production site is a replica in a different locale geared toward a different market, the example for which could be the automotive industry. The latter is a vertical integration model, where the production chain is divided into different stages that are strategically located in different settings for greater production efficiency, as is mostly seen in the case of the apparel and footwear industries (Mosley 2011: 31–32).

Mosley's comparative approach represents the liberal and the critical interpretations of the MNC-dominated production processes. The impact of

Table 1.1 Comparative analyses of transnational corporations

Internationalization Statistics of the 100 Largest Non-Financial TNCs Worldwide and TNCs from Developing and Transition Economies (billions of US $, thousands of employees, and %)

Variables	100 Largest TNCs Worldwide					100 Largest TNCs from Developing and Transition Economies		
	2011	2012	2011–2012 % change	2013	2012–2013 % change	2011	2012	2011–2012 % change
Assets								
Foreign	7,634	7,888	3	8,035	2	1,321	1,506	14
Domestic	4,897	5,435	11	5,620	3	3,561	4,025	13
Total	12,531	13,323	6	13,655	2	4,882	5,531	13
Foreign as % of Total	61	59	–3	59	0	27	27	0
Sales								
Foreign	5,783	5,900	2	6,057	3	1,650	1,690	2
Domestic	3,045	3,055	0	3,264	7	1,831	2,172	19
Total	8,828	8,955	1	9,321	4	3,481	3,862	11
Foreign as % of Total	66	66	0	65	–1	47	44	–3
Employment								
Foreign	9,911	9,821	–1	9,810	0	3,979	4,103	3
Domestic	6,585	7,125	8	7,482	5	6,218	6,493	4
Total	16,496	16,946	3	17,292	2	10,197	10,596	4
Foreign as % of Total	60	58	–2	57	–1	39	39	0

UNCTAD

Note: As of 2009, the fiscal year was taken to start on April 1 and end on March 31; therefore, some of the results for the 2013 fiscal year were preliminary at the time of research.

subcontracted production on labor processes and labor rights has been extensively discussed by several scholars. It is the horizontally integrated, MNC-operated production site that requires particular attention because of all the positive attributes it holds in regards to its labor impact. Why would MNCs seek best practices in their international branches? What are the costs and benefits of corporate social responsibility and enforcing corporate codes of conduct? To assume that MNCs act out of sheer altruism or even generate a positive corporate image would be a rather naïve interpretation of their actions. Harrington argues that "corporate social responsibility policies can be used to fill the common space which multinational corporations and labor interests share, ensuring that progressive labor standards that please workers and the public are used even where there is no legal obligation to do so" (Harrington 2012: 508). Best practices contribute to productive efficiency as much as they look good in public. MNCs pay higher wages than domestic companies to attract workers with advanced skills, which leads to greater productivity. A second motivation for paying higher wages is to control for technological spillover and further competition from domestic firms. Bernhardt and Dvoracek argue in their economic analysis that "the MNC is more willing to pay its workers wage premia to defend its technological superiority if more domestic firms would otherwise gain access to the MNC's technology. However, the MNC is less willing to pay the wage premia if there are more domestic firms in the industry" (Bernhardt and Dvoracek 2009: 728). A simple cost-benefit analysis of corporate social responsibility may reveal that a small amount of spending in a given campaign generates larger returns in corporate image and sales that will compensate for the initial spending. As for corporate codes of conduct, the idea that in the lack of governmental enforcement of labor standards corporations choose to enforce standards on their own is once again not representative of the general labor practice in a system that depends on surplus value for its existence. In evaluating the impact of corporate codes of conduct on labor practices, Barrientos and Smith state that "findings reflect a deeper disjuncture between a compliance approach to codes that focuses on technical outcome standards and a process approach that focuses on the empowerment of workers to claim their rights" (Barrientos and Smith 2007: 727). In an empirical study of the Ethical Trading Initiative (ETI) in the UK, Barrientos and Smith conducted a survey of 11 companies that have adopted ETI codes, 23 supplier sites, and 418 workers, which revealed that while corporate actors respond to civil society pressures by adopting corporate codes of conduct, they do little to improve social practices or business relations that undermine labor rights. Although civil society organizations prioritize labor rights and regulations, they have limited power vis-à-vis corporate power (Barrientos and Smith 2007: 727).

Numerous studies, models, and institutional and non-academic efforts have tried to formulate a regulatory framework in which corporate interests are reconciled with labor rights, none of which have the power to overcome violations of exploitation, informal or illegal employment, forced labor or even slavery. Verma and Elman focus on three major points in discussing the need for a new regulatory framework for labor standards: the long-term effectiveness of the regulatory approach that may require national government involvement; an all-encompassing approach to cover all workers in all sectors, including informally employed workers; and a public model that transcends consumer preferences for a major focus on labor rights and human rights: "When one begins examining labour standards, one fact becomes very clear – it is not a matter of resources but rather one of building a social and political consensus around the fundamental labour rights" (Verma and Elman 2007: 63).

While this evaluation of MNCs and their labor impact provides insight into corporate behavior and decision-making, there are other factors that contribute to the uniqueness of labor outcomes. First, the impact of openness and national policy outcomes plays a particular role in labor-related outcomes (Mosley 2011: 47). The particular mode of integration with the global economy and the policy responses to globalization at the national level generate unique labor conditions in different locales. Second, internal influences on collective labor rights require particular attention. Domestic economic conditions, unemployment rates, labor force demographics, worker skill levels, and the sectoral distribution of economic activity all play a role in the composition of labor rights (Mosley 2011: 47). The nature of domestic political institutions and ideologies, whether economic goals are prioritized over social ones, and whether voter behavior plays more of a central role than global integration are other aspects that need to be taken into consideration as well. Finally, whether there is room for the representation of worker organizations or labor, or whether these are oppressed under authoritarian governments plays a role in the overall construction and maintenance of labor rights.

The economy does not function under *ceteris paribus* conditions. A multivariate, dynamic analysis of MNC conduct and its implications for work and labor may expose the unique ways in which political, economic and social factors coincide; however, it will also expose persistent patterns of inequality among countries. Wall et al. review a number of variables in their empirical analysis of corporate connections and the structure of global corporate networks, covering home country, host country, and bilateral dynamics that shape corporate relations on a global scale. Their variables include gross domestic product (GDP), remoteness, openness and technology exports for both countries; stock market capitalization and credit provision in the home country; and fuel exports, quality of institutions and corporate taxes in the host country. In addition, physical distance, sectoral distance, common language and common history are included as bilateral variables. The results of their study show that the motivations behind corporate networking and the consequences of corporate networking reinforce the existing political and economic inequalities between countries:

> It was also shown that the number of connections targeted at poor countries is driven by low wage costs in these countries, whereas those

> targeted at rich countries are driven by low corporate taxes. Also, a country's market size is more important for connections targeted at rich countries than those targeted at poor countries. These findings reveal differences in economic activities conducted between countries, where connections into poor countries are primarily related to labor-intensive activities, and FDI into rich countries is mainly targeted at services. In addition, FDI into poor countries is more natural resource seeking and efficiency seeking than is FDI into rich countries.
>
> (Wall et al. 2011: 922)

The discussion so far exposes the fact that multinational investment patterns as a characteristic feature of neoliberal globalization transform work organization and accompanying labor relations. History has come to another turning point that challenges the corporate conduct that has been prevalent for more than four decades now. How will MNCs respond to the global economic crisis? What will be the impact of this response be on work processes, employment patterns and labor relations? Will MNCs remain the sole proprietors of the global economy? Is the MNC still the most optimal way of organizing the economy in general and production in particular?

Evidence shows that the MNC-dominated global economy has achieved a sustained growth rate; however, it was unable to escape recurrent and extensive crisis. MNCs generated increasing employment opportunities in less developed countries, yet this further polarized global inequality instead of diminishing it. A more focused review of corporate responses to the global economic crisis would reveal the unbalanced power relations in the economy and short-sighted decision-making at the corporate level.

Global value chains

The focus of inquiry in the previous section was the global organization of production and the multinational corporation. A major portion of the literature uses the MNC as the unit of analysis because of its dominant position in the political and economic organization of neoliberal globalization. The MNC is the center of attraction in the neoliberal context, whether one looks at it from a structuralist perspective or from an agency perspective. While this reveals much about the operation of economics under neoliberal globalization, a relational perspective toward MNCs will provide a broader picture in terms of cooperation and competition. An MNC may operate in several economic sectors and in multiple national settings, and its decision to invest may be a result of a number of different motivations, but here the major question is how all of these dynamics will relate to other economic and political actors.

This section aims to expose the expansion of production processes on a global scale with respect to network relations and nodes of concentration. The multinational organization of production requires networking relations, sectoral concentration, industrial clustering, geographical organization, and a legal institutional framework in which all of this geographically expanded production will function smoothly. There have been several different conceptualizations of the network relations that organize production on a global scale. The earlier analysis of commodity chains has led to the development of global value chains as a well-cited field of inquiry. Management literature in general and strategic management literature in particular, has focused on industrial clusters, or business clusters, and global production networks. The contemporary use of the term "global value chains" (GVC) rather than "global commodity chains" (GCC) will be scrutinized later on in this chapter. The evolution of terminology that defines global production parallels the intensification of production relations on a global scale.

The internationalization of production since the 1980s has been made possible by the fragmentation of the production process into smaller sub-processes, where different components of the final product were manufactured in different parts of the world. These components, generally referred to as the "intermediate goods," have since then comprised a major portion of world trade. These intermediate goods are traded in an extended manner and are finally assembled to be marketed in their final destinations. This interlinked production process and massive trading of intermediate goods led to the reformulation of the classical definitions of production, commodity, trade and market:

> A GCC consists of sets of inter-organizational networks clustered around one commodity or product, linking households, enterprises, and states to one another within the world-economy. These networks are situationally specific, socially constructed, and locally integrated, underscoring the social embeddedness of economic organization.
>
> (Gereffi et al. 1994: 2)

A GCC refers to a network organized around a commodity; this organization is not confined by the production process of that commodity and it includes labor employed in any link of the chain, households that earn their livelihood from the production process, and other political and social organizations that hold a stake in the maintenance of the network. It is not only the expansion of the production process on a global plane, but it is also an extended link between production and consumption, and the overall management of the network.

The analysis of commodity chains is not unique to the contemporary globalization of production. Hopkins and Wallerstein suggest that concentration and decentralization have to do with the cyclical rhythms of the world economy (Gereffi et al. 1994: 5). Defining the commodity chain as "a network of labor and production processes whose end result is a finished commodity" (Hopkins and Wallerstein 1986: 159), Hopkins and Wallerstein argue that commodity chains help trace the transformations of labor processes and the overall production system of the world economy. All separable components of a commodity chain are called "boxes," and their boundaries are socially defined. There are five major comparative dimensions in the analysis of commodity chains. First, the degree of monopoly in a box exposes whether the box, or the separate production process, has a core-like or a periphery-like nature. Second, the geographical spread of a box contributes to the analysis. Boxes stretched to a few countries are more core-like, whereas boxes that spread out across several countries are more periphery-like. Third, the number of commodity chains in which the box is located and the diversity of outlets are correlated with the structure of production in the box. The changes in production are responsive to the cyclical rhythms of the world economy. Fourth, property relations in the box, whether composed of petty owners, larger entities or lease-type relations through non-owner management, are another defining feature of the production process embedded in the commodity chain. In cases where production is organized by larger entities, boxes are vertically integrated. When production is organized by smaller economic units, ownership also becomes much more dispersed. The property relations are indicative of the extent of monopoly or competition in the world economy. Finally, modes of labor control, in the form of wage, non-wage or coerced labor, provide insight for comparative historical analysis (Hopkins and Wallerstein 1994: 18).

Hopkins and Wallerstein provide a historical analysis of the commodity chains with respect to the shifts in the world economy. Accordingly, the expansion phase of the world economy, commonly referred to as the A-phase, is characterized by vertical integration of the production process in which incentives for transaction costs are prioritized. In the contraction phase of world economy, the B-phase, there is an increase in subcontracting of the production process, taking after the incentive towards lower labor costs.

Gereffi's work has been a cornerstone of studies on network relations for the last three decades. Gereffi defines three major GCC dimensions: input-output structures, territoriality, and governance (in terms of power and authority). Gereffi's most important contribution to this field, however, has to do with the governance dimension and the distinction between producer-driven and buyer-driven commodity chains (Gereffi 1994: 97–99). In producer-driven commodity chains, MNCs or other large-scale enterprises control the production system. Production is capital- and technology-intensive, and profits come from scale economies under the management of the manufacturer. These commodity chains face less competition in the market, and states are more prone to intervene in sectors in which these chains are prevalent: hence in terms of governance, there is greater centralization of ownership, manufacturing and management. Aircraft, electric machinery and computers are some examples of producer-driven commodity chains, although they can be observed in a variety of sectors.

The production network is much more decentralized in the case of buyer-driven commodity chains. There is a definite detachment of the merchandizer and the manufacturer. Large retailers, brand-name merchandizers, and trading companies organize a network of contractors, who in turn organize the subcontractors in a chain-like manner, most of which are located in less developed countries. Production is labor-intensive, and profits come from a managerial system that comprises high-value research, design, sales, and marketing instead of scale economies. The decentralization and flexibility of the production process generates greater competition among contractors and subcontractors in less developed countries, and state intervention under these circumstances changes its character: it becomes more welcoming and accommodating in nature. Buyer-driven commodity chains are mostly seen in consumer goods, apparel, footwear and other labor-intensive sectors.

The analytical capacity of GCCs is more important, for the purposes of this research, than the descriptive and categorical features of GCCs. Gereffi et al. consider GCCs to be extremely helpful in better understanding spatial inequalities and contemporary development issues. As GCCs operate at levels below and above the nation-state, they expose micro- and macro-links between processes. This also enables a comparative analysis of the core and the periphery (Gereffi et al. 1994: 5). Hopkins and Wallerstein argue that the dynamics of commodity chains indicate two levels of accumulation in the capitalist world economy. The first level of capital accumulation results from the chain as a whole. The second emerges from each box in the chain, which is essentially the root of unequal exchange and hence global inequality. According to Korzeniewicz and Martin, commodity chains provide "a relational construct for investigating the structure of the world economy" (Korzeniewicz and Martin 1994: 68). It is possible to reveal patterns of global wealth distribution, long-term trends in zonal structures, and links between production processes by looking at the operation of commodity chains and then tracing a global and longitudinal approach to the operation of the capitalist world economy: "The GCCs approach explains the distribution of wealth within a chain as an outcome of the relative intensity of competition within different nodes" (Gereffi et al. 1994: 4). Relying on commodity chains in general or on one single commodity chain in particular to explain global patterns may definitely be misleading, as historical shifts may be counterintuitive. That is why a relational, comparative historical analysis has to be the order of the day.

The internationalization of production underwent noteworthy transformations in parallel to the structural transformations underwent by global production schemes. The transition from GCCs to GVCs may seem at first to have been purely conceptual; however, theoretically and methodologically this transition implies more than a descriptive shift. The GVC framework is an interdisciplinary approach to evaluating the impact of the global spread of industries on corporations and countries. GVCs function as the "world economy's backbone and central nervous system," given the increasing integration and interdependency of the world economy (Cattaneo et al. 2010: 7). Their focus is on value-added chains and the way they operate in specific sectors and industries, and in the production of specific commodities, standing separately from their world-systems predecessors and building largely upon international business literature. Major concerns are with the particular ways in which the chains are governed, the costs of organizing value chains in specific manners, and the possibilities of industrial upgrading through the value chains (Bair 2005). These concerns represent a major shift from the commodity chain approach in the way the structural and systemic context is largely omitted from the analysis, together with unequal exchange, capital accumulation and the labor regimes observed in specific production processes. In describing the theoretical and methodological shifts in the value chain approach, Bair states that

> it focuses more on the question of how inter-firm relations are shaped by the internal logics of sectors, such as industry structure and production-process characteristics that are more technical or organizational in nature, with lesser attention devoted in the value chain scheme to the external factors which shape chain dynamics and the distribution of value-added along the chain, such as the broader institutional environments in which chains operate.
>
> (Bair 2005: 164)

GVCs operate on the principle of trade openness, which may help corporations against domestic and regional shocks and which may shield against falling demand, but will make economies more vulnerable to external shocks at the same time: "Thus, if a shock occurs in one of the participating sectors or countries, the shock is transmitted quickly to the other stages of the supply chain through both backward and forward linkages" (Escait et al. 2010: 74). GVCs pursue flexibility in production and marketing with respect to demand fluctuations, including lean retailing, just-in-time inventory management control, and the use of accumulated inventories, full-package outsourcing, and modular production processes, in order to be more resilient to shocks of domestic or external origin (Milberg and Winkler 2010: 38).

The analysis of network relations in the world economy, whether conceptualized as commodity chains or value chains, is illuminating for a number of reasons. GVCs enable a deeper understanding of international trade, demand fluctuations in the world market and responsive policies for the maintenance of the world economy by providing insight into organization of production on a global scale. Second, the particular way in which countries participate in GVCs indicates a pattern of economic development; hence, countries shape their development policies by targeting particular sectors, industries, or stages within GVCs. On the micro level, commodity chains or value chains provide insight into the labor relations embedded in the production process. The shift from the commodity chain perspective to the value chain perspective suggests that there is a greater concern for firm-level analysis and market-level operations and a diminishing concern with development- and labor-related issues:

> In place of the abstract market of neoclassical economics, the GVC framework offers an empirically tractable model of the global economy as a field of overlapping value chains. In so doing, value chain frameworks have become central to constructing new generation private sector

> development policies that at once give pride of place to market integration and economic growth, while opening space for more active policies aimed at fomenting the participation of firms (and potentially other actors).
>
> (Werner et al. 2014: 1222)

So far the discussion on the network relations embedded in the world economy has covered commodity chains, global commodity chains and global value chains. The focus on chain conceptualization historically evolves in terms of its object of inquiry, theoretical framework and methodological approaches. Studies on global production networks, industrial clusters and input-output matrices outside the chain-like process have started to take on a new direction and carve out a unique niche in the management literature. Moving away from the critique of the chain approach conceptualizing production and distribution as vertical and linear, network analysis aims to explain production as a system which is complex and relational, forming links not only vertically but also horizontally and even diagonally (Henderson et al. 2002: 442). Networks are not permanent structures; they are subject to change with market fluctuations and emerging political crises compelling their relocation. However, under these circumstances each and every component of a network – whether in production or in business organization – can possibly be replaced:

> GPNs therefore slice through boundaries in highly differentiated ways, influenced in part by regulatory and non-regulatory barriers and in part by local socioeconomic conditions. This has a profound effect on the bargaining power of the actors involved. Consequently, local urban and regional development needs to be seen as a translocal, dynamic process of growth and change, with multiple actors operating at a variety of geographical scales shaping its trajectory.
>
> (Rainnie et al. 2013)

Henderson et al. define global production networks (GPNs) as multilayered and multidimensional phenomena, and they emphasize network organization, corporate power distribution, labor, value creation and transfer, and institutions – including government, labor unions and employer associations – and their impact on firm strategy and economic prosperity in general, and technological upgrading and value generation in particular (Henderson et al. 2002: 447). Along similar lines, Ernst has studied the impact of GPNs on international knowledge diffusion and the opportunities this creates for developing countries. Ernst's research mostly focuses on the high-tech electronics and IT industries, which are concentrated mainly in the Chinese and other Asian economies (Ernst 2000). The success stories emerging from Taiwan and South Korea, for example, where knowledge outsourcing has led to knowledge diffusion and the emergence of independent brands, are proof that GPNs may have spillover effects in developing countries. A more down-to-earth view of how these networks operate needs to consider the fact that the majority of the developing world in fact participates in commodity chains, value chains and production networks through labor-intensive production processes rather than capital- or technology-intensive production processes. The fundamental premise of efficiency, supported by competition in the global economy, is a major limitation of the "local capability formation" concept supported by the proponents of GPNs (Ernst and Kim 2001: 3). The possibility of GPNs actually enhancing local capability in labor-intensive and less value-added industries like apparel and footwear (and other manufactured goods) is rather low.

As economic actors have different priorities, so do researchers. Scholarly analysis, similar to the global production systems under focus – whether chains, networks or other interlinked mechanisms – is also multivariate and multiscalar. A simple methodological principle may help focus a research interest: a larger domain of inquiry may only provide shallow analytical coverage, whereas a smaller domain narrowed down with exclusive parameters will enable one to take a more in-depth view. For the purposes of this research, labor is the essential domain which operates in a multilayered production system and which links to the world economy by way of producing and, in return, consuming. This relational conceptualization does not necessarily have to emerge from a global context; it can come from a much smaller unit of analysis and link to the global:

> What all this suggests, we would argue, is that any investigation of the conditions of labour within small firms under capitalism cannot start from governance structures of commodity chains, managerial strategies, or similar concerns. Rather, it must instead start from an analysis of the organisation and control of the labour process in concrete settings.
>
> (Rainnie et al. 2013)

The focus on the small firm juxtaposed with the network structure exposes the practical implications of interdependent production relations for small producers. The sophistication of network relations and global value chains cater to the upper echelons of the social and economic hierarchies at the expense of the innumerable small producers they step on. All this sophistication has faced a huge backlash with the onset of the global economic crisis, which has forced networks to reconfigure themselves for minimal damage.

The global economic crisis

Some think the process of globalization has brought about the end of history; history, however, has proven otherwise. The postwar boom experienced by the capitalist world economy resulted in the full reconstruction of national economies to such an extent that profit margins could no longer be sustained within the borders of nation-states. Concomitant processes of globalization unfolded around the planet within the political backdrop of sustained peace under US hegemony, the Cold War era, the détente period in the 1970s, European integration and the despair of Third World developmentalism.

Postwar political objectives, however, regarding the building of nations, nation-states and national economies were undermined in favor of pursuing economic objectives centered on opening up and deregulating markets and leaving them to their own devices. The interstate system, with nation-states as its primary representatives, has meanwhile lost its crucial function of keeping international trade intact. The global economic system is now backed by a set of globally operating economic institutions – the World Trade Organization (WTO), the G-7, the International Monetary Fund (IMF) and the World Bank (WB) – which now have new roles to play thanks to the Washington Consensus.

The advancement of information and transportation technologies has enabled the reconfiguration of the global division of labor, where manufacturing based on the availability of cheap labor has moved to less developed parts of the world and services, particularly business services and other white-collar jobs, have been for the most part taken over the highly skilled labor forces of the advanced capitalist countries: "The integrated international production networks embodied in the twenty-first century corporate form now stand so much at the heart of global accumulation – and are so intimately related to the proletarianization of the Global South – that they effectively rule out extensive protectionism as a state response" (Panitch and Gindin 2010: 7–8). The global division of labor, based on the concentration of labor-intensive low-skill jobs in the Global South and capital-intensive, design-oriented, creative and high-skill jobs in the North also necessitated a rethinking of the labor theory of value, which will be further discussed in Chapter 4.

The historical, institutional and practical transformations brought about by globalization were followed and legitimated by a significant and overarching transformation in the idea world of political economy. The idea of neoliberalism renewed and expanded the use of the liberal paradigm by prioritizing the global economy over national economies, and international institutions over nation-states. Furthermore, it legitimized the integration of global markets and global production chains, and disregarded the social consequences of poverty, inequality and deteriorating social relations. Radice very appropriately distinguishes between the ideology of neoliberalism and its practical use in policy-making (Radice 2010: 35). The application of neoliberal policies was further diversified with the combination of local factors and state capabilities in different national settings. Saad-Filho provides a categorical definition of neoliberalism, which is applied in many ways and to various extents:

> In essence, neoliberalism is based on the systematic use of state power, under the ideological guise of "non-intervention," to impose a hegemonic project of recomposition of the rule of capital at five levels: domestic resource allocation, international economic integration, the reproduction of the state, ideology, and the reproduction of the working class.
>
> (Saad-Filho 2010: 242–243)

In policy terms, the advent of neoliberalism meant the retreat of states' economic role and control over the market by way of deregulation. The market, left to its own devices, overthrew national and social objectives associated with the postwar era and initiated a profit-oriented growth strategy as its fundamental basis. The hegemonic vacuum created with the declining role of the nation-state in economic matters was fulfilled by market actors – corporations and, more specifically, multinational corporations – that rendered the concept of the "nation" irrelevant. The relative concert between capital, labor and the state during the postwar era was heavily altered by neoliberalism, where the state lost its role as an arbitrator between the two classes. States, for the sake providing a profitable investment environment for global capital, cut down on various kinds of economic regulation, which ranged from taxes to trade barriers and from welfare provision to overall labor standards. The retreat of the state for the sake of the corporation resulted in an irreconcilable gap between economic growth and social development.

A comprehensive review of processes of and perspectives on globalization is beyond the scope of this book. The concept of globalization and the literature thereon will only be relevant for comparative purposes, so as to expose the historical continuities and transformations that characterize its current trajectory. Given that the current global crisis was initiated by the financial sector and that it had a butterfly effect on the real economy, a tracing of the process of financialization from the global era to the post-global era will expose the essential constraints of contemporary capitalism.

The financialization of the global system is an appropriate starting point for trying to get a better understanding of the culmination of the global economic crisis. This process can be traced as far back as the 1960s, and its effects can be seen in the economic crisis of the 1970s. Three separate yet interrelated processes can help us understand the way capital is reorganized on a global scale. The primary objective in a capitalist economy is to sustain high profit rates. In the real economy, this is done by seeking greater productivity through exploitation. In addition, demand generation by way of consumerism or crediting supports high profit rates (Panitch and Gindin 2010: 10). The devalorization of manufacturing and production in the real economy leads to further accumulation through innovation. Second, the spread of risk and the provision of risk insurance in a global economy further extend capital accumulation by commodifying the assets, risks and operations of the real economy. Radice regards the financialization of the global economy as "the 'production' of financial instruments," a process analogous to the production of other goods and services in the market (Radice 2010: 27). Corporations in general and multinational corporations in particular, with their recognition as legal persons, provide the institutional foundations of financialization: "What characterizes the recent expansion is the sector's ability to create and market legal claims on 'shares' in all manner of future income streams, such as repayment of student loans, rents on scarce natural resources, or future tax revenues" (Radice 2010: 27). Radice argues against the often-cited argument that the financial sector is detached from the real economy, maintaining that the real economy is heavily subsumed by the financial sector because money is made on the economic probabilities and risks that lie down the road. The third and final process of financialization is the institutional framework that surrounds it. The degree to which capital has been centralized and concentrated has reached such an unprecedented level, that financial institutions such as the IMF, the WB, and the US Federal Reserve have been compelled into a relationship of interdependency rather than one of regulation or administration. Firms have come to be regarded as "too big to fail," as they would take the whole economy down with them if they did. As a result, governments have resorted to bail-out policies for the sake of maintaining, or postponing, a crisis situation (Rohit 2013).

The process of financialization that has been going on since the 1970s has helped delay a major economic crisis. The capitalist world economy has experienced several sporadic mini-crises since then in Mexico, South Korea, Turkey and elsewhere, many of which have been governed by bail-outs and desperate measures at the expense of masses of people suffering at work, impoverished outside of work, and living without the basic means of dignity. The global economy received a last hit in 2008 with the US mortgage crisis. As Piketty appropriately points out, "the crisis of 2008 was the first crisis of the globalized patrimonial capitalism of the twenty-first century. It is unlikely to be the last" (Piketty 2014: 473).

Although the global economic crisis emerged out of the financial sector, the interdependency between the financial sector and the real economy suggests a massive spillover effect, where physical and material production processes take place and have a direct impact on the means of production. Extreme financialization in the system has skewed the distribution of value in accumulation and in redistribution; the real economy is directly influenced by financial processes in several ways. Problems regarding financial liquidity may be resolved by governments and central banks to a certain degree, but the lack of a secure and sustained investment environment prevents sustained production and growth in the real economy. The stagnation, if not shrinking, of the real economy directly affects employment in both qualitative and quantitative terms. Hence, the vicious circle of a shrinking economy interrupts sustained demand generation, and the inflationary interventions by governments and central banks do more harm than good – both in macroeconomic and socioeconomic terms.

Some quantitative indicators may be helpful in further explaining the nature of the global economic crisis. Table 1.2 shows the ratio of central government debt to GDP on a regional distribution. The data is only partial, as there were no aggregates available on Africa, East Asia, and Middle East and North Africa at the time of research. However, a crude exposition of the available data will be enough to demonstrate the impact of the crisis. There seems to be a steady and gradual increase in the government debt to GDP ratio from 2008 onward for all regions except South Asia. The most dramatic increase was in North America. The central government debt in the US,

Table 1.2 Central government debt, total (% of GDP)

Region	*2005*	*2006*	*2007*	*2008*	*2009*	*2010*	*2011*	*2012*	*2013*
Central Europe and the Baltics	.	.	.	24	34	43	42	43	.
Europe & Central Asia (all income levels)	43	42	39	38	42	49	47	53	.
European Union	49	46	42	49	53	59	61	70	.
North America	51	49	47	54	64	69	71	74	74
South Asia	61	59	56	.	.	51	.	.	.

World Bank

Note: Data on Africa, East Asia and the Middle East and North Africa was not available at the time of research.

where the crisis initially emerged, rose from 64% of GDP in 2008 to 96% in 2013. In the UK, the same rate moved from 56.5% in 2008 to 103.2% in 2012, which comes to mean that in 2012 the debt of the UK was larger than its GDP. Germany, as the dynamo of the European Union, was less affected by the crisis with regard to government debt, which rose from 43.1% in 2008 to 56.9% in 2012. One single indicator is definitely not enough to expose the repercussions of the global economic crisis. For a better understanding, further inquiry into the trickle-down effects of this crisis will be necessary.

Table 1.3 shows the ratio of the market capitalization of listed companies to GDP with respect to income aggregates. Market capitalization is calculated

Table 1.3 Market capitalization of listed companies by income level (% of GDP)

Income Level	*2004*	*2005*	*2006*	*2007*	*2008*	*2009*	*2010*	*2011*	*2012*
High income	100.3	105.8	118.2	118.6	62.1	86.3	93.5	76.1	86.4
Low & middle income	40.8	45.3	67.1	110.2	43.4	70.9	66.5	44	48
Low income	.	.	.	.	.	.	.	.	.
Lower middle income	38.6	47.9	59.7	98.3	36.4	56	62.9	41.3	48.4
Middle income	41.3	45.8	67.6	111	43.7	71.5	66.9	44.2	48.3
Upper middle income	42.1	45.1	69.9	114.9	45.8	75.8	68.2	45	48.2
World	90.3	94.7	108.1	116.8	57.8	82.4	86	66.7	74.9

World Bank DataBank, 2015

by multiplying the value of each share with the number of shares in trade. This calculation will only show the value of companies in the market by itself; the annual change in the ratio of market capitalization will reveal the extent of financialization in the market and, to a certain extent, the concentration of capital in the market. Market capitalization of companies at all income levels fell dramatically with the 2008 mortgage crisis. First, the crisis, despite having been initiated in the US, expanded both horizontally to different parts of the world and vertically to lower segments of society. Second, this loss of value had an impact on corporate decision-making, especially toward investment. Although the economy slightly improved by 2012, it can hardly be regarded to have made up for the damage it suffered as a result of the crisis.

Table 1.4 looks at market capitalization from a regional perspective. Market capitalization is generally lowest in Central Europe and the Baltics and the Middle East and North Africa, and both regions face difficulties in picking up after 2008. Comparing the distribution of data in Table 1.2 and Table 1.3, low- and middle-income areas hold a marginal position in the global economy with respect to the size of their assets, and they have been further marginalized with the impact of the global economic crisis. The potential of their economies to return to pre-crisis levels depends on whether they can be integrated into the global economy and the propensity of high-income regions like North America, Europe and Asia to invest in these rather marginal segments of the global economy.

Table 1.4 Market capitalization of listed companies by region (% of GDP)

Region	*2004*	*2005*	*2006*	*2007*	*2008*	*2009*	*2010*	*2011*	*2012*
Central Europe and the Baltics	24.6	26.4	35.7	41.8	15.9	24.4	27.2	18.8	22.7
East Asia & Pacific (all income levels)	78.5	90.5	109.1	137.1	69.9	93.6	91.8	65.1	68.3
Europe & Central Asia (all income levels)	72	75.7	94.9	95.7	41.5	63.5	67.5	52.8	61.6
European Union	71.4	73.7	91.9	91.9	41.4	60.2	64.6	53	62.5
Middle East & North Africa (all income levels)	71.3	108	71.9	90.6	43.8	55.8	55.1	40.2	40.4
North America	131.6	129.4	139.2	138.8	78.3	106.1	116.4	101.3	114.5
South Asia	47	58.8	74	127.1	44.9	73.5	82.6	47.9	59.1
Sub-Saharan Africa (all income levels)	120	128.7	149.4	.	.	.	80.2	60.4	68
World	90.3	94.7	108.1	116.8	57.8	82.4	86	66.7	74.9

World Development Indicators, World Bank

In terms of the real economy, globalization, financialization and geographical expansion are three concurrent and interrelated processes that generate interdependency and attribute a more important role to the actors they involve (Radice 2010: 33). These three processes cannot be treated as systemic dynamics operating at an abstract altitude; rather, they need to be grounded in social categories such as the labor market, social class and the state. The argument that trade liberalization will generate the global leveling of wages, especially for the benefit of low-wage workers in less developed parts of the world has been falsified, given the race to the bottom within the highly competitive global labor market (Milberg 2004). Little remains to maintain the initial optimism that many people had regarding neoliberal globalization and the ultimate end it sought to bring to history – and this can be shown by a panoramic view of the social and economic consequences of globalization through a comparative historical analysis.

Processes of globalization in general and financialization in particular expose a rather descriptive view of the dynamics behind the global crisis. How then, can we describe the crisis itself? First, the current global economic crisis is a crisis of accumulation caused by the inherent contradictions of capitalism. Similar to previous crises, it was preceded by financial speculation (Shaikh 2010). Some refer to these inherent contradictions as a tendency toward gradual stagnation (Rohit 2013), while others, in line with the Marxist view of capitalism, regard them as having the potential to generate an ever increasing gap of inequality. Increasing inequality results in a decline of purchasing power and hence decreasing demand on a macro level. Financial institutions then lend money to weaker segments of society to sustain demand, which consequently further contributes to rising inequality (Piketty 2014: 297).

Second, the crisis is not an isolated incident peculiar to the contemporary conduct of the global economy; instead, the crises of capitalism have a cyclical nature. Historical analyses of capitalism often refer to cycles (Hobsbawm 1994; Mandel 1972), either as cycles of accumulation (Arrighi 1994), or as cycles of expansion and contraction (Kondratieff 2010; Wallerstein 1974). The cyclical nature of the capitalist world economy does not necessarily imply simple recurrence: Arrighi (1994), in his *magnum opus*, refers to the way each crisis reflects peculiar aspects of capitalist conduct. According to Shaikh, the relationship between accumulation and profit reveals the recurrent nature of crisis in capitalism. All in all, the cost of it falls on the poor and the excluded (Shaikh 2010: 45).

Third, there are certain unique aspects in every crisis that are representative of the historical period in which it occurs in spite of its cyclical nature. In every crisis, there is a particular periodization and configuration that emerges, and this has to do with class relations and institutionalization. Capital-labor relations in general and the degree and nature of proletarianization in particular indicate a pattern in which capitalism leads to crisis (Panitch and Gindin 2010). A comprehensive understanding of the global economic crisis necessitates macroeconomic indicators to be complemented by socioeconomic indicators and other variables regarding the class and state dimensions of economic relations. The dramatic increase in wealth since the 1990s, the shareholder revolution of the 1980s, an increase in the dividend-payout ratio, and, finally, sub-prime lending are major factors that characterize the current global crisis as more of an extended staggering rather than a sudden collapse (Rohit 2013). The financial nature of the crisis has been variously interpreted as bringing about skewed wealth generation, an increase in inequality, and increase in aggregate international asset positions and in the capital-income ratio (Piketty 2014).

There have been several attempts to compare the current global economic crisis with the Great Depression of the 1930s. While the similarities are easier to notice than the differences, it is in fact the latter that expose the unique nature of the contemporary crisis. For Piketty, one major difference is that the current crisis suggests a "Great Recession" rather than a "Great Depression" (Piketty 2014: 472). Output levels are lower and government finances deteriorate when future economic growth is uncertain; the efforts of governments and central banks in bailing out financial corporations for the sake of maintaining the global economy at large is one unique aspect of the current crisis. Rohit refers to the maintenance of overconsumption – three prolonged booms with savings and loans in the 1980s, the dot-com economy in the 1990s and the real estate boom in the 2000s – leading to a "prolonged period of tranquility with deep crisis" (Rohit 2013: xxv).

The transition from neoliberal globalization to global economic crisis has been discussed on the basis of structural dynamics and long-term historical analysis. Little has been said, however, about the impact of this transition on actors, institutions and the relations between them. How does the relationship between the market and the state transform as the prediction that globalization would bring about an end to history fade away? To what extent does the capital-labor dichotomy hold its explanatory value regarding the impact of the global economic crisis? Finally, what kinds of new issues might be raised about the existing structure of actors, institutions and the relations between them?

The golden age of capitalism in the postwar era witnessed relative congruity between capital, labor and the state (Esping-Andersen 1990). Esping-Andersen's oft-cited *The Three Worlds of Welfare Capitalism* vividly illustrates the consensus established under welfare regimes of the highly protected national economies of the time. The solidarity between capital, labor and the state was altered by the processes of opening up, outsourcing and overall deregulation of the economic system from the 1970s onward with the onset of neoliberal globalization. The disintegration of the collective bargaining system in Sweden, the weakening or even vanishing of welfare provision under the Reagan and Thatcher regimes in the US and the UK, respectively, and the emergence of rustbelt towns in the US are some examples of the institutional challenges posed by globalization. Globalization led to the strengthening of capital's position vis-à-vis labor and the state, as the primary concern for states was the maintenance of the economic system through profit-generating resolutions and reconfigurations.

A significant portion of the globalization literature focuses on the retreat of the state under the process of globalization. Two poles of the discussion refer to the withering away of the state and the ever-increasing importance of the state. The first approach regards market actors and institutions as the central governing bodies of the global order and support a minimal role for the state in the economy. To a certain extent, the argument is operationally valid, given the changing meaning of state sovereignty, the meaninglessness of national borders vis-à-vis capital and to a lesser extent labor mobility, and the emergence of new jurisdictions outside of the realm of the state judiciary to govern disputes among global parties. The shrinking of the state as such seems nothing but natural under circumstances where state regulation and arbitration lose their utility, and where the heavy-handed bureaucracy cannot meet the needs of globally operating systems. The second approach toward the existence and role of the state under globalization argues otherwise, namely, that increasing inequality within and between countries suggests an ever-increasing need for states. The social and economic polarization between the countries of the North and the Global South, the intensity of competition among the countries of the Global South to attract further capital investment so as to incorporate themselves into the global economy, the enforcement and pressure coming from global actors, whether they are multinational corporations or supranational organizations, suggests a need for the state to represent the interests of its constituents. Globalization discourse focuses heavily on liberal objectives of growth and development in general and investment and profit in particular, yet there is hardly any reference to redistribution and reallocation mechanisms. Deteriorating income in the lower and middle ranks of all societies proves that inequality is not to be resolved by corporate social responsibility or non-governmental charity. The state, despite the presence of several organizational and jurisdictional challenges, remains to be a relevant actor in the global order.

The current state of the global economy suggests a comeback for the state rather than a retreat. The primary source of security during global economic crisis has been state intervention, even if the term "bail-out" is preferred. States have been instrumental in the management of the global economic crisis in two respects. First, states have intervened in financial affairs by bailing out banks and financial institutions that were in collapse. This was done by taking over their debt and pursuing the necessary monetary policies for the maintenance of the system. Second, several countries affected by the global economic crisis have observed their governments use austerity policies. States have contributed to the management of the global economic crisis by resorting to austerity, albeit in an indirect manner. States have deliberately and inadvertently intervened in the market for the sake of avoiding a massive collapse. The particular mode of intervention the states have chosen worked to the benefit of capital at the expense of labor, including those in and out of the labor market, the working poor, and immigrant labor: the wretched of the market.[3] Why have states chosen to intervene in this particular manner? What does the combination of the bail-out of large corporations and the austerity policies imply about the changing role of the state? How will the state position itself vis-à-vis capital and labor in the future? How will the state re-regulate the market? Is it possible for the state to take back control of redistribution in the future?

The conventional dichotomy of the state versus the market, state capitalism versus the market economy, or the free market versus state intervention will provide limited insight into the nature of the contemporary global order. There are diverse efforts at social and economic reorganization that have taken and continue to take place outside the realms of the market and the state. Despite their unstructured and sporadic nature, these efforts suggest the possibility of the non-capitalist market and non-state redistribution. With further intensification, what may be in the making is an unconventional regulation of the market through the very "visible hand" of the people. For a better understanding of this, one only need look at the way the global economic crisis challenges the conventional capital-labor dichotomy.

Panitch and Gindin refer to three major shortcomings in the Marxist analysis of economic crisis. First, Marxist crisis theorists fail to see the long-term impact of the complementary relationship between domestic consumption and capital accumulation. The postwar boom is one good example of how domestic consumption fed capital accumulation and undermined a potential class conflict between capital and labor. Second, the rejection of the state's relative autonomy and its perception as an instrument of capitalist class prevents the Marxist analysis from understanding the consequences of state intervention in times of economic crisis. The way states have intervened in the economy during the global economic crisis is totally different from the way they intervened during the Great Depression. This difference requires an in-depth analysis of the causes and the consequences of economic crisis. Finally, a focus on the concentration and centralization of capital that a disregards underconsumptionist tendencies provides only a partial analysis of economic crisis. For Panitch and Gindin, these limitations of Marxist crisis analysis remain to this day and hence prevent a deeper understanding and opening up of Marxist theory with the inclusion of new variables (Panitch and Gindin 2010).

There has been considerable consensus on the inevitability of class analysis in exposing the political and social consequences of the global economic crisis. In Marxist analysis, this kind of analysis is central in explaining historical progress on a macro level, and the social and material underpinnings of this progression at various lower levels of social organization. The concept of class as a social structure and the constituents of class as being categorized on the basis of their relationship to the means of production in Marxist terms, or to party and status in Weberian terms, has been significantly modified to represent more than the conventional capital-labor dichotomy. To stick with class analysis only and disregard factors intensifying the meaning of this binary opposition may lead to reductionism in Marxist thinking. The definition of class needs to be renewed in such a way as to encompass contemporary social and material relations surrounding it and move past the regarding of class relations as a categorical imperative. A number of social and economic challenges to the current system make it important for the concept of class to be incorporated, as a variable, into the analysis of economic crises.

Four major issues require attention for a comprehensive approach toward understanding the global economic crisis. Although these issues are interrelated, they need to be handled separately for analytical purposes. The first issue is the growth of the world's population at a rate never seen before and the consequences of this for the management of the global economic crisis. A second issue is the immigration currently taking place on a global scale and the changing size, range and nature of immigration. This also has significant implications in terms of labor mobility, wealth generation, redistribution and other policy responses necessary on more immediate grounds. Third, consumption, whether seen as a derivative of the growing world population or as a demand-generating economic activity, holds significant political, economic, and social consequences. The question then comes down to "to consume or not to consume?" without a clear answer. Finally, increasing awareness of these issues and more, including growing inequality, increasing authoritarianism, governmental weaknesses, and the militarization of police forces against civilians, generate sporadic occurrences of social movements and subsequent demands for democracy. Political challenges may seem unrelated to economic crisis, but in the end politics serves an economic function as a means to maintain the dangerous classes.

With regard to the first issue, the world's population has reached an all-time high and continues to grow, albeit at a slower pace. Life expectancy has more than doubled in the last few decades due to improved healthcare systems. The high fertility rates of the 1960s were effective in generating population growth around the world on a global scale. Next to this massive growth, the regional distribution of the world's population significantly influenced the global distribution of wealth – hence the existence of income inequality. However, at present, the aging of the world's population together with a declining fertility rate poses major problems for the global economy. In only a few decades, a massive portion of the world's population will be in need of a whole host of financial and health-related services, whereas the manpower in productive capacity to maintain these services will diminish, which dims hopes for the question of distribution. Brooks maintains that demographics together with productivity growth have an impact on international capital flows. The saving behavior of the aging population is has a direct impact on capital flows, especially for countries where a major segment of the population is aging (Brooks 2003). There are two major consequences of currently changing global demographics. First, the future will see a decline in long-term economic growth due to an aging population and a declining workforce. Second, consumer spending is expected to slow down for the same reasons, leading to a decline in demand and severe challenges for businesses (Lee and Mason 2010).

Precautionary measures against these demographic challenges have to take into account generational and regional variations: "These demographic pressures can be substantially offset only if both rich and poor countries undertake profound and far-reaching changes in working arrangements, lifestyles, business practices, and government policies" (Eberstadt 2010: 54). The policies that need to be pursued cannot be universal or macroeconomic; instead, they have to cover basic elements of human development, including improvements in education, widespread access to healthcare advances, and the voluntary extension of working life through healthy aging and knowledge production. According to Eberstadt, "such an approach must focus on augmenting human capital by expanding education, improving health conditions, and creating an economic environment in which greater returns can be generated by the world's precious human resources (Eberstadt 2010: 64).

The second issue that requires attention in regards to the global economic crisis is global migration. Despite the well-known argument that labor mobility is rather limited vis-à-vis capital mobility, technological improvements of the global era have enabled faster and more efficient means of transportation for individuals. More people are able to travel greater distances in shorter periods of time and at much more affordable rates compared to a few decades ago. The improvements in information technology and surveillance techniques have further contributed to the easing of individual mobility. Sources of motivation for immigrants have diversified with globalization; better economic standards and human security remain primary pull factors for migrants. It becomes much more difficult to trace migration networks with respect to pull and push factors given the outreach of the global economic crisis and the penetration of networks around the world with the aid of advanced technologies.

Several observations are noteworthy regarding the relationship between the global economic crisis and global migration. As the global economic crisis has meant a decline in employment opportunities and a fall in income levels, this has a negative impact on migration flows (Ghosh 2010). Koser draws attention to three major changes in global migration patterns: a reduction in overall migration flows, a slowdown in the growth of remittances, and an acceleration of brain drain (Koser 2009). As economic conditions deteriorate, host countries tend to limit migration flows by tightening border controls, establishing immigrant quotas, conducting tests for occupational backgrounds or granting work permits more selectively (Ghosh 2010). Also, anti-immigrant public opinion intensifies during an economic crisis, as has recently been seen in Greece, Spain, and the US (Dadush and Falcao 2009). It is also important to note that when legal means of immigration are limited, those seeking better a better future for themselves and their families resort to illegal means of immigration, as is commonly the case of those currently fleeing Syria, Afghanistan, Iraq, Egypt, and Libya.

Much remains to be investigated regarding the relationship between the global economic crisis and immigration. For the purposes of this book, the status of immigrant labor requires particular attention for three major reasons because of how it has been affected by the global economic crisis. First, immigrant labor in the host country occupies a unique position in the labor market, predominantly in low-skill, low-income positions. The number of immigrant workers in the labor market may decrease competition among native workers. Second, migrant remittances making up $200 billion each year is a significant contribution to the economies of home countries (Koser 2009). Finally, the acceleration of brain drain during economic crisis requires focused immigration management and policymaking on both sides of the migration network.

Consumerism has been deliberately used as an instrument of demand generation for the sustaining of profit maximization since the heyday of globalization. One major outcome of consumerism has been the widening gap between the rich and the poor. Consumerism has increased the dependency of less developed countries on advanced capitalist countries on a macro level. The overvalorization of innovative technologies and designer goods from advanced capitalist countries to be consumed by masses in less developed countries is suggestive of this dependent relationship. The privatization of public services, including healthcare, pension systems, education and even infrastructure-related services such as water and electricity, has expanded the margins of consumerism. Given the outreach of the global economic crisis, falling unemployment and declining incomes, together with austerity measures that limit government spending, the main question becomes: How will the system recuperate under conditions of declining consumption? The use of consumption for demand generation has to change if there is to be a more socially conscious and environmentally sound understanding of consumerism that will support the rearrangement of production.

How do corporations respond to economic crisis? What are their priorities in building responsive strategies? How do these priorities impact workers, and further, the households that depend on these businesses for their welfare? The premise of neoliberal globalization has been capital's increasing ability (through increasing mobility) to expand its profit margins, access cheaper resources, whether natural or human, and benefit from ever-expanding marketing opportunities in the remotest corners of the world. A variety of business strategies have been employed with an end to expanding business networks since the onset of globalization. Capital mobility was realized in the form of mergers and acquisitions, company buyouts, the establishment of subsidiaries in cost-effective geographies, and franchising as a means of expanding both production and marketing capacity. Outsourcing and subcontracting have been less formal and more cost-effective outlets of expansion, where companies have further diminished production costs and their liability against possible market fluctuations. The concentration of capital in the hands of a few MNCs in each sector together with the centralization of capital in core countries, with only a minuscule portion being invested in the periphery, indicates what has been called the "unequal development" by Frank (1978) and the "ceaseless accumulation of capital" by Wallerstein (1974). A critical view on capital mobility exposes the illusion of development, employment and skill formation, and the reality of structural dependency, and it belies the mainstream liberal creed on capital's contribution in generating development and employment on the periphery.

Corporate responses to global economic crisis are important in exposing the capacity of market actors to intervene in the current state of affairs and the more immediate challenges their responses may create for labor. To what extent these responses result in long-term structural transformations in the capitalist world economy remains to be seen. More important here is the extent to which they have been able to reverse the impact of the crisis.

An in-depth evaluation of the corporate strategies and the response alternatives has to take into consideration a combined set of exogenous and endogenous factors defining the corporate setting. The former will refer to government initiatives, labor market structure, the nature of world demand, sector-based market dynamics such as competition, seasonality, and links with auxiliary sectors, while the latter will cover the organization of the corporation, its geographical outreach, the combination of its financial assets, and the nature of the labor input it requires in both qualitative and quantitative terms. One can hardly expect a coherent typological model of corporate responses from such a multivariate analysis. Therefore, a labor perspective will help refine the analytical basis of this overview.

Panitch underlines three major characteristics of the global economic crisis on a macro level that can be regarded as the cause, which in return generates an effect on the corporate side.[4] For Panitch, the crisis is not one of capitalist profitability, nor does it generate massive unemployment as was the case during Great Depression. Also, the crisis did not lead to the breakdown of capitalist globalization (Panitch 2014: 8). The macro-level outlook does not necessarily indicate a retreat of corporations from the global networks they operate in, nor does it halt the operation of business. The corporate objective is to achieve immediate remedies to overcome the profit-related challenges and demand fluctuations in the market. The global economic crisis in its current state does not hint at a structural transformation of the system; instead, it is more suggestive of geographical, sectoral and corporate level shifts.

Corporate strategies can also be distinguished as short-term and long-term approaches beyond the level of the responses themselves. While short-term approaches may include temporary lay-offs, tighter management of product cycles, and increased flexibility in wages and benefits, long-term approaches may include shifts in the choice of subsidiaries and heavier reliance on temporary and contract labor, and they may even go as far as including plant closures or sell-outs. All this diversity of possibilities is further complicated by industry-specific dynamics, such as the geographical dispersion of the division of labor, the impact of the economic crisis on industry-specific demand, and the availability of alternative strategies to cope with the crisis. Both short-term and long-term approaches can be feasible in the case of the textile industry, but the same cannot be said in the case of aviation. There is little room for managerial maneuvering in industries where production dynamics have long been saturated and stable on the basis of production and market demand.

The causal relationship between the global economic crisis and the corporate strategies that have devised against it is much more complex on the corporate level. Grewal and Tansuhaj compare the impact of market orientation and strategic flexibility in confronting the economic crisis by evaluating the impact of the Asian economic crisis in Thailand. Market orientation proves to be of utility under conditions of "high demand uncertainty or high technology uncertainty," while strategic flexibility is more efficient in dealing with "high competitive intensity" (Grewal and Tansuhaj 2001: 76). The former is more of a pre-crisis approach and the latter is more effective during the crisis. The utility of different strategies during different phases of crisis suggests that a complementary approach is best in confronting major crises such as the Asian crisis or the current global economic crisis.

The impact of the global economic crisis on corporate performance is yet to be seen. There are signs of recovery in world trade and investment, as well as in growth rates. Still, the macroeconomic performance of some national economies has yet to improve, and many demand-related challenges lie ahead. It is very difficult to have a full understanding of post-crisis corporate behavior, but one can benefit from certain analytical parameters in evaluating the existing data. The essential premise of corporate actors is to sustain their profit margins, which can be done by decreasing costs and generating demand. Two tasks will be undertaken in the rest of this section: first, cost-cutting responses to the global economic crisis will be evaluated; and second, management strategies regarding market expansion and demand generation will be scrutinized. The gradual recovery of FDI from 2009 onward indicates that investment continues to grow globally, with significant regional and country-based variations. The following is an effort to trace both qualitative and quantitative changes in corporate behavior.

How do corporations manage their finances in times of economic crisis? Three major interventions stand out when it comes to corporate alternatives: they will close down international plants because of management, transaction and transportation costs; they will let employees go; and they lower the wages being paid to their employees. What may be the most rational alternative in terms of finances may not be so in terms of the overall operation of the corporation. The environment created by economic crisis is not necessarily a limitation on the internationalization strategies of corporations. Corporations often resort to new strategies of internationalization instead of completely abandoning the idea internationalization altogether. They rely less on the institutional and legal reliability of governments and the macroeconomic stability of national economies, and they rely more on global indicators, the possibility of finding joint venture partners, the working out comparative costs, and the geographic dispersion of target markets (Williams and Martinez 2012: 75).

Boyle and McDonnell (2013), drawing upon an empirical analysis of MNCs in Australia, found out that the most stated impact of the global economic crisis on MNC activities was the reduction of international travel followed by a reduction in recruitment. Plant closures, outsourcing and off-shoring were other responses, albeit at lower frequencies. The authors compare the behavior of corporations within liberal market economies and coordinated market economies, and suggest that the organizational responses of firms such as plant closure, relocation and outsourcing depend on whether they operate in a purely competitive and market-dominated institutional context or whether they operate in one that includes non-market relationships and networks. Burgess and Connell refer to human resources strategies against the global economic crisis and distinguish between hard responses and soft responses: "Where hard responses are associated with labour shedding and major organizational restructuring, soft responses are associated with labour retention and investment towards productivity improvements" (Burgess and Connell, 2013: 163). Shen and D'Netto studied the human resource management of 184 Chinese export-oriented enterprises following the global economic crisis. The most common response observed in a majority of cases was retrenchment in the form of cutting down off-the-job training costs for low managers and other employees, and reducing individual performance goals and fringe benefits (Shen and D'Netto 2012). Whether a corporation opts for hard or soft responses depends on a number of factors, including demand fluctuations, network relations with suppliers and other producers in the value chain, and various macroeconomic indicators regarding the economic crisis. Shifts in government policy toward labor market regulation and the provision of subsidies are also relevant in shaping corporate responses to crisis.

As far as financial adjustments are concerned, corporate responses may differ based on region and sector as well as the nature of the corporation itself. Lower profit margins or lower productivity rates may lead to plant closures, although many companies see this as a last resort considering the damage this may do to their image and the need for resource relocation. Employment-related cost-cutting may come in various forms, such as cuts to training expenses and benefits, temporary layoffs, or permanent layoffs. There are two very important limitations on corporations' liberty to employ cost-cutting measures. The less important limitation has to do with corporate image and the negative publicity generated by plant closures and layoffs. The second and more serious limitation has to do with the impact of cost-cutting on market performance and on demand generation. There is a very delicate balance between profits and demand, which needs to be the premise of business strategies in times of crisis:

> Profits and rents need outlets for investment and large capacity needs increasing demand for its absorption: unless the absorption problem is solved potential capacity cannot be realized into actual capacity and actual income. As potential and actual capacities grow, equilibrium can only be maintained if demand grows accordingly in order to absorb the

growing capacity. For demand to grow in line with potential capacity there must be a congenial income distribution.

(Ietto-Gillies 2010: 912)

Although our focus has been more on the response of MNCs to the global economic crisis, these responses have a spillover effect on domestic firms of various sizes. The spillover effect may generate more closures and unemployment, as production costs would have priority over corporate image. As domestic firms depend more on local factors and have less mobility opportunities, the spillover effect would result in more dire social and economic consequences for labor in domestic firms.

The spatial organization of the capitalist world economy is largely shaped by MNCs. In this economic network, governments may choose to promote and lubricate the functioning of the system through capital mobility, or they may intervene in ways that will cause friction and expel international investors. In either case, the corporations will be the dominant actors, at liberty to move their capital to profitable geographies. Harris summarizes this situation in one straightforward research question: "Has there developed a nationally centered recovery policy, or has the crisis been used to reconfigure corporate combinations that strengthen the transnational character of the global economy?" (Harris 2010: 395). Returning to the political economy of national protectionism of the Great Depression era can hardly be apprehended under the current global state of interconnectedness. Harris draws upon empirical evidence from the global automotive industry and exposes the interrelations of TNCs: through joint ventures, manufacturing plants in numerous national settings, targeting multiple national markets irrespective of the brand's country of origin, and employing labor on a transnational scale. The growing monopoly of MNCs over the world economy indicates that the national identity of companies or the national context of labor or demand does not necessarily determine the flow of capital from one location to another. This monopoly is not limited to the automotive industry; it also applies to pharmaceuticals, electronics and footwear (among others). HSBC's recent decision to cut up to 25,000 jobs globally to concentrate their assets and activities in Asia is another example where capital reaps the benefit of relocation irrespective of the costs to labor (Pylas 2015).

Economic crises generate risks for corporations, but they also bring new opportunities for reinvestment, accessing new markets, and product differentiation. The smaller firms that barely survive economic crises become affordable deals for larger corporations like MNCs that have more resilience to the effects of economic crises due to the domino effect from the financial markets to the real economy. Wan and Yiu looked at the relationship between corporate acquisitions and firm performance during the Asian economic crisis, and point out that firms that are more aggressive during an economic crisis regard acquisitions as an opportunity (Wan and Yiu 2009). Business approaches such as strategic management or, more specifically, strategic flexibility focus on the way negative environmental factors can be translated into business opportunities (Chung and Beamish 2008). The flexibility coming from international investment comes both in the form of FDI and export investments: "Consistent with the nature of these investments, a primary benefit of firms' foreign direct investments is the ability to shift production from one location to another in response to negative changes in the environment, while an essential advantage of exporting investments is the ability to rapidly identify and sell to new customers in foreign locations" (Lee and Makhija 2009: 552). Lee and Makhija evaluated the international investment of South Korean firms after the Korean economic crisis, and they conclude that both forms of flexibility improve the chances of corporations in coping with economic crisis. Economic crises do generate challenges for corporations, yet the sustained continuity of GPNs, GVCs, and the global division of labor, and the unlimited mobility of capital provide an ample amount of risk-hedging and reinvestment opportunities for corporations.

Several studies show that the impact of the global economic crisis has not been as detrimental in Asia, Latin America and developing countries as it has been elsewhere. Zhao et al. studied the impact of the global economic crisis on the financial performance of MNCs in an extensive empirical study that covered 729 multinational and 2,625 domestic firms. They concluded that firms which relocated their sales in Asia and China after the economic crisis received an increase in returns on their assets (Zhao et al. 2015). The resilience of these economies to the negative impact of the current economic crisis has been attributed to a number of factors including macroeconomic management (Alvarez and De Gregorio 2014: 521) and governments' support of the market, labor subsidies, and austerity measures. The relatively better performance of developing economies comes as no surprise in a system which heavily relies on the availability of cost-cutting resources and ravenous markets. Corporations making use of the most efficient instruments of strategic management and flexibility face no difficulty in relocating to areas that will be profitable on both accounts. The perseverance of the Chinese economy during the global economic crisis is due not only to the capital it has attracted for the last few decades but to the size and nature of its domestic market.

GVC approaches may once again become instrumental in analyzing corporate responses to economic crisis. GVCs help expose the functional and the spatial shifts in corporate organization during and after crisis. Sass and Szalavetz argue that the financial crisis and the consolidation of GVCs, both geographically and organizationally, have led advanced capitalist economies to specialize more in high-skill sectors, and less developed economies to continue to remain in low-skill, low-wage sectors (Sass and Szalavetz 2014: 65). When this outcome is combined with the increasing outsourcing and offshoring preferences of MNCs, it is hardly surprising to see the rise of global inequality after economic crisis, GVC consolidation, and MNC managerial choices.

The solidarity economy as an alternative

Alternative production systems are the primary components of the solidarity economy. These systems differ from corporate structures and rely primarily on the real economy, irrespective of the latter's sectoral composition. These production systems are based on the principle of local focus, and they benefit from the resources that are locally available, whether in terms of natural resources or human resources. The solidarity economy was defined in the Introduction as a non-market, non-state entity, and the most important reason behind its rejection of existing entities is its objective of maintaining an independent, autonomous code of conduct. Being dependent on the public sector or the market actors for economic reasons would sacrifice social objectives at the expense of economic premises. The state may be relevant in regulating the economic sphere or providing a legal framework for organizational purposes, but dependence on the state for any reason would jeopardize the solidarity economy's political cause. Establishing an autonomous stance in the economic sphere, however, requires a firm stance against interventions from existing institutions.

This section will discuss cooperatives, community-building corporations, profit-sharing alternatives, employee buyouts and the idea of economic citizenship as an alternative production system, where a solidaristic production scheme may flourish. All of these cases have existed before the onset of globalization. None of these examples are completely non-market or non-state alternatives. Governments in some countries have provided a legal framework and socio-economic incentives for the flourishing of these economic alternatives. In others, these alternatives have transformed into capitalist enterprises, although they have maintained their commitment to pillars of social responsibility, redistribution and cooperation. The task undertaken here is by no means to state the obvious or reinvent the wheel; rather, it is to understand to what extent these alternatives may be a remedy to the detrimental impact of neoliberal globalization.

One of the most important alternatives to existing production systems are cooperatives. They can hardly be regarded as a novel invention. Given the limitations of contemporary economic organization, their importance and relevance as a viable alternative is increasing day by day. There are a number of guiding principles of cooperatives: they are voluntary and seek open membership. They are democratically controlled, where each member has one vote, with relative autonomy and independence from state and other institutional mechanisms. Economic participation does not only take place in production but also in ownership, decision-making and distribution. Socially, cooperatives pursue community development at the local level (Quijano 2006). A significant component of this development agenda is the provision of education and, more specifically, to cater to the effective participation of members. Cooperatives are understood to be local and small-scale; in successful cases, part of their agenda is to promote cooperation on the national and international levels (Santos and Rodriguez-Garavito 2006).

Cooperatives can be established in various economic sectors and with the purpose of fulfilling of a number of community interests. The aforementioned principles of cooperative operation are definitive, yet the field on which this operation takes place shows variation. Agricultural cooperatives are the most common form of cooperative, where producers in one locale form a cooperative to market their harvests in a collective manner. Especially when agrarian produce is very much locally harvested, cooperatives provide their members the advantage of accessing the external market and the relative protection of being middlemen at different nodes of commodity chains. Coffee and cocoa producer cooperatives are important examples of this. Similarly, fishing cooperatives are also important for communities that rely heavily on the sea and the earnings they make from fishing. These cooperatives help ensure all members have a steady income, steady trade with continuous demand from a set number of customers and overall financial stability regardless of seasonal shifts and natural challenges. The interests in such cooperatives are not exclusively economic. This kind of solidarity also helps generate awareness about issue such as the environment and sustainability.

There are also cooperatives that are more about community needs than production processes. Housing cooperatives are established, where members create an income pool to be used in the construction of low-cost homes to overcome housing problems, especially in urban settings. The most well-known example of a housing cooperative is Coop-City in Bronx, New York. The construction of Coop-City began in 1964, and the project was completed in 1973. The main concern was to overcome the housing problem in the city by providing low-cost housing to those working in the city. Although Coop-City is known to be the largest housing cooperative in the world to this day, there are various other examples around the world where housing cooperatives were established to provide affordable housing to their members.

There are a growing number of cooperatives beyond the more common producer cooperatives and the consumer cooperatives that cater to economically marginal groups. The most common examples are women's cooperatives, where goods and services produced by women are collectively marketed and sold based on cooperative principles. The best-known example of this form of cooperative is the Self-Employed Women's Association (SEWA), which will be discussed in Chapter 5. However, there are other women's cooperatives in Turkey, Uganda, Niger and elsewhere. Once cooperatives organize and settle for a certain time, they tend to generate a spillover effect into new locations, new cooperatives or new economic sectors. An agricultural cooperative may lead to a transportation cooperative, where the produce would be collected and transported to the external market. A producer cooperative may lead to a retail cooperative, or a worker cooperative may form a housing cooperative to help its members access better housing. The spillover effect, after the success of the initial cooperative, may lead to a cooperative or a credit union, where the constituents seek to control their own finances. In this sense, the way cooperatives move from single entities to networks indicates that the most immediate, local, and grassroots organizations become the building blocks of a whole new economic structure.

In fact, cooperative enterprises are not new. Currently, they employ more than 250 million people worldwide, with a turnover of $2.2 trillion. In the G-20 countries, 12% of total employment is in cooperatives. The number of cooperatives exceeds 30,000 in the US, and they provide more than 2 million jobs (International Co-operative Alliance 2015). The numbers could very well be extended: cross country analysis would reveal more as to the industrial distribution of cooperatives and the functional diversity they serve. Cooperatives in advanced capitalist countries like the US or France operate in industrial sectors, and those in less developed countries like Indonesia and Kenya are clustered in agricultural production. Therefore, more than the size of the economy or the level of economic development, local factors are central to the building of cooperatives.

There are four major advantages of cooperatives vis-à-vis existing corporate structures. First, the coexistence of non-capitalist principles with market economies requires a social concern for production alongside an economic one. Second, worker cooperatives cut down on managerial costs and are more adaptive to flexible, segmented and changing market conditions. Third, the fact the redistributive mechanisms are more efficient in cooperative systems decreases inequality, and in return it generates economic growth. Finally, cooperatives provide non-economic benefits to their members; therefore, what corporate social responsibility seeks to do on a limited budget and as a complimentary function is organized as a central component in cooperatives (Santos and Rodriguez-Garavito 2006).

The community development corporation (CDC) is another alternative economic model to corporate capitalism. The definitive features of CDCs is that they are non-profit and they focus on the social and economic well-being of the community. The CDC also operates within the market economy rather than as an alternative to it. A major portion of CDCs in the US operate as instruments of urban regeneration and revitalization programs or as mechanisms for improving the infrastructure of the community (Johnson 2004); they also provide benefits beyond the material, such as empowerment, bonding (through social capital), and the creation of a sense of "responsible citizenship" (Serlen 2011: 351–355). Outside of the US, development banks or development corporations work to organize and market the local production of agricultural produce and arts and crafts. Andhra Pradesh Handicrafts Development Corporation in India is one such example, where a state-initiated corporation organizes arts and crafts production at the local level to generate community empowerment.[5] Similar projects are initiated by governments and development banks in a number of developing countries. These programs prioritize community development and skill formation only as a pathway to global integration and market integration. Therefore, community development is not an end in itself, but rather a means to an end.

Cooperatives and CDCs emerge outside of the corporate setting. There are also alternative production and ownership models emerging from within the corporate world. Profit-sharing provides relative immunity to workers from market dynamics. Weitzman argues that profit-sharing schemes have "some natural tendencies towards sustained, non-inflationary, market-oriented full employment." Weitzman's conclusions regarding wages in a profit-sharing economy are not as optimistic. The wage structure in profit-sharing schemes lacks stability and therefore requires monetary intervention to stabilize incomes (Weitzman 1985). The literature on profit-sharing also concentrates on two other arguments. According to Blanchflower and Oswald, these are the morale and productivity argument, and the wage flexibility argument (Blanchflower and Oswald 1987: 3–5). The morale and productivity argument suggests that workers who become a part of a profit-sharing scheme will be sharing risks and responsibilities; therefore, their commitment to work and their loyalty to the business will be greater. The wage flexibility argument suggests that in times of market fluctuations workers will face fluctuating income yet will be secure in their jobs, for there will be a trade-off between steady employment and steady income.

It is beyond the scope of this study to evaluate the whole set of theoretical and empirical studies on profit-sharing. Profit-sharing helps control market risks for employment, but it can hardly be conceptualized as part of the alternative economy. Most importantly, profit-sharing operates under the assumption of a capitalist economy. It is not a non-market alternative. Second, the premise of profit-sharing is less social and more economic. Loyalty to the workplace and the possible increase of productivity has a social dimension, but the primary objective is not labor amelioration but the stability of corporate capitalism. When considering the intensity of competition under global capitalism, the clash of interests between the profit-sharing workers and the profit-seeking company will be more apparent. Questions regarding autonomy at work, workplace democracy, and employee empowerment have not been central to the discussions of profit-sharing schemes. There are references to co-determination, yet it can hardly be thought of as a prerequisite for profit-sharing. Hence, profit-sharing does not challenge the conventional inequalities at work, whether on an economic or social basis.

Several other possibilities and arrangements can be discussed that challenge corporate ownership and encourage employee financial participation. Employee stock ownership plans (ESOPs) are one way that employees financially participate in ownership. While the ESOP may generate further loyalty to the company, increase productivity and serve as an alternative redistribution mechanism, it may also serve as a financial outlet for the corporation, and hence prioritize the financial well-being of the company rather than its redistributive impact. There have been numerous instances where ESOPs have failed in terms of generating greater employee involvement or loyalty to the company (Trewhitt 2000; Sengupta et al. 2007; McCarthy and Palcic 2012). Challenging corporate ownership by way of employee shareholding or employee ownership imply two different paths. In employee shareholding, the employee becomes an equity holder sharing the revenues and the expenses of the corporation. In the case of employee ownership, the employee enters the equation by way of labor input. Therefore, the crux of the matter lies in redefining ownership in such a way that labor will translate into governance (Boatright 2004).

Companies running into financial difficulty or an uncertain future due to succession issues are often bought by employees and transformed into worker cooperatives. Successful examples can be traced to Argentina (Monteagudo 2008; Vieta 2014), Greece or Turkey. Especially in times of economic crisis, where one tends to see company close downs, employee buy outs may become the last exit before the road to unemployment. Employees focus on long-term gains instead of short-term benefits (Bradley and Gelb 1985). For worker cooperatives to become a viable alternative to company closures, there has to be a developing infrastructure to promote their economic existence together with a legal institutional framework to promote their existence (Nolan et al. 2013).

Davis comes up with four major principles in his discussion of post-corporate economic organization that may serve as the pillars of future ownership models. The first principle is that "the size and location of the institution should match the size of the project" (Davis 2013: 299). The corporate conduct of the global economy has always been in favor of the bigger organizations; however, bigger is not necessarily better. Considering the extra management costs, transportation costs, and the detrimental impact on the environment, bigger businesses become more costly both economically and socially. The labor impact runs much deeper and has been discussed in some detail earlier. Davis argues instead that the organization of production should remain local. In his second principle, Davis argues that form should follow function. Formal organizations and corporate structures may not necessarily be the only viable options for a successful economic organization. Third, Davis states that high-level carbon emissions imply a return to the local level. It is not only the carbon emissions *per se*, but the whole environmental degradation emerging from the global economy through transportation, consumerism and pollution that forces the economy to return to its local origins. Finally, local control must preside over central control within a larger global network (Davis 2013: 299–300).

Industrial citizenship or occupational citizenship stands as another conceptual intervention on alternative production systems. In reformulating the concept of citizenship, the focus is more on the definition and framing of rights and responsibilities associated with work and employment status than on building an alternative production system. Marshall's reference to industrial citizenship remains a seminal beginning to this discussion (Marshall 2009); the literature on the issue has moved along in parallel to the transformation of work and labor relations. For Zhang and Lillie, "industrial citizenship is both a status, granting rights within a defined territorially based (political) community, and a process and relationship between workers and employers" (Zhang and Lillie 2015: 95). The idea of industrial citizenship as a more nuanced derivative of social citizenship or economic citizenship underlines the importance of the right to work, the sharing of work and the access to appropriate compensation and benefits in return for work. The underlying assumption of industrial citizenship is the existence of a nation-state and a market economy because of its relational and spatial definition. The concept of industrial citizenship, even if backed by a legal framework or enforced through an institutional structure, offers limited space for the precariat – those in non-standard employment situations and the marginalized groups in the labor market – who are already deprived of their basic citizenship rights, let alone industrial citizenship rights, given the weakening of the nation-state in terms of its sovereignty and territoriality together with the overriding domination of market interests (Crouch 1998).

Bertocchi and Strozzi's empirical analysis on the evolution of citizenship provides noteworthy conclusions as to how citizenship transforms with respect to endogenous factors. The authors define citizenship as a legal institution and by doing so they underline the way this legal structure responds to changing social and political dynamics, such as migration, border stability and the dominant legal tradition in a given country: "By showing that citizenship laws are shaped not only by the broader legal origins but also by other institutions, such as the internal system of political rights and the international system of relations as reflected by state borders, we also establish that different institutions are interrelated" (Bertocchi and Strozzi 2010). The growth of illegal immigration and the informal employment of illegal immigrants is a major challenge to the debate on industrial citizenship, and it raises the question of the extent to which citizenship, as a legal institution, can face the challenges that illegal immigration poses.

Standing's conceptualization of occupational citizenship develops from a well-known discussion of precarization at work and the accompanying struggles at work (Standing 2009). Standing traces the roots of occupational citizenship in Durkheim's idea of professional groups becoming the source of social solidarity, and he distinguishes between two paths of social organization, the occupational view and the labor view:

> Thinking of occupation builds in consideration of inter-worker and "horizontal" relationships, between peers and between networks who share common interests. The labourist model focused on hierarchical or "vertical" relationships, between capital and labour, bosses and workers, employers and employees, managers and the "shop floor."
>
> (Standing 2009: 253)

The roots of the occupational model go back historically to the guild structure, where occupational association provided a framework for the quality of goods, the artisanship, and the value and quantity of trade. Occupational associations and chambers of commerce still undertake similar tasks on the basis of occupational membership and networking.

Standing emphasizes a number of normative issues in occupational citizenship. Occupational citizenship will carry an element of authenticity within a multicultural setting of identity, and hence will serve as an outlet for individuals to move among and interact with different identities. Education should provide both specialization and skill formation for individuals to be able to do several kinds of work and not simply to be put into the labor force. Occupational citizenship allows for an improved social organization of time so that activities of work and non-work, work and leisure, and the production and reproduction of labor are distributed to all rather than granted to a few. The progress of one's career need not be imposed from a mainstream business approach; instead, universal socioeconomic rights and basic income may ensure the appropriate pace of progress. Finally, citizenship is about rights. Therefore, occupational citizenship pursues developmental freedom: "freedom from the power of others, and freedom to retain the capacity for choice itself" (Standing 2009: 262). This, according to Standing, will provide individuals with the right to determine their own motivations, paths, and progress in their work lives.

Although occupational citizenship is described here in a general framework, the universalism implied in this framework is highly doubtful. Whether in terms of the universal basic income discussed earlier, or in terms of the lacking of a code of ethics in the capitalist system, this type of conceptualization at a high altitude of abstraction can hardly translate into structural transformations in the capitalist world economy. Unfortunately, one can hardly speak of occupational citizenship in geographies that lack the very basic framework for citizenship. Although there is an extended discussion of occupational regulation among scholars, institutionally and legally, on both national and international levels, the way in which the transition from a labor approach to an occupational approach to the economy would take place remains a mystery.

The alternatives to the mainstream organization of production could be extended. Solidarity economies stand out among other alternatives in terms of their outreach to workers and their potential to reorganize the production process in order to channel returns to the workers. Reorganizing the production process outside of the domains of the market and the state will generate the opportunity to transform employment relations in ways that are responsive to and reflective of the needs of the workers and the structures of local communities. They may not hold the potential to become the dominant mode of production on a global scale, yet the search is not toward one universal model to replace the other. Instead, the objective is to provide the option of production outside the realm of the market whose own objectives are not necessarily economic but social.

Notes

1 For Convention 177 and 122 (and others), please see http://www.ilo.org/dyn/normlex/en/f?p=1000:12000:0::NO:::.

2 The distinction between multinational corporations and transnational corporations may be regarded as discursive for the purposes of this research. It is the role and

function of these corporate structures and their operations as indicators of the global economy that are more relevant at this point.

3 The allusion made to Fanon's *The Wretched of the Earth* (1963) is indeed intentional, as globalization reproduces the colonial relations between advanced capitalist countries and less developed parts of the world. The forms of oppression may not be as blunt; they may be hidden under the discourses of human rights, multiculturalism, and equal opportunity, but the oppression of neo-colonial networks and relations are maintained nonetheless – even if in more subtle forms.

4 Although the cause and effect relationship is not limited to corporations and also includes governments and international financial institutions, this chapter only covers the corporate response to crisis in order to expose the labor implications of policymaking.

5 Please see this development corporation's website: http://www.lepakshihandicrafts.gov.in/.

2 Redistribution

The question of redistributive justice is even more relevant under neoliberal globalization. One reason for this is the rise in global inequality and the changing nature of social inequality. It is no more a question of poverty in its basic form, but of income polarization within and between societies. Redistribution affects social indicators beyond income polarization, including indicators that pertain to human development, gender development and other indicators aggregated in millennium development goals. The mechanisms that are instrumental in fighting inequality have been significantly weakened since the 1980s, and the erosion of welfare regimes and social safety nets has further materialized in the form of austerity measures. It is in this context that alternative solidarity mechanisms are utilized as buffers against global inequality. This chapter will focus on the role of solidarity networks in fulfilling a function that was previously the responsibility of the state and the market. These networks emerge in an unstructured manner and make use of different methods and models. Functions of production and redistribution are complementary pillars of solidaristic alternatives.

Rising global inequality

Global inequality refers to the social and economic inequalities within and between nations that have become more severe with the onset of neoliberal globalization. As economic aspects of global inequality focus on income inequality and wage differentials, social aspects of global inequality refer to human development indicators and the differentials regarding living standards: "Inequality comparisons will yield very different results depending on whether we concentrate only on incomes or also on the impact of other economic and social influences on the quality of life" (Sen 1997: 389) According to Amartya Sen, evaluating inequality on the basis of income provides only a partial explanation of its structural aspects; instead, a broader conceptualization including interpersonal utility and quality of life will reveal the social and possibly more heterogeneous aspects of inequality.

Amartya Sen's critical approach toward inequality is exposed more openly when contrasted with conventional indicators of inequality. Table 2.1 shows

Table 2.1 GNI per capita PPP (current international $) by income level

Countries	*1990*	*1995*	*2000*	*2005*	*2010*	*2012*
High-income	16,335	19,503	24,517	30,464	36,006	38,841
Low-income	696	708	822	1,008	1,310	1,442
Middle-income	2,225	2,855	3,650	5,184	7,668	8,678
Upper-middle-income	2,728	3,703	4,945	7,177	11,032	12,680
Low- and middle-income	2,101	2,674	3,399	4,790	7,028	7,929
Lower-middle-income	1,741	2,065	2,480	3,451	4,848	5,369
World	5,337	6,342	7,820	9,984	12,728	13,926

World Bank Data Bank, 2015

purchasing-power-parity-(PPP)-adjusted gross national income (GNI) per capita for countries of different income levels. Time series data indicates an overall increase in GNI per capita for countries of all income levels. Two critical points stand out in this evaluation. First, the overall increase in per capita incomes does not indicate a shrinking of the gap between the high-income and the low-income countries. Second, the increase could also be attributed to an inflationist tendency in the world economy, which can generally be expressed in relation to financialization and the emergence of an economic bubble. Also, a more commonly known critique is that per capita income represents an average that does not exist in real life, as individual incomes vary based on a number of factors.

Table 2.2 shows PPP-adjusted GNI per capita distribution on a regional basis. The regional disparities remain structural as the steady increase in income levels continues over time. The regional disparities are important in showing the spatial boundaries of inclusion and exclusion in the global economy, where transition economies of Central Europe and Central Asia face a significant increase in income levels as opposed to those of South Asia and Sub-Saharan Africa, which remain structurally excluded from the global economy. Still, the mean distribution of income assumes homogeneity, which obscures the downward penetration of inequalities.

Apart from the temporal and spatial dimensions of income inequality, the polarization between the richest and the poorest countries is noteworthy. The most recent GDP per capita ranking indicates that the poorest nation has 164 times less wealth than the richest nation. Income polarization by itself demonstrates the heavily distorted nature of distribution on a global scale. Further descriptions of this polarization refer to the "top 1%," the "bottom billion," and the distribution of global wealth in these top and bottom segments of the world's population (Ortiz and Cummins 2011: 20). This polarization primarily affects the poor, women, and children.

Table 2.2 GNI per capita PPP (current international $) by region

Region	*1990*	*1995*	*2000*	*2005*	*2010*	*2012*
Central Europe & the Baltics	.	7,683	9,915	13,927	19,754	21,733
East Asia & Pacific (all income levels)	3,147	4,432	5,582	7,895	11,576	13,273
Europe & Central Asia (all income levels)	11,305	12,380	15,754	20,312	25,710	27,592
European Union	14,806	17,861	22,548	27,796	33,269	35,019
Latin America & Caribbean (all income levels)	5,712	7,169	8,369	10,092	13,077	14,355
Middle East & North Africa (all income levels)	7,433	8,488	10,283	13,062	16,360	17,492
North America	23,289	27,951	36,093	43,814	47,939	51,719
South Asia	1,202	1,550	1,997	2,812	4,127	4,646
Sub-Saharan Africa (all income levels)	1,509	1,578	1,770	2,311	2,945	3,156
World	5,337	6,342	7,820	9,984	12,728	13,926

World Bank DataBank, 2015

Table 2.3 GDP per capita ranking, PPP (current international $) in 2014

Richest Ten Countries		*Poorest Ten Countries*	
Luxembourg	97,662	Togo	1,429
Singapore	82,763	Guinea-Bissau	1,386
United Arab Emirates	67,674	Guinea	1,221
Norway	64,856	Mozambique	1,129
Switzerland	57,235	Niger	938
Hong Kong, SAR China	55,084	Liberia	841
United States of America	54,630	Malawi	822
Saudi Arabia	51,924	Burundi	770
Ireland	48,755	Democratic Republic of Congo	746
The Netherlands	47,663	Central African Republic	594

World Bank DataBank, 2015

The problem of global inequality is not new. The causal relationship between neoliberal economic globalization and the rise of global inequality has been debated for the last four decades. The liberal proponents of globalization have argued for a gradual decline of global inequality as the lower-income economies would benefit from technological spillovers and increasing employment opportunities due to global integration. More critical perspectives have argued for the rise of mechanisms of exclusion and interdependency due to the expansion of the globally integrated market. Castells' notion of the Fourth World is representative of the latter view, which argues that marginalization and exclusion will be the main results of globalization (Castells 2000).

The novelty about global inequality is the way it has been transformed by global processes. It is no more a simple gap in income distribution or level of development. There have been significant qualitative changes in inequality with the advent of globalization. Castells distinguishes various forms of inequality on the basis of redistribution and relations of production: "On the one hand, *inequality, polarization, poverty* and *misery* all pertain to the domain of relationships of distribution/consumption or differential appropriation of the wealth generated by collective effort. On the other hand, *individualization of work, over-exploitation of workers, social exclusion* and *perverse integration* are characteristic of four specific processes vis-à-vis relationships of production" (Castells 2000: 348). This is a very clear description of the nature of inequality under neoliberal economic globalization – it is not simply that one has more than the other, but that the distance between the two ends of the income spectrum is getting wider. Those at the lower end of the income spectrum will their standard of living continuously decline. Beyond the conventional distinction between rich and poor, Castells introduces a distinction between poverty and misery, where someone experiencing the latter is worse off (materially) than someone experiencing the former. This qualitative transformation of inequality is not only due to the distorted mechanisms of redistribution but also to the severe working conditions and labor relations emerging in the changing relations of production.

The key issue in Piketty's highly praised analysis is not simply how capital operates in the twenty-first century, but the way in which the capitalist system continuously reproduces inequality. Piketty, contrary to the mainstream argument about economic growth, states that "growth can create new forms of inequality: for example, fortunes can be amassed very quickly in new sectors of economic activity" (Piketty 2014: 96). The size or the extent of inequality requires particular attention together with the way inequality is justified in the capitalist system. This justification enables the continuous reproduction of inequality in a systemic manner. Piketty attributes the source of this justification to a structural distinction between a hyper-patrimonial society, where wealth is by and large inherited, and a hyper-meritocratic society, where the top ranks in redistribution are taken over by high-income labor, which he calls a "society of superstars" (Piketty 2014: 264). While wage inequality is increasing with the expansion of a wage hierarchy, wage mobility is not increasing at the same pace; hence, one either earns a very high salary or becomes a low-wage worker.

The expansion and qualitative transformation of global inequality parallels that of the global division of labor. The deindustrialization process and the rise of service industries in advanced capitalist economies has been the basis of post-industrial, middle class societies. The transfer of outdated industrial production to less developed countries, which operate on cheap labor, led to a widening wealth gap between nations based on their mode of integration into the global economy. The widening wage gaps between industry and agriculture, and the much wider social and economic divergence between industry and services indicate that contrary to the liberal argument that globalization will generate growth and employment – and hence decrease inequality – new forms and margins of inequality have been observed at all levels of social organization. On a structural level, global inequality is an issue within and between nations. Its impact is not limited to material well-being: it can also be seen in access to education, healthcare, and social safety nets.

Increasing global mobility and changing global migration dynamics also contribute to the expanding margins of global inequality (Massey et al. 1993; Korzeniewicz and Moran 2009). The mass exodus of refugees from conflict zones such as Afghanistan, Libya, Egypt and Syria to Europe has created a reserve army of labor in its most desperate state; these people take up the worst available working conditions and the least amount of income to survive. Illegal immigrants from several Latin American countries entering the US via Mexico have also become the primary source of a growing precariat, catering to the construction industry and sweatshop production in a crisis-ridden US economy. The widening developmental gap and the inattentiveness of governments to emerging social needs have pushed the marginalized masses to the illusion of a better future in a Western destination. The host societies do provide a safe haven for those running away from conflict zones, but the possibility of an economic uplift through migration is rather dim.

There has also been significant academic scrutiny over the causal relationship between the global economic crisis and the increase in global inequality. Stockhammer argues that rising inequality contributes to the emergence of global economic crisis, and he defines four major channels through which it does so: "a downward pressure on aggregate demand;" extended periods of current account deficits in some countries; households maintaining social consumption standards despite significant decline in real wages (hence a massive increase in household debt); and, finally, an increasing tendency among richer households to make risky investments (Stockhammer 2012). Income inequality does translate into different economic choices and decisions for unequal households, yet the causal link between inequality and economic crisis only provides a partial explanation of the whole economic picture. There is more of a reciprocal relationship between economic crisis and inequality, and this relationship of reciprocity repeats itself in a cyclical manner. Economic crises in general are risky settings in which market actors, mainly corporations, decrease their investments as a way of avoiding risk, something which in turn generates a falling employment rate. A decline in investment coupled with rising unemployment has a direct impact on households' economic decisions, as a result consumption, and overall demand falls. Governments, as administrators of economic policy, may resort to investment-generating policies in the market to reverse the plunging economic cycle, or they may increase their spending on social safety nets to attack inequality. Either market functions are restored for a stable and secure market economy, or public spending secures greater social solidarity. The response to crisis is at least as important as the causal relationship between inequality and crisis, whether the former is geared toward the market or toward the public. The adoption of austerity measures in several countries irrespective of their development levels suggests that governments have chosen to forsake social safety nets in order to maintain market functions. The policy choice of governments also contributes to the continuity of inequality in a structural manner.

The rise in global inequality indicates an ever-increasing need for efficient distributional mechanisms locally, nationally and globally. A multilevel approach to distribution may employ different mechanisms at each level. The local availability of public education and healthcare services may limit domestic and international migration and may serve to be an initial attempt to enhance human development. The retreat of the nation-state from the economy both as an employer in the public sector and as the regulator in the market has led to a weakening of public economics in general and welfare systems in particular. Given the consequences of excessive deregulation and the social ills that nation-states have to face, it may be the right conjuncture to revive the defunct divisions of public economies. There have been several different discussions about a global intervention against increasing inequality. The idea of a cosmopolitan citizenship to overcome the fallacies of democratic governance and the pressures of the market economy provide a broad yet very liberal framework for doing just this (Held 2010). The possibility of a universal basic income discussed by many is another attempt to overcome inequalities generated by the market economy. Economic citizenship, or occupational citizenship, extends the social rights already embedded in the conventional citizenship definition to incorporate the right to decent work and earning a livelihood. The liberal institutional resolutions toward global inequality could very well be extended. It is the practical limitations and the social and political gaps that have put off these alternatives.

The privatization of public services and welfare regimes

The postwar reconstruction period under US hegemony was characterized by an environment of political stability and economic growth that promoted the redistributive functions of the nation-state. States under Keynesian consensus supported the reconstruction of national economies through industrialization and protectionism. The golden age of capitalism generated sustained economic growth through industrialization and demand generation, high employment and high wages, and an overall consensus between capital, labor and the state. This was a historical moment when the welfare state, despite the variation in its implementation (Esping-Andersen 1996), became the ideal-typical model of state in the economy.

The postwar reconstruction period reached its peak in the 1970s, when the capitalist world economy entered a new phase of overproduction and declining profitability. The efforts of using advanced technology and low-cost labor at the same time to increase competition and profitability postponed a sharp fall for a limited time. However, according to Brenner,

> by the end of the 1970s, the manufacturing sector on an international scale was at an impasse, as was the Keynesian programme of demand management that had been implemented to revitalize the world economy. Ever greater government stimulus had been unable to prevent the further fall of manufacturing profitability *system-wide.*
>
> (Brenner 2002: 34)

The reconstruction period under US hegemony came to a gradual end as the industrialization process reached its limits of profitability, and the domestic markets became obsolete in generating demand that could absorb further production. The historical conjuncture that enabled the active involvement of the state in the economy was replaced by a new political-economic environment where capital, in search for further accumulation capacity, sought greater mobility, and the state, in need of capital to maintain its economic functions, gave greater concessions to capital. In between the two, labor faced a significant loss of bargaining power against capital as well as against the state, as the state ceased to function as the arbitrator between the two.

The central question at this point is the way redistribution policies have transformed from the postwar political setting to the era of neoliberal globalization. The postwar welfare state was characterized by relatively high levels of public social benefit provision and extended social safety nets, especially by way of public education and healthcare, as well as by sizeable public pension plans. The provision of these benefits was enabled by high tax rates, which were readily accepted by capital and labor at a time when the domestic market generated sufficient demand toward sustained production, and hence surplus generation. The administration of the welfare state also required a sizeable public sector, which was mainly, but not exclusively, devoted to education and healthcare. Not all states were economically involved to the same extent. Esping-Andersen's seminal work on welfare states distinguished between the liberal, conservative and social-democratic welfare states. The difference between these three models depends on the role of the state, the degree to which the market is a source of welfare, and the political objectives behind welfare provision (Esping-Andersen 1990). The welfare state model emerged as a response to the unique historical conjuncture of postwar Europe, during which the reconstruction of national economies through industrialization compelled the market and the state to make a compromise, where capital, labor and the state were able to achieve a delicate balance:

> Welfare states are social systems of human reproduction which provide public goods and four kinds of private goods: regulations and/or provisions/prohibitions of market externalities; provisions or promotion of merit goods following from problems of market choice with regard to certain goods for human reproduction; extra state wages (special payments for services rendered to the state, including loyal suffering because of state actions, such as wars); state supply of other private goods. Public goods and the first two kinds of private goods derive from intrinsic failures and deficiencies of markets. The last two sorts of private goods from markets coming into conflicts with the different rationalities of states, classes, and citizenship [sic].
>
> (Therborn 1987: 244)

The primary function of the welfare state was not redistribution. Therborn states that the welfare state was not about providing equality on the basis of citizenship; rather, the high tax rates were a way of generating revenue to fund compulsory education and other instruments to help the state maintain cohesion. The primary function of the welfare state was to compensate for market problems, market controversies, and market failures. Once the compromise of the market and the state disintegrated through deterritorialization and opening up, there was no longer a balancing act against the inherent contradictions of the market.

The world economy saw a retreat of welfare provision with neoliberal globalization, even in the most egalitarian, extended welfare states. States were faced with increasing capital mobility and were unable to generate the revenue necessary to maintain the public provision of pension plans, public education and healthcare. The famous saying "There is no alternative" was not a symbolic expression, but was actually realized with the privatization of public enterprises, gradual budget cuts for public services, and the deterioration of public pension plans. States are significantly altering processes of redistributive justice and possibilities for social cohesion by quitting almost all means of social policy and public provision (Korpi and Palme 2003). These services did not cease to exist; rather, they were transformed from social rights into market goods. The emergence of private pension plans, private hospitals and private schools have been primary forms of this commodification of social rights. The deterioration of welfare provision and social safety nets expanded the margins of inequality. The increasing and deepening poverty levels necessitated greater intervention from the state in the form of social policy, which created a vicious circle of declining welfare and increasing poverty. The welfare state retrenchment under the Thatcher administration in the UK and the Reagan administration in the US brought about a reduction in the material benefits and social safety nets in the healthcare and housing sectors; a reduction in disability programs; and a decrease in old-age pensions. There was also a political retrenchment beyond the material incentives that altered public opinion about the possible negative consequences of welfare cuts, dividing potential opponents to these cost-cutting policies and breaking down their resistance by providing compensation to those affected (Pierson 1994: 19). The possibility of social upheaval against deepening social inequality was offset by the weakening of the labor movement in general and the unions, as its institutionalized form, in particular. The particular historical milieu of neoliberal globalization embraced diversity socially and economically, which led to the domination of identity politics over class-based politics.

The transition from the welfare state to the neoliberal minimal state was not exclusive to the advanced capitalist countries. The earliest attempts at privatization in the public sector were seen in Chile in the 1980s (Silva 1993). In a similar fashion, neoliberal restructuring in Turkey relied heavily on the privatization of the state's economic enterprises and social services. The structural adjustment program under the supervision of the IMF was implemented in January 1980 and was followed by a military coup in September of the same year (Onis 1999). The transition from state-led capitalism to a neoliberal economy was backed by a political attack against the left, particularly the working class. The privatization of public services across the board, irrespective of developmental differences between countries, was contrary to the modernization ideals and developmental models of the previous era. The disregard for developmental gaps further deepened the inequality between nations.

The main impact of neoliberal globalization on welfare regimes was the incapacitation of the state as an economic actor, as an arbitrator of class relations, and as a guarantor of social rights. According to Harvey, "the state, once transformed into a neoliberal set of institutions, becomes a prime agent of redistributive policies, reversing the flow from upper to lower classes that had been implemented during the preceding social democratic era" (Harvey 2007: 38). This retreat of the state was very much in line with the decline of the political and social functions of the state. The emerging void was pragmatically taken over by the market as a new domain to expand and generate surplus. Institutionalist and policy-oriented approaches toward social upheavals caused by the retreat of the state gained momentum as poverty and social exclusion became structural problems in both the developed and the developing world. The discourse on poverty emerged as a consequence of the inevitability of neoliberalism. Efforts at resolving poverty were geared more toward market resolutions than seeing a welfare state comeback.

Austerity measures

The global economic crisis directly affected the economic capacities of governments in managing their revenues and budgets for the remaining public services and social safety nets. The post-crisis buzzword became "austerity," which can be crudely defined as governments' tightening of expenses and economic provisions:

> The welfare state now faces a context of essentially permanent austerity. Changes in the global economy, the sharp slowdown in economic growth, the maturation of governmental commitments, and population ageing all generate considerable fiscal stress. There is little reason to expect these pressures to diminish over the next few decades. If anything, they are likely to intensify.
>
> (Pierson 2002: 370)

The liberal creed justifies austerity measures on the basis of the sovereign debt crisis and governments' inability to generate the financial means necessary to maintain public services and social safety nets. This is a time when states either go bankrupt, as in Iceland and Argentina, or are unable to pay their debt to creditors, as in Greece. The primary areas of retreat in the recovery process have been public services and social protections. The increase in income taxes and revenue-generating value-added tax (VAT) has led to the shrinking of purchasing power; the decrease in value of pension plans; the deterioration of public education systems (as the number of teachers in schools has declined); and the significant privatization of national healthcare systems.

Amartya Sen argues that European financial leaders' reinvention of austerity as a response to global economic crisis has relied on the historical analogy of social expenditure cuts during the Great Depression. The problem, in his view, is that such a response would bring more harm than good, especially in the currently interrelated and interdependent state of the global economy: "Austerity could do little, since a reduction of public expenditure adds to the inadequacy of private incomes and market demands, thereby tending to put even more people out of work" (Sen 2015: 30).

The scope and intensity of austerity policies differ according to national contexts. At first glance, demographics and the penetrating impact of the global economy – the economic crisis – have a determining impact on the unique combination of austerity measures being promulgated across the world. Bob Jessop approaches the issue from a cultural political economy perspective and provides a typology of neoliberal models along with their associated austerity approaches. The first type of neoliberal regime shift can be seen in the radical transition of post-Soviet countries to the neoliberal system. The second type is the mainstream transformations of liberalization, deregulation, privatization, internationalization and the concurrent cuts on public spending and taxation. The third type is neoliberalism imposed from outside, as it is observed in the developing world. Finally, the fourth type is the pragmatic policy adjustments toward neoliberalism that have been seen in the Nordic countries (Jessop 2015: 93–94). This classification exposes the extent of neoliberal penetration and the potential of the state in controlling for adverse effects. From a comparative angle, a pragmatic yet controlled transition to neoliberalism may retain the state's capacity to intervene in adverse conditions, whereas an imposed integration, as seen in the developing world, may result in the state's inability to manoeuvre under the strains of neoliberal globalization in general or during global economic crisis in particular:

> This ramping up of the politics of austerity occurred in part because the response of financial capital to this crisis intensified the state's fisco-financial crisis. [...] This is used to justify a state of economic emergency that is presented initially as a "temporary" response to immediate and chronic problems but then acquires more permanent form through cumulative and mutually reinforcing institutional change, routinisation of exceptional measures and habituation.
>
> (Jessop 2015: 98–100)

The commitment of contemporary governments to austerity policies is the most important consequence of this routinization. The media depiction of impoverished masses, homeless families seeking survival in cheap bed and breakfasts or even in cars, stretching lines at food banks and soup kitchens, the embarrassment of living on benefits, and great social decline is the habituation that Jessop is referring to.

The first half of this chapter discussed three major historical trajectories that occured in a continuum. The global economic crisis of the new millennium cannot be understood in isolation from the crisis of 1970s. The rise and fall of the welfare state model fits into this historical continuum as a conjunctural response to the reconstruction processes of the postwar era only to be omitted in accordance with the recent expansion of the global economy. The overarching implementation of austerity measures is an extension of welfare state retrenchment, leading one to question the utility and function of the state in the first place. The detachment of the state and the public, of polity and policy, forms a new domain of inquiry as to what the agents, principles and mechanisms of redistribution and sharing could be.

Redistribution through solidarity networks

What kind of redistributive alternatives can be utilized in the absence of formal institutional mechanisms? The consequences of globalization and the following global economic crisis for labor were discussed above. The current state of the global economy exacerbates existing social inequalities. The accompanying weakening of the nation-state in general and welfare regimes in particular further polarize social segments, whether they are defined on the basis of class or some other category. The aforementioned austerity measures compel citizens to seek alternative social safety nets through the market or through civil society initiatives. Private provision of welfare and social security depends on the sustenance and level of household income. Civil society initiatives, irrespective of their level of organization, mostly operate on a voluntary basis and provide temporary reparation rather than structural resolution. The objective of redistributive justice becomes a fundamental objective of the alternative economy due to the weakness of institutions and the lack of alternative mechanisms to fight against ever-increasing inequality.

What could the principles of alternative redistributive justice be? The first principle is the rationing of managers' salaries and workers' wages in such a way so as to avoid expanding wage gaps. This will target the income gap but not necessarily social and developmental gaps. The second principle is the sharing of earnings on the basis of work investment rather than capital investment. Linking redistribution with work may result in equality being a precondition in the production process, and any income becomes returns on work rather than rent or interest on capital. This overrides the economic and social distinction between the boss and the worker, putting the former on the same plane as the latter.

Not all principles of redistributive justice have to do with income adjustment. Rationing of wages and salaries or work-based income determinants are outcomes of the production process. Certain transformations in consumption patterns also work against social inequality. The third principle of redistributive justice has to do with fair trade and fair labor practices. There are numerous examples of fair trade practices in the cocoa industry, in the coffee industry, in carpet weaving, and in labeling practices and a variety of public awareness campaigns (Lyon and Moberg 2010). The success of fair trade practices is debatable; however, the pricing and the marketing of products in an alternative economy is as relevant as the valorization of labor in wages and salaries. Finally, the fourth principle has to do with local exchange trading systems (LETS), which help local communities produce and consume locally in such a way as to minimize their dependence on the global market as producers and as consumers (Papavasiliou 2010). Individuals increasingly rely on a diverse set of goods and services in the global economy, which makes LETS sound relatively utopian. It becomes hardly feasible to consume in purely local terms, since high-technology commodities are produced by a few yet consumed by many. Prices may not always be competitive for consumers, as small-scale local production is not as profitable as industrial mass production. This may render the LETS as a purely ethical outlet, rather than an economic one. However, it would become a significant detachment from dominant market relations once it becomes a collective effort. The strength of redistributive mechanisms in general and LETS in particular lies in their collective character. The greater the number of their constituents, the greater the returns they keep from capitalist economic relations.

Redistribution processes need to be interconnected with production on a broader scale. As production is locally organized on the basis of local resources and demographic factors, local organization of redistribution would have to be structured on the basis of revenue generation from local production processes. The centralized administration of redistribution would be inefficient in addressing immediate needs at the local level; therefore, redistribution agents and organizations would have to organize horizontally in a structure that would be more responsive to local needs and problems.

There is a dire need to define the agents and procedures of alternative redistribution systems beyond the level of general principles. The state and the market have proven to be inappropriate agents of redistribution. The former has been functional in a specific conjuncture, while the latter refrained from forming a balance between the private interests of capital and public interests of labor. The rejection of the state and the market as efficient channels of redistribution leaves civilian initiatives as the last resort of organization. These civilian initiatives are not necessarily charity organizations or traditional mechanisms of solidarity; instead, the active participation of recipients in the production and redistribution processes is organized on a local basis.

One of the most commonly cited examples of redistributive justice and local development is that of Kerala, India. Also known as the Kerala Model, the unique development model initiated in the early 1970s followed a "basic-needs-first" approach to prioritize the needs of the locals, and hence focused on human development rather than economic development. Land reform has been one way to attack poverty; and further mobilization in organized and unorganized sectors led to a responsive relationship between public demand and a pro-active state (Justino 2006: 1266). Kerala has the highest female literacy rate, the lowest infant mortality rate, and one of the highest life expectancy rates in the country. The matrilinear tradition enables women to inherit and hold property, which is an important aspect of gender equality. Parayil's conceptual analysis of the Kerala experience indicates basic principles of sustainable development in its most concrete, prototypical form:

> Kerala's ability to undertake public action through the mobilisation of peasant farmers, tenants and industrial workers by leftist parties; the spread of literacy, particularly among women; maintaining women's rights (though these rights were mostly a result of historically contingent factors); reducing social inequality and decreasing inequalities in income and consumption; and indigenous evolution and popularisation of social movements concerned with environment and development issues.
>
> (Parayil 1996: 950–951)

For Oomen, Kerala's success was based on certain unique characteristics of the region. The linguistic homogeneity in Kerala led to high levels of literacy and education. The multi-religious structure forced different segments of society to embrace secularism. The lack of a rural-urban dichotomy, the caste-neutral nature of entrepreneurship, and the sustained inflow of migrant remittances all contributed to local development in Kerala. At least as important, however, has been the role of social movements in Kerala that used news media, literature and cinema as instruments of social transformation (Oomen 2009).

The most important lesson one can learn from the Kerala Model is that redistributive justice is not necessarily a monetary issue. Kerala partially fulfills the criteria of non-state, non-market operation as a unique model. The awareness and the social transformation that this redistribution needs to generate are at least as important as the redistribution of resources. Redistributive justice is not only about giving people money or increasing their income. It is also about a qualitative change in lifestyles and standards.

A more formal and relatively institutionalized redistributive model is the LETS, which are locally organized exchange mechanisms that directly link producers with consumers. They hold several advantages as non-market exchange systems and are immune to the externalities of capitalist exchange relations. First, cash nexus is excluded from the exchange relationship. In certain instances, alternative currencies are utilized to facilitate the exchange relationship; however, monetary exchange is not a compulsory instrument. Second, both goods and services could be exchanged, and this enhances local productivity. This is especially important in times of economic crisis, when cash flows are limited and unemployment rises. LETS become significant outlets during times of crisis, both for producers and consumers, as they enable economic sustenance and social solidarity. LETS have become an integral part of the anti-globalization movement outside of times of economic turbulence as a response to the consumerist culture fueled by corporations for the sake of demand creation. A derivative of LETS in this case has been swap groups that get together in informal markets for an exchange of vintage or used goods. Swap groups (also known as swap meets) serve more of a redistributive function than a productive one. The extensity of information technology provides the necessary infrastructure to link producers, consumers and LETS in different settings to enable further networking opportunities. The Internet and social media play a central role in the organization and collaboration of members and the outreach toward participants.

One major limitation of LETS is that the amount and variety of goods and services is limited in a local exchange system. The potential to expand the exchange network is confined geographically, demographically and economically. LETS operate mostly as community-level organizations in rural economies. Their sustainability depends on the commitment of the locals to an exchange system that is based on local produce. The initial motivation gradually fades away in many cases. One can hardly imagine a structural transformation or a systemic overtake on the basis of LETS, which could only be a viable alternative under specific circumstances. It is more appropriate to think of LETS as a complementary facility rather than an anti-systemic alternative. They could be easily and efficiently incorporated into cooperative systems, inter-cooperative alliances, and community development programs.

The Magnesia Exchange and Social Solidarity Network emerged in Volos, Greece, in 2010 as a local response to the Greek economic crisis. The network operates on its own currency, the TEM, in its own location, the TEM Market. The number of those involved in the exchange network was as high as 1,300 as of 2013 (Smith 2013). The exchange includes local produce, services such as childcare and language courses, as well as used goods. It has been an important outlet for women as producers and as consumers, and it provides an opportunity for small-scale home-made goods to be marketed without the associated business costs. The network operates on three major principles.[1] The principle of equality and parity refers to the equal status of members, who gather in assemblies to make decisions in a collective manner. Information dissemination and communication among members is facilitated through its website and is guaranteed under the principles of openness and transparency. The most important principles, however, are participation and social solidarity, which underline the collaborative aspects of the network. The TEM Network is a small local response to Greece's economic crisis. The TEM Market is more of a meeting place for local buyers and sellers than a competitive capitalist market. The alternative currency provides members with relative immunity from the macroeconomic management of the government.

Post-crisis Greece experienced a flourishing of local exchange systems and the emergence of local markets as alternative domains of the economy. These local markets may be in urban or rural areas, providing whatever is locally produced. Xoris Mesazontes operates as a network of small-scale agricultural production. The network is located in the small town of Dionysos, slightly north of Athens, and markets local products on the Internet through the Farmers Republic website.[2] The Time Bank of Athens and Syntagma is an urban network, which uses time as a currency in the exchange of certain services: a one-hour private Spanish lesson equals one hour of childcare; or one hour of guitar lessons equals one hour of domestic labor.[3] The primary function of LETS is to provide their constituents with relative immunity from the global economy, especially from monetary challenges and financial fluctuations. As expressed by OVOLOS, a financial cooperative established in Patras, Greece, as a response to financial crisis in the country,

> the difference and the power of OVOLOS CENTER OF STUDY AND DOCUMENTATION OF SOCIAL CURRENCY is that while the monetary value of the euro may fluctuate [due] to enhancements or depreciation, the "Ovolos" remains [a] stable endpoint within the limits of the economic union, thus protecting its members from revaluations and economic crisis.
>
> In this way, the logic of supply and demand as we know it does not change, but it is transferred onto a sphere of intranet transactions where the currency is valid in the context of the economic system in which [it] is protected and from [sic] which it is powered.
>
> ("How Does It Work?" 2015)

The definitive features of the nation-state have been significantly jeopardized under neoliberal globalization. The deterritorialization process, as a natural extension of neoliberal restructuring, has brought the monopoly of power and state sovereignty into question. The diffusion of market ideology and corporate discourse through global trade regimes administered by supranational organizations has further limited states' capacities to administer or intervene in the economy. The weakness of the state when it comes to responding to emerging social problems, whether in terms of inequality or social conflict, has led to the flourishing of civil society approaches to economic well-being. It is in this context that governance has become a more inclusive term to overcome the limitations of governments in transforming themselves with respect to the challenges of neoliberal globalization.

Before discussing local solidarity governance, it is important to distinguish governance from government. In the face of neoliberal globalization and the subsequent incapacitation of the nation-state, a new institutional configuration has emerged as certain functions of the nation-state have been taken up by new actors ranging from supranational organizations to agents of various social movements. This institutional diversification will affect the mechanisms and procedures of policymaking. Newer approaches may be advantageous in overcoming the bureaucratic lags of centralized governments and may benefit from new media and information technologies – though they may also suffer from distorted interest representation. Along with this rather vague structure of administration, one must also look at the question of the source and proper use of available resources.

Local governance, whether as local democratic governance or local participatory governance, has been on the agenda of mainstream supranational organizations and non-governmental organizations as a more inclusive approach toward socially and economically marginalized groups. The United Nations Development Program (UNDP) recognizes the contribution of subnational institutions in providing "inclusiveness and accountability" and defines four major areas of operation that can help improve local governance: the provision of services towards millennium development goals, state- and peacebuilding, democratic representation, and environmental sustainability ("Local Governance" 2015). The National Democratic Institute (NDI) promotes local governance and seeks to strengthen it by providing technical assistance with regard to the management and coordination of tasks, enhancing citizen participation, and forming associations between local authorities with the aim of facilitating networking opportunities and the exchange of ideas ("Democratic Governance" 2015). These and other mainstream approaches could very well be extended. One major critique of mainstream approaches is that they do not refer to developmental goals, economic inclusiveness, or the construction of a local economy through mobilizing locally available resources. Economic organization at the local level is left to its own devices at best, but it is mostly left to market incentives, however diffusive they may be. Local governance must be democratic and participatory, but it must also be conceptualized beyond the dynamics of mainstream institutionalist approaches. Problems of social exclusion, poverty and economic degradation are not necessarily the consequences of institutional deficiency. They may very well be consequences of an overarching bureaucracy. The top-down approaches toward the local ignore the idiosyncrasies of different locales, and they are inefficient at addressing the specific needs of the local. It is the material and economic circumstances that local solidarity governance expands upon, as opposed to the institutional possibilities. The Council of Europe (CoE) defines twelve principles of good governance at the local level (Council of Europe 2015). The first six principles are geared toward ensuring efficiency in political administration through fair elections, transparency, the rule of law, ethical conduct, accountability, and enhanced capacity and conduct. These principles are broadly and superficially defined, with little consideration for the distinction between central governance and local governance. The remaining six principles frame the provision of social rights and the sustained production of public good. Policies have to be responsive to the needs of citizens in a timely manner. They need to be effective and sustainable, and in this regard innovation becomes a primary strategy. Financial management becomes a key instrument for expanding productive capacities locally. Finally, the ultimate objective is to create a socially inclusive, culturally diverse environment at the local level. The principles of local governance conceptualized by the UNDP or CoE represent the institutional paradigm of local governance. They emerge out of an underlying assumption that institutions are representative of populations, and that locals can equally and fully access institutions. Governance becomes a means to an end rather than an end in itself.

Regional Development Agencies (RDAs) have been a prominent model in local governance. This model has been widely implemented in both the developed and the developing world. Partnerships have been built with government agents, non-governmental organizations and, in some cases, supranational bodies. The primary objective of RDAs has been to overcome regional developmental gaps. Their conceptualization of development, however, is mainstream: RDAs seek investment to generate employment and restart the economic cycle of investment-growth-development. Yet this kind of model ignores the changing dynamics and the nature of competition in the global economy. The Rostowian model of "catching up" is not only outdated but is incongruent with the current market environment. Kevin Cox evaluates the impact of globalization on local and regional development thus: "The emergence of the idea of 'business climate' and correlative benchmarking likewise make little sense outside of the increase in FDI and foreign trade and the increased exposure of local economies to competition from outside" (Cox 2004: 187). While Cox's comparison of US and UK approaches to local and regional development does not expose the dangers of integrating backward regions into the global economy, a developing country perspective clearly exposes the extent of exploitation and socioeconomic inequality, and threats to the local economy.

Local solidarity governance as conceptualized in this study is contrary to the "business climate" model geared toward the global economy. Instead, the primary objective is economic viability and subsistence on a local level. It is not seeking a competitive edge in the global market, but an economic stance that is independent from the global market. Its viability depends very much on the resources available locally, whether as productive input or as labor power. Local solidarity governance is distinct from a mainstream governance model in the way it incorporates small, informal groups in the decision-making process. Relatively more marginal groups are being represented on the basis of their input and their interests. Local solidarity governance is about defining needs on a local basis and meeting those needs by way of local input. This simplistic approach also generates employment and economic growth and development, albeit at a very slow pace compared to the market approaches discussed above.

It is worth reiterating that redistribution has to be locally organized, non-state and non-market in principle. It has to respond to and reflect solidaristic production systems. The relationship of production and redistribution determines the material basis and availability that may be channeled to redistribution. Exchange relations need to be an integral part of this material basis. Solidaristic redistribution does not come in a single form. It may rely more on traditional mechanisms in some societies, and it may be articulated through modern, technological media in others. Forms and structures may be renewed and adapted to changing conditions; it is the principle of solidarity, however, that will provide direction to the nature of that change.

Notes

1 For more information, please see https://www.tem-magnisia.gr/en.
2 http://farmersrepublic.gr/.
3 For more information, please listen to the Dialogos Radio interview at https://soundcloud.com/kvrxaustin/dialogos-radio-interview-with-christina-papadopoulou-of-the-time-bank-of-athens.

3 Workplace democracy

The relationship between capitalism and democracy was for a long time regarded to be a rather harmonious one. The former was a systemic representation of economic liberalism, and the latter served as its political justification and institutional framework. The inequalities generated by the former were relatively suppressed by the provision of political liberties to the dangerous classes for the sake of maintaining the capitalist grid. The gist of the capitalist state was a derivative of economic liberalism in the way it promoted elite alliances at the expense of the laboring masses.

This congruence of capitalism and democracy has been deeply scrutinized for some time, as the holy alliance of the economic and the political elite has deprived the masses of their civil and political rights of interest-seeking and representation under democratic systems. Several reasons could be marshalled for the divergent paths of the capitalist system and democratic practice. The former operates in a transnational manner, whereas the latter is predominantly confined to the national setting. The supranational institutionalization of capitalism overrides the national institutions of democracy, rendering interest-seeking and representation at the national level all but obsolete. The attacks against the labor movement, unions and labor parties since the onset of globalization in the 1980s and the disintegration of class-based alliances have created a political vacuum, which has come to be occupied by global social movements and identity politics. This has led to a qualitative transformation in the causes embedded in democratic struggles and the processes undertaken to fight for them.

The objective of this chapter is to critically analyze the limitations of current democratic practices for representing labor rights and demands. The first half of the chapter will present the contemporary setting in which labor struggles are embedded. The decline of class-based politics and the rise of identity politics will be a starting point. Global social movements in general and global justice movements in particular will expose the diversity of interests and the potential for alliances. The second half of the chapter will conceptualize workplace democracy as an alternative to the predominant parliamentary form of democracy and the systems espoused by global social movements.

Class-based movements versus identity-based movements

One of the most important challenges posed by globalization is the decline of unionism as a major organizing force and the rise of identity politics as a mainstay of political discourse. An earlier divergence of social movements from the more conventional political parties and labor movements took place in the late 1960s, when more particularistic issues became sources of mobilization. There has been a deepening of this bifurcation with the increasing intensity of identity politics and a further weakening of the labor movement with the onset globalization: "The group-based 'identity politics' of the 'new social movements' that arose after the 1960s still exist, but the recent period has seen more diverse mobilizations in which individuals are mobilized around personal lifestyle values to engage with multiple causes such as economic justice (fair trade, inequality, and development policies), environmental protection, and worker and human rights" (Bennett 2012: 37). The dominant ideology that is neoliberalism operates not only in the realm of economic policy, but in the realm of political organization as well. Individualism has become the organizing principle in both realms, where the individual, ripped away from public support from the government and social institutions, has been left to the mercy of the market. Political representation has little meaning in a system in which the state has become a mere administrative structure undergirding the market. One recent line of debate has centered on the possibility of creating a global civil society, where shared concerns regarding globalization, social problems and identity politics would be broached concomitantly in different parts of the world (Kaldor 2003; Keane 2003). Castells' notion of the network society has served as a milestone in defining a globally active civil society and the global outreach of social movements (Castells 1996). The conceptualizations of cyberspace, electronic space and spaces of flows are central for understanding the operation of contemporary social movements and the waves they generate as ideas are transmitted from one locus to another (Castells 1999). Another line of debate has focused on anti-globalization movements, the turning point for which was the protests against the WTO in Seattle in 1999 (Cockburn and St. Clair 2000). Such movements have been sporadic and unstructured; however, they have had a tendency to grow and expand: the World Social Forum (WSF) as an alternative organization to the World Economic Forum (WEF) started out in South America, but eventually grew to cover three continents (Santos 2006), and global justice movements operate in several European countries in different capacities (Della Porta 2007). Two major differences, however, are noteworthy in the changing dynamics of social movements under globalization. First, in quantitative terms, the decline of unions has been compensated for by a growth in civil society movements organized around a diverse set of issues. Second, in ideological terms, class-based movements that traditionally relied on issues of inequality and material well-being were replaced by movements based on identity politics, which focused on issues of discrimination, social exclusion, and representation: "Social movements, throughout history, are the producers of new values and goals around which the institutions of society are transformed to represent these values by creating new norms to organize social life" (Castells 2012: 9).

A comprehensive analysis of global transformations surrounding labor relations has to incorporate the power of social movements and their demands for greater democracy. First and foremost, the global economic crisis was a major blow to the dominant ideology of neoliberalism, and it compelled contemporary social movements to reconsider the individualist, identity-based micro-demands that served as their organizing principles (Bornstein 2009: 106). Second, economic motivations are once again a core concern due to increasing inequality, expanding margins of poverty, and massive unemployment rates that await already vulnerable groups such as women, youth and immigrants. Calhoun draws attention to the way Occupy Wall Street attacked the financial elite and their apparatuses of power (Calhoun 2013), and the protests in Greece, Spain and other European countries emphasized the impact of austerity on the material well-being of their citizens. Third, although global social movements in the North had a different character than those of the Global South in the heyday of globalization, current movements are similar in terms of the centrality of economic issues, their demands for transparency and democracy, and the strategies used by their members (Calhoun 2013). The movements include a wide array of parties, ranging from ethnic and indigenous groups to women's organizations, LGBT groups, student groups, and worker organizations (Mew 2012: 99). Contemporary movements are highly diverse and unconventional in terms of strategy; occupation has become a common tactic in different parts of the world, and the use of electronic space and digital media has become instrumental. In short, the way social movements respond to the impact of global economic crisis will determine the way society will organize politically, economically and socially in the future.

The labor movement in general has always been political. Militant labor movements seek to gain power through democratic systems; for this, they usually form alliances with labor parties. Second, labor movements seek to pressure governments through militant activism, that is, through strikes, protests and other high-profile tactics. Labor has lost political ground and bargaining power vis-à-vis capital and the state with the diffusion of neoliberal globalization. Labor strategies during this period were less militant because of significant legal and political obstacles; they were also more responsive to the increased competition in the global labor market, and they were designed to enhance workers' qualifications through training and skill formation. Seidman elaborates on the detachment of citizenship and labor rights, and the labor movement's loss of political clout; he also criticizes the transnationalization of the movement, which occurred because of the diverse range of experiences and issues that existed within labor and because of labor's repeated dependence on traditional hierarchies of power in the international system. The international system, institutionalized on the basis of nation-states, inter-state relations and supranational organizations, is already dominated by a neoliberal discourse. Seeking a resolution in this kind of a system would further subordinate the labor movement: "Unless international mechanisms are thoroughly reconstructed, organized labor will, almost inevitably, return to strategies that emphasize strengthening workers' citizenship rights and strengthening local states rather than looking to global institutions for enforcement and protection" (Seidman 2004: 110).

The historical conjuncture that brought about capitalist restructuring and welfare state retrenchment under neoliberal globalization heavily undermined the labor movement. Both labor parties and labor unions have lost ground in terms of membership, representation and interest-seeking. Labor unions have been heavily attacked by the neoliberal state through legal limitations, and through sectoral or industrial lines of division. Labor unions lacked a substantive response to and stance against neoliberal globalization. The weakness of the labor movement was set off by a growth of alternative social movements, which focused on cultural identities as opposed to class identity. The transition from a labor-dominant public sphere to one characterized by a diversity of identities has led to many comparative analyses of class-based politics and identity politics. One such analysis posited that the relative homogeneity of class identity contributed to the strength of the labor movement. Classes, however, are not static structures that maintain homogeneity; on the contrary, classes are dynamic, constantly changing structures:

> Let us accept once and for all that classes are not social super-individualities, neither as objects nor as subjects; in other words, they are not castes. Both structurally and historically, classes overlap and become meshed together, at least in part. In the same way that there are necessarily bourgeoisified proletarians, there are proletarianized bourgeois. This overlap never occurs without there being material divisions. In other words, "class identities," which are relatively homogeneous, are not a result of predestination but of conjuncture.
>
> (Wallerstein 1988: 179)

Following from Wallerstein's argument for the conjunctural homogeneity of class, the institutional forms of class-based movements, namely labor parties and labor unions, need to be scrutinized in terms of their ability to reflect the changes in the aforementioned conjuncture and their capacity to adopt new strategies to better incorporate emerging issues from contemporary trajectories. The labor movement has historically focused on workers, workplace issues, collective bargaining, wages, and benefits; it has traditionally held a male-dominant position, and gender issues have always been subordinated to workplace issues. Interest representation was exclusive to formal sector workers, and in this regard it is important to note that the onset of flexible specialization and the precarization of work led to tensions between formal and informal workers that was not handled well by labor unions. Beyond the exclusion of the precariat, the traditional labor movement has had difficulty incorporating cultural diversity and identity politics into its bailiwick.

Several factors played a role in the rise of identity politics. The saturation of middle-class values and democratic practice enabled civil society networks to flourish in advanced capitalist countries. The collapse of the Soviet Union and the emergence of new national and/or cultural identities encouraged new social movements to organize along the lines of identity politics. The emergence and the growth of "anti-globalizers" was a result of the resentment generated by neoliberal globalization, particularly the increase in capital mobility, "McDonaldization" (Ritzer 2000), and associated global inequalities. More importantly, the rise of identity politics in different parts of the world, which was caused by a variety of political, economic and social issues, intensified and became more representative for individuals than class-based movements.

Class-based movements and identity-based movements could be compared on the basis of their respective agendas, their constituencies, their strategies, and the nature of their struggles. Class-based movements propose a universal agenda, yet their practice is more confined to their national context. This national mode of operation generates diversity within the movement. Identity movements are more particularistic, but they form international alliances in practice. They are ideologically diverse, as interests and objectives are determined within the local and/or national context. Therefore, in both cases, irrespective of whether their starting point is universal or particularistic, these movements are confined to the contexts from which they emerge. The constituencies of class-based movements are traditionally male-dominant and represent formal and fully employed workers, rather than socially diverse, non-standard and/or informal workers. The constituencies of identity-based movements represent different social groups with various interests.[1] There are intersections, overlaps and sometimes even clashes of interest among different movements. In terms of strategy, class-based movements struggle through labor parties in parliamentary democracies and through labor unions in collective bargaining systems or strikes; they may be organized by sector, by company, or as general associations. Identity-based movements benefit from global transformations in communication and transportation technologies and are an integral part of the information society.

There have been attempts to revive the labor movement in all these comparative dimensions. Labor parties and labor unions are joined by alternative organizational forms that may override the legal and institutional limitations that traditional structures now face. There have been attempts to join forces with informal workers, illegal immigrants who are the pariah of the informal economy, as well as other groups that have been marginalized in both the labor market and the labor movement. Cobble, writing on the American labor movement, makes a statement that applies not only in the US context but the global one as well:

> The industrial form of unionism dominant today may continue to be viable for some groups of workers in some sectors of the economy, but if

> the labor movement is ever to appeal to the majority of today's workers, it must transform itself radically. New models of unionism must be invented – specifically, models more appropriate for a mobile, service-oriented, and knowledge-based economy in which women, immigrants, and people of color are in the majority.
>
> (Cobble 2001: 83)

The pertinent issue is not only an institutional limitation, but one of representation and commitment. In the context of neoliberal globalization, individuals regarded identity politics as a more viable, more representative venue for interest-seeking. This does not suggest a competition of social movements; instead, it suggests a need for alternative configurations of identities, representation and social mobility. The distinction between class-based movements and identity-based movements does not necessarily lead to a confrontation, for they can be reconciled: "Resisting essentialism, this politics of cultural identity crosscuts different forms of social struggle; these intersections in turn create bases for cooperation. Identity politics of this kind intersects with the formative process of class consciousness in the space of culture" (Chuang 2002: 137).

Global social movements

Several factors contributed to the proliferation of social movements on a global scale. Identity politics and the cultural by-products of intersectionality created an atmosphere of motivation and mobilization. This, in turn, enabled the strengthening of alliances between different movements. The spread and penetration of information technology allowed the free flow of information and further enhanced the instruments of mobilization. Castells' concept of the "space of flows" refers to the multilayered structure that combines a technological infrastructure with networks of interaction connecting through nodes and hubs, all of which facilitate the operation of financial markets, manufacturing, entertainment, media, and more (Castells 1999: 295). The public sphere has been transformed from a physical space into a virtual one, in which acts of deliberation, protest and participation connect remote participants in delinked geographies.

Tilly and Tarrow, writing on contentious politics, discuss the conjunctural transformations that lead to the flourishing of global social movements. They seek to overcome the analytical limitations of globalization by proposing to use internationalization as their conceptual basis of their research. Globalization, briefly defined as the process of economic integration, the penetration of a high-technology infrastructure, and the emergence cultural universalism, provides limited insight on intervening processes and can only partially explain global social movements, some of which are not directly related to globalization at all. Instead, internationalization suggests that there is an internalization of domestic issues and a diffusion of domestic conflicts on an international plane. Social movements become transnational through the efforts of transnational agents facilitating transnational alliances between actors, agents or movements, leading transnational protests such as anti-globalization protests, and finally resulting in coalitions being formed between domestic activists: "To the extent that transnational movements displace domestic contention (and we hasten to add that there is not yet much sign of such a development), they will *deactivate the boundaries* between states and *activate new boundaries* across broader constellations of states" (Tilly and Tarrow 2007: 177).

Seidman analyzes the relationship between globalization and social movements in terms of the changing nature of activism and the way this has been scrutinized academically. The movements are becoming increasingly global in terms of their constituents and the alliances they are forming. International legal frameworks and sources of pressure are used as supporting mechanisms. Yet social movements still operate locally, especially when it comes to the policy changes they are demanding. The globalization of social movements may be strategic in outreach and recognition, yet the settlements remain local. The complexity of the global-local diversity in social movements is reflected in the conduct of academic inquiry. First, social movement theory tends to focus on local or grassroots movements and their development in a bottom-up manner. This generates an emphasis on collective histories, local identities, and movements' local legitimacy. Second, social movement studies define movements on the basis of political targets instead of universal appeals, which is very much consistent with the local focus (Seidman 2000: 345). The tension between the global and the local requires particular attention from activists as well as theorists. Seidman compares two important examples in this regard: First, the labor movement, despite its universal internationalist origins, has remained nationally organized and historically has been forced to reconcile national labor issues with universalist claims on an international plane. Second, while social movements are increasingly becoming more global, they represent a local resistance to the very globalization process that makes them global: "In the late twentieth century, globalization often appears to be the result of a hegemonic project, a process largely driven by those who are powerful and wealthy. Global social movements, on the other hand, often seem to embody local resistance to that project. What does that mean for the development of a transnational collective identity?" (Seidman 2000: 356).

Global social movements also come across serious limitations, despite transformations and improved facilitations, especially after the global economic crisis. While challenging material conditions and social degradation has been reason enough to organize, civil society organizations have been constrained more than ever. One source of pressure has been the erosion of funds and the limited ability to generate resources in a world where the state and the market both face financial difficulties. Another limitation has been the weakness of the response to the global economic crisis. Civil society organizations, including labor unions, have generated partially useful responses to the crisis, which have nevertheless been far from successful in formulating a viable economic alternative. The material and political weakness of movements resulted in deeper divisions and, to a certain extent, rivalries between civil society organizations. What had seemed to be profitable alliances soon became costly competitions in a time of crisis (Clark 2011: 243–245).

The main question in this historical context is how to juxtapose nationally organized labor movements and global social movements. The labor movement was essentially internationalist. Despite the long historical background of the Internationals, the International Confederation of Free Trade Unions (ICFTU) and the International Trade Union Confederation (ITUC), the labor movement operates by and large in the national context. The vertical integration of organized labor on a global scale may open up opportunities for new alliances and for an extension of bargaining power, but it may also run the risk of trivializing locally pertinent issues. The horizontal integration, whether as a geographic extension through alliances with other national labor movements, or as a thematic extension through cooperation with other social movements, may also empower national labor movements and generate solidarity, yet they also run the risk of making compromises that may override the interests of their local members. Finally, movements of all sorts have been forced into a trade-off between short-term compensations to meet their demands and long-term structural transformations. Not all movements have the same life span. This is another aspect that the labor movement has to incorporate into its revival strategy, among many others.

Global justice movement

Global civil society, global social movements and global justice movements are three interrelated yet separate concepts that need to be laid out clearly for further analysis. Global civil society refers to a domain which is integrated on a global scale through international cooperation and alliances. This domain is further facilitated with the advancement of information technology, which allows for the faster and more efficient exchange and dissemination of information. The global nature of this domain is free from potential interventions by the state or the market, although it is subject to legal frameworks and material limitations. Global social movements operate within the domain of global civil society; they are composed of civil society organizations, non-governmental organizations, networks of organizations, and strategic alliances of various sorts. Although they are thematically separate, in many cases alliances become resourceful in terms of increasing membership and participation, awareness, and recognition.

Global justice movements stand at a particular juncture in the midst of global social movements. They operate within global civil society, and they are also social movements. However, they are distinctly organized against neoliberal globalization and the consequential inequalities it continuously generates:

> Although a great variety of different mobilizations can be identified in this area, we will refer to them with the general term of global justice

> movements, for at least three reasons: first, all of them share values and identities opposed to neoliberal globalization; second, they have woven together an increasingly tight network of coalitions and campaigns; and finally, they have regularly met and planned initiatives at major global events.
>
> (Pianta and Marchetti 2007: 31)

There is an element of ambiguity in the definition of global justice movements (as opposed to civil society and social movements) in the national context. In the national context, demands were made to the state against the economic actors dominating the national economy; therefore the national domain would have a class dimension and the possibility of a compromise between groups. The state in this context would serve the function of arbitration between interest groups. To what extent a compromise between confrontational groups is desirable or functional is debatable. In global civil society, the struggle of global social movements and global justice movements are against a vague, amorphous body of global markets, globally operating capital, and other economic actors, such as the IMF, the WB and the WTO. The mechanisms of interest representation and arbitration are much more diffuse in global civil society; the achievement of these movements and the extent to which it reflects upon the lives of their members is more difficult to observe. The richness of the causes and interests pursued and the diversity of alliances made through global networks is noteworthy and carries the potential of generating alternatives, if not a complete structural transformation. Global social movements and global justice movements interlink the local, national, regional and global levels of organization for a diverse and comprehensive representation of issues and search for policy options. Global movements increasingly seek cross-country alliances beyond the vertical layer of organization in order to unite different social groups that target a common cause. The difficulty in horizontal integration is due to geographic limitations, a lack of available resources, and differences in political cultures and political consciousness (Pianta and Marchetti 2007: 47).

The question now becomes: Where does labor fit into in this picture? The labor movement is essentially international, so how does it relate to contemporary global social movements in its struggle against neoliberal globalization? Are alliances with women's movements, environmental movements or humanitarian movements beneficial for labor? Della Porta argues that the heterogeneous social base of the global justice movement enabled the labor movement to make horizontal alliances with other movements against the backlash that the organized labor movement faced during the 1990s due to declining membership and a loss of bargaining power. It enabled the labor movement to renew its strategies – with the potential to protest rather than make unlimited concessions against a business coalition – and to construct collective identities that incorporate interests other than material ones. Over and against the neocorporatist paradigm of highly institutionalized hierarchical mechanisms for the representation of material interests, the labor movement as part of a coalition of movements operates in a new paradigm of social organization as an agent of a less political but more civic struggle:

> Moreover, in the movement, unions act according to a different logic than that prevailing in neocorporatist agreements: they protest more than "concert," they build horizontal networks with other movements instead of developing hierarchical organizations, and they construct encompassing collective identities instead of focusing on the defence of economic interests.
>
> (Della Porta 2005: 16)

Labor interests consist of an integral part of a coalition of interests borne out of the detrimental impact of neoliberal globalization. These interests include economic interests that have emerged from class inequality, and social interests that have emerged from inequalities in human development: access to decent standards of living and to proper infrastructure, protection against the impact of environmental degradation created by global production systems, and political rights for disadvantaged groups that have hitherto been deprived of representation. The people subject to economic inequalities are the same people who suffer from social exclusion, who are deprived of decent infrastructure and services, and who are subject to environmental degradation on a daily basis. It is possible to mobilize the same constituency for labor causes and for social causes. The divergence of unions and non-governmental organizations can be reconciled through cooperation and networking from an organizational perspective (Roman 2004: 107). The moment of reconciliation will motivate and help non-governmental organizations to overcome the divergence of class politics and identity politics, and the labor unions to seek more than material interests for their members. This may mean the passing of legal resolutions for illegal immigrants or informal workers, the extension of women workers' rights beyond the workplace, and the recognition and representation of LGBT identity in the labor movement.

Workplace democracy

The discussion of alternative production systems covers the material basis of the alternative economy. The inequalities associated with the capitalist economy are not limited to the material. A major cause and component of inequality is the lack of room for the representation of a wider set of issues, especially labor issues. Inequalities of power distribution and decision-making are at least as relevant as material inequalities. The most visible example for this is the hierarchical management systems that corporate structures are founded upon. These management systems, whether categorized as "operations management" or "human resources management," deal with data in its most secluded, abstract form to optimize the production process in the most asocial manner.

Highly specialized measurement techniques are adopted without even considering their efficiency in many cases. The exclusion of the productive masses from the decision-making process and the rank and file of the corporate structure diminishes their motivation and loyalty at work.

The concept of workplace democracy, sometimes used interchangeably with the terms "industrial democracy" and "economic democracy," is not new. Mason traces the European and the American origins of this concept in the context of a critique of liberalism (Mason 1982). The European tradition of workplace democracy seeks to unravel the legitimate constituents of workplace democracy. Historically, these may be found in cooperative work efforts, and medieval communes and guild systems. While the utopian socialism represented by Owen, Engels and Fourier focused on the material and the organizational basis of workplace structures, the anarchist tradition of thought represented by Kropotkin and Proudhon argues for communal solidarity and mutualism in production, consumption and decision-making along with a fundamental rejection of the state (Mason 1982: 137–142). These major lines of thought suggest that the practice of workplace democracy has been prevalent since early industrialization in Europe and in the US. Initial forms of workplace democracy were hardly separable from unionization, collective bargaining and other conventional forms of labor struggle. However, for a meaningful contemporary analysis, one needs to distinguish outlets that are immune to the neoliberal onslaught, the weakening labor movement and the declining union struggle.

Guest and Peccei (2001) evaluate the possibilities of partnership at work and the structure of employer-employee relationships. They distinguish three major approaches to these issues. The pluralist approach seeks a legal framework that defines the basis of interest representation through co-determination and communication, rather than through the direct participation and action of workers. The unitarist approach focuses on the direct participation of workers in daily work-related issues. This approach has more room for worker involvement in and contribution to the decision-making process with regard to work-related issues. The limitation of direct participation parallels those of direct democracy: they can only be effective on a certain set of issues and not on a broad spectrum of issues. A third approach is the hybrid approach, which seeks "a formal joint governance system" for long-term commitment to workplace democracy (Guest and Peccei 2001: 210). European Works Councils (EWC) could be a very efficient example of this formal joint governance system. Although EWCs are primarily concerned with economic efficiency and promote workers' input on organization and work-related issues, they also promote political democracy and social cohesion (Hardy and Adnett 2006: 1025).

In addition to the legal framework and the organizational structure of workplace democracy, the scope and range of the issues undertaken in the workplace is another important dimension of democratic practice. Guest and Peccei came up with eight factors undertaken in partnership practices in their empirical evaluation: the first two are on direct participation in decisions about work and personal employment issues, and the next two are on representative participation on both employment and organizational issues. The last four issues consist of flexible job design; job quality; performance management; and employee ownership, communication, and security (Guest and Peccei 2001: 221).

Melman identifies five major categories where workers seek change, also which unions adjust in their contract demands, basing his argument on Lawrence B. Cohen's unpublished book on workers and production (Melman 2001: 281–283).[2] The worker group includes those who produce, those who perform clerical duties, and those who bargain and negotiate on the side of the workers. Work time refers to any time dedicated to work, whether regular or not. Melman identifies deployment as changes in the place, department and grade of a worker's position as spatial dimensions of the worker's mobility. Although deployment is bound by seniority, the flexibilization of the work process suggests that alternatives will be numerous. The last two categories Melman focuses on are performance and compensation. Performance refers to the workload, work standards, and procedures regarding the production process. Compensation refers to the wage and non-wage payments and benefits a worker receives or demands from the employer.

Melman's framework of worker demands and challenges is very comprehensive in representation. The worker group is hardly a monolithic unit, given the temporal and spatial variation in the organization of the production process. Work time shows variation with respect to the nature of the employment contract in a time when temporary, casual and contractual employment becomes the norm rather than the exception. Deployment, despite the limitations imposed by seniority, can hardly be traced on a structural level, given the decentralization of the production process. The last two categories of performance and compensation are especially important as they relate to the workplace and beyond the workplace, that is, to the social conditions of the workers. If these are the major areas of struggle, how then are workers going to have an input in the decision-making process? How can participation be defined and operationalized?

Mason defines participation with respect to five major dimensions: the number of participants (extensity); forms of input, face-to-face communication, and voting (mode); types of issues covered (scope), psychological involvement of participants (intensity), and impact upon decision-making (quality) Mason 1982: 153). All of these dimensions remain relevant in evaluating workplace democracy. There is still need for further features to be specified in response to the corporate strategies that operate on the neoliberal pillars of the global market. The corporate perspective approaches employee participation as an expression of competence and self-actualization, as part of democratization and industrial citizenship, but more importantly as an instrument of organizational efficiency (Markey 2001: 4–5). Workplace democracy conceptualized as part of the alternative economy is more of an end in itself rather than a means to an end. This is one other reason why it needs to be conceptualized and specified according to the limits of corporate capitalism.

So far, the discussion has focused on the legal framework of workplace democracy, its organizational aspects, and the issues that it affects. The cited literature mainly refers to the challenges awaiting workers in the workplace. They all stress the need to incorporate social issues into workplace management. At this point, a theoretical and a practical intervention are needed. The problems that workers face today are not limited to the workplace. The community, as a dimension of workplace democracy, needs to be added to the foregoing discussion. The community here represents the social and the material circumstances in which workers find themselves with regard to work and the workplace. The community includes the legal problems (i.e. legal status) of immigrant workers, the housing problems of low-wage workers, the environmental problems that affect workers who live along the borders of major industrial centres, and the infrastructure problems workers face due to their marginalization in the public economy.

The existing literature on workplace democracy conceptualizes it as a practice to improve the decision-making process in such a way that it will both increase worker input and increase worker productivity due to a psychological effect (their self-esteem) and an economic effect (industrial reorganization). Workplace democracy as a component of the alternative economy has a different value and meaning compared to its role in the capitalist world economy. Collective management or participatory management in the alternative economy implies more than the vertical organization of the workplace. Collective ownership schemes that directly include workers give them the opportunity to vote on matters such as profit-sharing and re-investment, and whether to open up to new members or remain small in production. Workplace democracy as one of the four pillars of the alternative economy considers the workplace and the social context surrounding it as a whole. Any decision taken in the workplace needs to be evaluated for its implications outside of the workplace simply because the outside world is an extension of the relations of production. Expanding a production plant will have dire social, environmental and/or infrastructural consequences for the workers and their extended communities. Making decisions on the basis of workplace dynamics will not necessarily improve the stakes workers hold outside of the workplace.

Collom, in an empirical study, analyzes the impact of race, gender and class on support for economic democracy. The research is representative of the American labor market and incorporates Latino and African-American men and women. The findings suggest that African-Americans are more supportive of economic democracy due to their race position, whereas race and class seem to be the motivation for Latino support of economic democracy: "The superexploitation of people of color under capitalism is perhaps the best explanation for their greater support of economic democracy" (Collom 2001: 492). The relative conservatism of Whites does not come as a surprise. Collom appropriately concludes:

> Overall, labor is strengthened through workplace democracy as issues of wages and benefits are superseded and the nature of work itself is brought into question. Transformations of the relations in production offer the most to those who are most subjugated under contemporary capitalism. As all workers are empowered, women and people of color gain the most.
>
> (Collom 2001: 495)

Workplace democracy embraces class and other sources of social inequality as an alternative organizational form and frame of action. The demands for the democratization of the workplace are not simply geared toward the enhancement of material benefits; they also include greater control over the labor process, greater room for representation in the decision-making process, and an overall concern for the well-being of workers in and outside of the workplace.

Rothschild examines the possibility of enhanced workplace democracy and introduces four major interventions that are not necessarily revolutionary, but that, taken as a whole, provide a coherent framework for workplace democracy. First, Rothschild maintains that a flatter, team-based model – as a basis for organization – bridges the gap between management and production (Rothschild 2000). It eliminates bureaucracy; it is less costly; and its innovative high-performance systems enable continuous renewal. Second, full democratization of the workplace requires the incorporation of women, minorities and others in the lower echelons of society into organizing teams. This will help overcome wage gaps between different groups and eliminate gender and racial bias during and after the recruitment process. Third, unions stand out as an essential component of workplace democracy. The weakening union density and the loss of bargaining power is a limitation for unions in pursuing alternative strategies or focusing on new recruitment, yet pushing for greater workplace democracy and the incorporation of more marginal segments of workers may serve as a way for the unions to revitalize their ranks. Finally, the use of technology in the workplace is more important in the contemporary global setting. Rothschild states that those who make decisions about the use of technology in the workplace do so according to the needs of their position in the workplace. Management uses technology to exert more pressure and control over workers and the labor process in hierarchical managerial systems. If the decision about the use of technology is made by the horizontally integrated teams instead of management, the use of technology will be geared toward productivity and efficiency rather than surveillance and control:

> New institutional forms do not arrive de novo. They are born and grow inside of old institutional forms, and they can grow a long way before people notice that something very basic has changed. The involvement and the influence of working people from all levels of the organization and on all kinds of teams –on the shop floor, in hospitals, in offices – will be pivotal in shaping the outcomes of this process.
>
> (Rothschild 2000: 211)

The potential of workplace democracy as an alternative model carries democratic practice beyond the political domain to that of the economy and society. This necessitates an overall transformation of the way democracy is understood in terms of rights, practices and procedures. The changing perception and practice of democracy will gradually be reflected in organizations as well. New organizations will form, and the old ones will transform. The undertaking of workplace democracy is an effort to appropriate the right kind of means toward the most immediate ends.

Notes

1 This is not to overgeneralize in a way that would override reform attempts in unions. Workers employed in non-standard forms did find room for representation either in existing unions or in groups they established themselves. Gender issues were partially addressed by unions, but not to the extent that gender inequalities were resolved. Gender issues that became part of the union agenda targeted women but not necessarily members of the LGBT community.

2 Melman refers to *Workers and Decision-Making on Production* by Lawrence B. Cohen, Professor Emeritus of Industrial Engineering at Columbia University, which was unpublished in 2001, when Melman's own book came out. For a more accessible reference on Cohen's work, see Cohen 1976.

4 Rethinking employment relations

This chapter will set out to construct a conceptual framework for understanding and analyzing empirical discussions. A number of overarching points, however, are worth repeating. First, the evolution of labor studies to include a growing number of methodologies and perspectives necessitates a moment of clarification as to how these methodologies and perspectives will be operationalized here. The divergence between the literatures of work and occupation on the one hand and labor relations on the other has generated a plethora of ways in which basic concepts have been used, operationalized and even measured. Second, the historical transformations brought about by neoliberal globalization, the advent of flexibility as the dominant mode of production, and the ongoing global economic crisis require a re-evaluation of concepts such as work, labor, employment, occupation and job. Third, inherent transformations in the essence of work, labor, employment and other related concepts require a moment of clarification. In the case of work, the conventional understanding of this term has been that it refers to tasks undertaken outside of the home and produced in a separate spatial setting for the market. Today, home-based work is a significant component of global production. What was essentially physical labor – as in the case of blue-collar workers – has now come to mean physical, mental and even emotional labor employed in the production of tangible goods and intangible services. Employment has traditionally referred to a continuous relationship under a formal contract in the case of lifetime full proletarianization, whereas now, with the rise of contingent employment, the form and the contract of employment have been radically transformed. The conceptual discussion, then, will be followed by a review of the implications of technological developments and economic crisis on employment relations, and a close examination of the labor movement and its potential to form a firm stance in the faces of contemporary economic challenges.

Conceptual challenges

The distinctions underlined here will help clarify the blurred boundaries between work and non-work, weakening institutional formations and cultural connotations of occupations and jobs, and the persistence of labor as a component of the production process in spite of intensifying technological progress. This conceptual clarity will help better expose the social consequences of the contemporary transformations in the world of work that will discussed below. The concepts are ordered in a deductive manner, starting from the most general and abstract term (labor) and moving on to the most specific term (job). The concepts will be defined and discussed in a comparative manner so as to be easily incorporated into the analytical discussions that will follow.

The most appropriate beginning for a conceptual review of labor is a look at the writings of Karl Marx. Labor refers to the efforts of a person excluded from the means of production – a person who takes part in the production process through his or her physical effort: "We mean by labour-power or labour-capacity, the aggregate of those mental and physical capabilities existing in the physical form, the living personality, of a human being, capabilities which he sets in motion whenever he produces a use-value of any kind" (Marx 1990 [1867]: 270). For Marx, labor is an abstraction that is instrumental to the understanding of the way the capitalist mode of production operates to generate accumulation and form class. Marx makes four major distinctions with regard to the conceptualization of labor. First, the distinction between productive and unproductive labor is based on the distinction between the use of labor to produce capital and the nature of labor as use-value in and of itself:

> It is possible for work of one type (such as gardening, tailoring etc.) to be performed by the same working man either in the service of an industrial capitalist or on behalf of the immediate consumer. He is a wage-labourer or day labourer in either situation, only he is a productive worker in the one case and unproductive in the other, because in the one he produces capital and in the other not; because in the one case his work is a factor in the self-valorization process of capital and in the other it is not.
>
> (Marx 1990 [1867]: 1045)

Second, the concept of alienated labor refers to the way labor is subsumed in the production process and the worker as a human being is impoverished by the loss of reality he produces through his labor, namely, the commodity: "In political economy this realization of labour appears as a loss of reality to the worker, objectification as a loss of the object or slavery to it, and appropriation as alienation, as externalization" (McLellan 1977: 78). Third, discussing wage labor Marx explains that the commodification of labor in the market and the exchange between the capitalist and the laborer is in fact an exchange of two commodities, namely, labor and wages (money). Wages are determined with respect to supply and demand in the market, the cost of the reproduction of labor (the means by which the laborer will find the effort to work again), and the gain of the capitalist (McLellan 1977: 249–260). Fourth, the division of labor, in both its economic and social definitions, situates labor in larger structures and contexts:

> The division of labour in society is mediated through the purchase and sale of the products of different branches of industry, while the connection between the various partial operations in a workshop is mediated through the sale of the labour-power of several workers to one capitalist, who applies it as combined labour-power. The division of labour within manufacture presupposes a concentration of the means of production in the hands of one capitalist; the division of labour within society presupposes a dispersal of those means among many independent producers of commodities.
>
> (Marx 1990 [1867]: 475–476)

The essential and the relational definitions pertaining to labor reveal the functioning of capitalism as a system; more specifically, the labor theory of value exposes the extraction of surplus value from labor. The whole capitalist cycle from the shop floor to the global economy operates on the value of labor, irrespective of the form it takes in the market. Almost one hundred years after the publication of Marx's *Das Kapital*, Karl Polanyi very appropriately names labor, together with land and capital, as fictitious commodities (Polanyi 1967). In their crudest form, all three are fictitious, as they exist prior to the market and neither is produced for the market; labor as a fictitious commodity is an exceptional category because of its abstract nature and because it is part of human existence. Labor in this sense is not an economic category but a social one.

While an exclusive reliance on Marx may lead to an essentialist view of labor, it may also exclude the impact of contemporary economic transformations on labor. These contemporary transformations include the spatial expansion of the division of labor under globalization; the increasing use of informal and casual labor; especially in less developed parts of the world that integrate into the global market by using cheap labor; flexible specialization becoming the dominant mode of production on a global scale; the increasing use of female labor as the cheapest and the most flexible source of labor for global capital; and, finally, the qualitative and quantitative weakening of unionization, which has made labor much more vulnerable vis-à-vis capital (Munck 2002). For Standing, "labour's function is to produce marketable output or services," whereas "labor power is the bundle of capacities one possesses" (Standing 2009: 7). Standing takes the definitions of Marx and Polanyi one step further and defines labor in the market and extends its function to include the production of intangible commodities such as various kinds of services.

The historical transformation of the way in which labor is conceptualized reveals certain continuities and discontinuities. As for the continuities, the prevalence of the capitalist world economy assures the continuous commodification of labor. The ceaseless accumulation of capital suggests that labor will continue to generate surplus value that will translate into profit for the capitalists. As for the discontinuities, they will emerge from the expansion of the capitalist market both in size and in scope to include both goods and services: tangible and intangible products that were previously not commodified.

As a result, labor is not only a physical effort employed in the production of tangible goods, but labor is also a mental capacity, an emotional input in the making of intangible commodities, namely, services. The diversity of labor power employed in the capitalist economy challenges the male-dominant nature of the labor force, as physical labor loses its centrality in the market. Women become a more competitive segment of the labor force given the diversity in the market and in labor demand.

Gorz argues that the labor theory of value is losing its explanatory power because use-value does not represent the amount of labor input; exchange value is not reflected in the current price system. For Gorz, prices are political (Gorz 1999: 90). The movement of capital to less developed countries with cheap labor is supportive of the political pricing argument. Gorz's observation on the current pricing bias is accurate, yet his analysis of the utility of the labor theory of value is rather off-track. If the overvalorization of the system due to extreme financialization were to be reversed, price adjustments in the market would enable a return to the essential labor theory of value, given the financial nature of the global economic crisis.

Standing defines employment as "stabilized labour based on subordinated labour security" (Standing 2009: 6). He defines labor in the market mechanism and uses a similar relational approach to define employment as a contractual relationship within a political and an institutional framework. Employment locates the exchange between capital and labor within a framework of rights and responsibilities; more specifically, employment entitles individuals and their dependents to certain social protections and safety measures within their state's existing welfare regime.

The concepts of unemployment and underemployment are at least as important as the concept of employment itself. It has been a while since social scientists in general and economists in particular have taken full employment off their agendas. Lifetime full employment has become a rare experience for the contemporary global labor force, irrespective of geographical location. As flexibility has become the *modus operandi* of contemporary capitalism, underemployment has become the norm. The advance and the deepening of global economic crisis made unemployment become a structural component of austerity-driven economies:

> These changes in employment relations create challenges – and opportunities – for sociology. There is a greater urgency to explain: how various kinds of employment relations are created and maintained; their consequences for job quality, productivity, and other essential outcomes; and the kinds of public policies that might be implemented in order to reduce precarity and other negative outcomes associated with nonstandard employment relations.
> (Kalleberg 2009)

Kalleberg draws attention to the need to study organizational structure as part of managerial strategies concerning different forms and relations of employment. The spatial expansion of the production process and improvements in information technology have transformed the priorities of organizations and challenge them to adopt precise managerial techniques to structure employment relations in the most optimal manner. Organizational and managerial challenges in employment relations are beyond the scope of this book for two main reasons. First, the business perspective on employment relations focuses on the efficiency and productivity of the organization at the expense of worker relations. Second, the focus here is on transformations that concern the inherent dynamics of employment, that is, the way employment is defined, operationalized, structured and embedded in various social contexts inside and outside of the workplace. The external factors of management and organization are part of the larger setting defined with respect to neoliberal globalization and flexible specialization. It is flexibility itself that organizes employment in the most optimal manner for the sake of capital.

The conceptual comparisons provided by Standing help clarify the distinctions between terms that are otherwise used interchangeably in scholarship. When comparing labor and employment with work, the former has no room for reproductive activity, whereas the latter includes productive, reproductive and creative activity. Labor and employment operate on the basis of an economic imperative that aims at maximizing efficiency through competitiveness, whereas work is a space for stillness and pressure from within, where control over the "worker" assures productivity and efficiency only with the imposition of an external agent. In terms of personal outcome, "labor intensive" production generates "stress, burn out and loss of control" as opposed to work that generates "necessity, surviving and reproducing, and personal development" (Standing 1999: 6–7). Labor is alienated and abstracted from the social relations that surround it, and hence lacks agency. Work has agency and a feeling of self-determination that is embedded in the social relations that surround it.

The centrality of "work" in social organization is changing. The place of work in people's lives is to be filled by other social components, as fewer workers are needed for the capitalist economy. The blurred boundaries of work and non-work require a "radical reform" in social organization, the political mechanism, and culture. For Gorz, "wage-labour has to disappear and, with it, capitalism" (Gorz 1999: 77). Gorz proposes three major resolutions along this line of argument. The first concerns guaranteed basic income for all, which is also supported by Standing and other labor scholars. The second is the redistribution of work and the collective control by individuals over time. The benefits associated with work and non-work have to be redistributed according to changes in the production system and consumption patterns, and should not be defined by the conventional patterns of economic organization and redistribution. The third covers all three areas of "radical reform" and underlines the need for new areas of social solidarity and exchange beyond the wage relation. Hence, Gorz sees "a future with less employment and less selling of labour and services, but with a growth in collective facilities and services, in non-monetary exchange and self-providing" (Gorz 1999: 83).

Standing defines occupation as "creative and dignifying work around a self-chosen set of activities" (Standing 2009: 10). The building of an occupation as a structural entity, as an institution and identity that reflects upon class, culture, and technology, is in fact a historical process, "an evolving set of related tasks based on traditions and accumulated knowledge" (Standing 2009: 10). Labor in its most abstract form refers to the capacities and skills a person holds that enable him or her to hold a position in the production process. Work refers to specific areas in which labor is subsumed to produce goods for the market. Occupation, different from work, refers to a specialized form of work where tasks, production processes, and the social relations surrounding them are also uniquely expressed.

Kalleberg states three major reasons for the centrality of occupations in the twenty-first century. They are the primary source of "affiliation and identification" in a world where the definitions and boundaries of work and labor relations are becoming more and more blurred (Kalleberg 2009). Second, workers get a chance to become a part of a collective agency across multiple employers and organizations through the process of identity formation associated with occupations. Third, occupations have become the foundation of unionization in some settings, especially under circumstances which strictly limit unionization and membership. Occupations serve as benchmarks that provide relative predictability and stability in a setting where employment is flexible, high turnover rates characterize labor markets, and occupational categories are continuously challenged by on-the-job-training and fragmented production processes.

According to Standing (2009: 6), a "job is a manipulated limitation of skill." The difference between an occupation and a job is that the former represents a long-term, institutionalized position in the world of work that implies continuity, an identity as a member in an occupational category, and a cultural framework in which this identity can be built. The latter, however, is a more transient category, which is only externally defined and which is imposed on the individual participating in the labor market. An occupation consists of a set of activities making a career and a career structure – a civic friendship based on respect, ethics, and identity – that is altogether solidified in occupational circles or occupational guilds. A job holds none of these features but is defined in such a way so as to encompass certain tasks and features geared toward labor market competition. A good example of this distinction between an occupation and a job is the process of on-the-job training. The amount of skill embedded in the job is so limited that it can be learned and performed at the same time, irrespective of previous experience. Hence a job does not necessitate a long-term commitment or a cultural dedication as is the case with an occupation.

A conceptual framework built to represent the contemporary transformations in work and labor relations has to be complemented by a contemporary research methodology. A number of issues complicate the process of measurement in labor studies. The field of labor studies does not have an exclusive research methodology as a discipline would have, since it produces an interdisciplinary body of literature. The interdisciplinary character of the literature can be its richness in perspective and theoretical analysis, but it may also be a challenge in terms of methodology. Disciplines as scientific structures are roughly defined on the basis of the unique issues they focus on from a particular perspective using research methods that are specifically designed to link empirical data with said perspective. Labor economics, the sociology of work and labor, labor history, and labor law stand as distinct disciplinary categories. The multidimensional nature of labor issues requires a multivariate interdisciplinary analysis and greater cooperation between different segments of labor studies.

The field of labor studies by no means produces a monolithic body of literature, since it has its own diversity with respect to the study of work and occupations on the one hand and industrial and labor relations on the other. The former focuses on workplace dynamics, working conditions, skill formation and deskilling as variables, whereas the latter looks at employment issues, labor struggles in organizations, union membership, and the prevalence of strikes. There is a greater tendency toward qualitative analysis in the former and a strong emphasis on quantitative analysis in the latter.

Most labor studies fall into the subfield of labor economics, where macroeconomic evaluations, monetary policy, and even welfare economics include a labor dimension, even if they touch upon it tangentially. One major issue in labor economics is the problem of unemployment and the way that it can be controlled in economic terms. Econometrics as a subfield also deserves particular attention in regards to labor studies, as the advancement of quantitative methodology applied to large sets of data in a multivariate and longitudinal manner enables a broader analysis of existing dynamics (Heckman and Singer 2008). Econometric modeling and computation provide an opportunity to funnel massive aggregate data through a dynamic analysis so as to be evaluated at a higher level of abstraction (Valenzuela 2007).

In business studies, labor studies falls within the field of human resources management (HRM). Even a simple nominal evaluation of HRM suggests that labor in business studies is separated from its social constituents and its contextual and relational components, and is merely reduced to a resource. The primary goal of the HRM perspective is to benefit from human resources in the most productive and efficient manner so as to contribute to the profitability of business. Labor market forecasting, especially with respect to demand fluctuations in the world market, labor scheduling in different industries, and performance evaluation with respect to optimal productivity, are some of the issues undertaken in HRM in this pursuit. HRM methodologies used with regard to employee-related risk management are so meticulous, that even the health-related risk factors of employees are taken into consideration, including their smoking habits and, in the case of women, their maternal responsibilities. Drug tests for potential employees during the recruitment process have nearly become a standard procedure, and it has been the result of HRM methodologies and their efficient use.

The focus of studies on labor in sociology is more on the social dynamics and the processes of social change in regards to labor. Sociological inquiry operates on three levels of analysis to investigate issues of labor, work and employment in a relational manner. On a macro level, global or national transformations are under a microscope. The study of corporations that operate on a global scale, for example, employs a macro-level analysis. On a micro level, sociological inquiry evaluates the experiences of individuals united in the smallest social categories, namely, the household and the family. Household labor force surveys are important examples of micro-level analysis, where the immediate experiences of individuals regarding work, employment, income and labor relations are gathered through fieldwork. Between the two ends of the research spectrum lies the meso-level analysis. Research in urban sociology on immigrant labor, community labor organizations, worker centers, and cooperatives and worker-owned businesses are conducted on the meso-level; they are neither as general as macro-level studies nor as specific and focused as micro-level studies. The third part of this chapter will benefit from meso-level analysis in evaluating the responses to the repercussions of the global economic crisis.

Aside from the aforementioned disciplinary diversity in the research literature, the use of official data further complicates the methodological concerns about labor studies. Official data is heavily political, despite the extensity of networks, instruments and resources behind it. This political dimension shows up in the way variables are defined, samples are drawn from the universal set under focus, and the way variables are measured. The most vivid example of the politicized nature of gathered data is seen in unemployment rates. In many countries, a person has to apply to government agencies for jobs and not be able to enrol in employment training programs to be counted as unemployed. Then the massive numbers of people who are also excluded from formal job search mechanisms are excluded from the aggregate data. Labor force participation provides a more accurate view of labor markets, yet is less popular in quantitative research. Similar experiences are true in the measurement of the informal economy and informal employment. Massive numbers of illegal immigrants and undocumented laborers working in various settings also obscure labor market data. Official data is further politicized by the dominant ideology in government: the way statistics bureaus and/or departments of labor manipulate data so as to portray a well-functioning government. Finally, bureaucratic limitations and corruption in countries with a transparency issue prevent the accurate statement of labor issues. Strikes become classified as "social unrest," the unemployed are not counted, and inflation is miscalculated to make minimum wages look good. International organizations' heavy reliance on official data in their databases conceals rather than exposes labor problems. Cross-country analysis based on official aggregate data may be biased due to the dominant ideology of ruling governments.

The use of quantitative as opposed to qualitative methodology also generates diverse results in labor studies. Questions of labor productivity and efficiency are examined at the global level, which necessitates a cross-country analysis due to the emergence of a global division of labor. Increasing capital mobility with staggering labor mobility intensifies competition in the global labor market; this allows labor market forecasting and evaluation of wage differentials to be examined on a global plane. Diversity in labor market conditions and the local repercussions of the global division of labor requires a more focused, in-depth analysis of work and labor relations. Quantitative analysis enables a larger domain to be studied in a comparative manner; it will provide limited insight, however, into the internal variations and inner dynamics of the relevant variables. When thinking about the global labor market, it may be possible to compare productivity, efficiency, or labor cost for a multiple set of countries, while it may be more difficult to see the social and material consequences of employment in the global labor market. This is the case in a major portion of economic, econometric and management studies. Qualitative analysis will provide greater insight into the variables that are being studied and will bring a vivid understanding of the causalities between them. Qualitative analysis may be operational only in smaller domains that researchers can access for practical purposes. There is also a growing idealization of quantitative methodology because of its computerized foundations and its ability to analyze temporally and spatially extended data sets. One has to regard this idealization with caution, as qualitative methodology is at least as meticulous and labor-intensive as its quantitative counterpart. The process of preparing and conducting fieldwork is more time-consuming and labor-intensive than the process of running aggregate data through a computer program (that has already been written and developed).

The most appropriate approach to research in labor studies, given its interdisciplinary nature, has to be the employment of mixed methods. The availability of aggregate data on a number of labor issues in the form of official data or through other institutional resources such as household labor force surveys or census data relatively simplifies the use of quantitative methodology, at least in basic comparisons. Supporting macro-scale structural information with field data will establish a complementary approach in labor-related research. The two approaches will hold different units of analysis and focus on different levels of analysis. Quantitative methodology is more appropriate for macro-level analysis, and qualitative methodology is more appropriate for micro-level analysis. The data from two different methodological sources will enrich comparative analysis. In some cases that have a more specific area of research, both conceptually and geographically, the aforementioned meso-level analysis may prove to be a middle ground on which both qualitative and quantitative approaches can work.

For the purposes of the research presented in this book, macro-level quantitative data will be combined with a meso-level analysis to expose the reciprocal relationship between the global and the local. In evaluating the local alternatives of production, redistribution and labor organization, qualitative methodology may prove to be useful in exposing the immediate circumstances that led to the development of these alternatives and the consolidation of their social relations.

The focus on empirical aspects of labor studies in general and this study in particular is by no means to underestimate the importance of theoretical contributions to the existing body of literature. The social sciences in general suffer from a heavy reliance on empiricism due to the expansion of publication opportunities and publication requirements in academia. Any empirical investigation has to do more than state the obvious: the responsibility of scientific inquiry is to take the existing interpretation and analysis one step further and generate more questions and shed light on future research possibilities. One question that has been posed is on the future of work, which is the issue undertaken in the next section.

The economy without work

Two decades have passed since the publication of Jeremy Rifkin's *The End of Work: The Decline of the Global Labor Force and the Dawn of the Post-Market Era* (Rifkin 1995), and there still is a lot of "work" being done. The market maintains its present status and the post-market era is still an uncertainty. The nature and the definition of work have changed, and the whole social organization of work – along with the political and economic changes surrounding it – has been reciprocally responsive. Rifkin's foresight regarding the doom of work has yet to be proven correct (and some doubt that it ever will be). This section looks at the externalization of work, rather than the end of work, by examining the process by which corporations externalize work and by examining the social, political and economic consequences of this externalization. These consequences can be observed on multiple levels: at the micro level for workers and corporations, at the meso level for industries and for local development, and at the macro level for national economies and governments (with respect to the possibility of a consensus between capital, labor and the state). A comparative analysis on the nation-state level may provide insight into the functioning of the global economy; however, the heterogeneity of observations about the global economy may make it impossible to come to an overarching conclusion about the externalization of work.

Corporations push jobs and workers out of their domain by investing in improved technologies. The concept of technological unemployment, rising unemployment as a result of improved production technologies, can be traced back to the early period of industrialization and the Luddite Uprisings (1811–1817). Since then, Luddism, or neo-Luddism in its contemporary form, has been taken as an anti-technology movement. Although improved technologies diminish the dependency of the production process on labor, they do not necessarily lead to the disappearance of work or the total abandonment of labor as an input in economic organization. The Luddite Fallacy refers to the theoretical understanding that technological change leads to structural unemployment, but this remains a highly debated issue. Technological innovation may improve product efficiency and diminish labor dependence, but the adoption of such innovations also depends on other external factors such as the cost of labor versus the cost of technology, and the impact of the former and the latter on competition and long-term returns. Economics does not operate under *ceteris paribus* conditions, where all other social, political, historical and geographical factors can easily be externalized.

Brynjolfsson and McAfee evaluate the structural transformations generated by the intensive penetration of technology into the production process. In what they define as humans' "race against the machine," "there is a growing mismatch between rapidly advancing digital technologies and slow-changing humans" (Brynjolfsson and McAfee 2012). Examples such as Geofluent, the electronic translator, Google's driverless car, or Watson the *Jeopardy!*-winning computer show the range of computers' digital pattern recognition capabilities. The winners and losers of technological change are highly skilled and low-skilled workers, respectively, at the micro level, and capital and labor, respectively, at the macro level. As a result, as Brynjolfsson and McAfee suggest, humans need to pursue structural transformations, or even adaptations, in fields such as education, entrepreneurship, investment, law, regulation, and taxes, to keep up with the exponential pace of technological progress.

Marchant et al. state that there are several dimensions of contemporary unemployment that have soared due to technology. The impact, according to them, is multilayered, starting from the individual in terms of psychological stress and the deterioration of self-worth and identity (Deane 2013), moving onto the family with the decline of income and the weakening of the household, and finally reaching to the macro level, where falling demand due to unemployment affects the whole economy (Marchant et al. 2014: 29). Technological unemployment affects society in an intergenerational manner and is unevenly distributed in terms of gender and skills. Marchant et al. propose several policy options to fight against technological unemployment, such as slowing innovation, work-sharing, making new work, redistribution, extended education opportunities, and fostering a new social contract. Yet none of these policy options are targeting unemployment emerging as a consequence of technology. If technological unemployment leads to a polarization of jobs by deliberately eliminating semi-skilled positions, then policies need to address specifically those groups that are affected. A multivariate analysis and a socioeconomic policy approach may be crucial to appropriate policymaking.

While technology is a crucial variable in analyzing employment and unemployment in the labor market, it can by no means be isolated from the dominant neoliberal economic policy and the leftist opposition to it:

> Neo-liberal dogma holds that there will never be unemployment if wages are allowed to find their natural level by eliminating minimum wage laws and social welfare measures, and if state-imposed restrictions on the economy were removed to unleash the power of the market. If we have reached a tipping point where humans are losing the race against

> the machine eventually even having an employee with zero wages would produce less profit than owning a robot, and unleashing capitalism and slashing job protecting regulations will simply speed up the process of job displacement. But the prescriptions of left economists, for more job-protection and higher wages, will simply increase the cost of human labor compared to automation.
>
> (Hughes 2014: 4)

The policy responses to technological unemployment will challenge the position of the state vis-à-vis labor and capital. More unemployment will come to mean less revenue from taxes and more provision for the unemployed and all those requiring a basic income (Gajewska 2014). To what extent a universal basic income will be probable across the board is highly debatable. Whether from a structural perspective or an actor-based perspective, technological unemployment requires a relational, comparative, and historical analysis that will encompass the diverse impacts of technological change on society in general and labor in particular.

The tension between technological progress and employment can be further elaborated. A number of points are worth reiterating before extending the laborious task of comparing the pros and cons. The current state of technological progress may be faster than it has ever been and it may display greater diffusion that it has ever shown, but it is not new. The way horses were replaced by machines, telegram by telex or fax, and mail by email, is to a certain extent part of the historical progress of science and technology. The impact of this technological progress is diverse. Despite all the scientific and technological progress that has been made, a major portion of the world's population still lives on technology that would be called primitive by Western standards. It can hardly be assumed that a new technology will be available and adopted across the board. Examples and analysis emerging from the most developed settings do not necessarily represent a universal course of conduct. Mandel refers to outdated technologies being transferred to less developed parts of the world to generate income and dependency at the same time. As such, one would need to differentiate between the instrumental impact of technology and the role of technology as a commodity in the capitalist system (Mandel 1972).

The process of industrial upgrading is generally analyzed with respect to the organization of global value chains. Trade liberalization and the expansion of the production process on a global scale would lead to a spillover effect with the expansion of GVCs, resulting in industrial transition toward more capital-intensive industries that require high-skilled labor. Milberg argues that industrial upgrading "involves fitting into existing corporate strategies and, given the increasingly liberal international trade and investment environment, establishing close ties to a potentially diverse group of leading firms" (Milberg 2004: 3). Therefore, labor from the developing world aims to integrate itself into constantly renewing industrial production within a highly competitive market. Industrialization would gradually shift toward capital-intensive sectors, generate more added value, and increase labor productivity and wages. The expected impact on labor would be higher skills and higher wages.

Empirical evidence in the form of cross-country data presents the diverse consequences of industrial upgrading. Akyuz et al. argue that the pace and pattern of industrialization depends on the pace and pattern of capital accumulation and participation of a country in international trade. Productivity growth depends on the concomitant developments in investment, technological progress, and the learning process which will dictate how this technological progress will be utilized (Akyuz et al. 2004: 29–32). As a result, Akyuz et al. come up with a five-tier categorization of countries experiencing various degrees of industrialization – a scheme which in fact parallels the long-term historical analysis of dependency theorists and world-systems analysts.[1]

This illusion of the universal linear progress of industrial upgrading is more than optimistic, given the current discrepancies regarding industrialization, labor productivity and wages within and between countries. There are several limitations to the industrial upgrading myth. The first has to do with the immediate experiences of the workers. What will happen when the pace of skill formation among laborers cannot catch up with the process of industrial upgrading? What will the intergenerational impact of industrial upgrading be? Even if structural responses such as educational reform, labor transformation, and further regulation are pursued punctually and extensively, there will be massive numbers of workers who will be excluded from the labor market.

The second limitation, which starts on a higher level of analysis, is the fact that industrial upgrading cannot be a universal experience. There are two reasons for this. First, older technology continues to be of use for certain segments of society despite the transfer of technology or the move to capital-intensive, high-value-added sectors. Technological innovation in its initial stages of invention is too costly to be applied in a widespread manner. Second, industrial upgrading will benefit only some of the labor force as long as it accounts for some industries in some economies. Even if success stories will pop up on a sporadic basis, one can hardly talk about structural transformations in a general sense. The counter-argument will be based on the newly industrialized economies (NIEs) of East Asia or to a certain extent those of Brazil, China, Russia, and China (the BRICs), which did go through significant social and economic transformations. But these examples are to be regarded more as exceptions than the rule, which brings us to the third important limitation to the myth of industrial upgrading.

The basic rule of the system is unequal exchange between people, between enterprises, and between countries. Mandel, in his seminal work *Late Capitalism*, explains in great detail how the transfer of older technologies from the core capitalist countries to the periphery is used as a form of industrial upgrading to extract further surplus value and intensify the dependency of the periphery on the core (Mandel 1972). This dependency is observed both at the moment of production and the moment of consumption. In explaining the "absolute inner limit of the capitalist mode of production," Mandel states that

> it lies in the fact that the mass of surplus-value itself necessarily diminishes as a result of the elimination of living labour from the production process in the course of the final stage of mechanization-automation. Capitalism is incompatible with fully automated production in the whole of industry and agriculture, because this no longer allows the creation of surplus-value or valorization of capital. It is hence impossible for automation to spread to the entire realm of production in the age of late capitalism.
>
> (Mandel 1972: 207)

The underlying assumptions of an analysis of the relationship between variables, whether between technology and employment, or industrial structure and employment, must be clearly stated and understood before undertaking such an analysis. The primary assumption is that the ultimate objective of production or efficient production is to maximize profit, that is, that profit, as Mandel states, can only be maximized in a system of inequality, which continuously reproduces inequality by way of extracting surplus value from production and absorbing profit from consumption. Methodological and topical constrictions in an analysis may create myopia toward the bigger picture.

One major proposal has been the provision of a universal basic income based on the idea of economic citizenship. Several scholars have contributed to the development of this idea. Wright provides a basic definition of universal basic income:

> Every legal resident of a country receives a monthly living stipend sufficient to live at a culturally defined respectable standard of living, say 125 percent of the "poverty line." The grant is unconditional on the performance of any labor or other form of contribution, and it is universal – everyone receives the grant as a matter of citizenship right, rich and poor alike. Grants go to individuals, not families. Parents are the custodians of minority children's grants.
>
> (Wright 2010: 153)

The idea of a universal basic income is not only a monetary instrument but it is one component of a larger agenda of social organization, where spheres of work and non-work will have to be reconstituted. For Gorz, the unconditional guaranteed income has to be supported with other resolutions, namely, the redistribution of work, the collective control over time by individuals, and the establishment of new areas of social solidarity and wage relations (Gorz 1999: 83–87). It is not only a transformation of the material basis of production, but a transformation of the social context in which material dispositions are meaningfully constructed. And this is the reason why voluntarism and maximization of free time are to be included in the new equation. Gorz uses voluntarism as a mechanism of checks and balances against the free rider problem that may arise from the implementation of an unconditional guaranteed income.

Standing analyzes the changing labor dynamics in the developing world and supervises pilot projects in Africa and India that aim to implement a universal basic income as a social right attached to citizenship:

> I believe we must see basic income as a question of emancipation, a question of building freedom, building control over life and of social justice, not just as a measure for dealing with poverty. We must understand that the debate on basic income must be seen in the context of a global transformation taking place in which inequalities are becoming unsustainable and we are turning our European economies into "rentier" economies where a tiny plutocracy is gaining income from the system while the growing precariat is facing falling wages, unstable labour and a loss of rights. They are being turned from citizens into "denizens," losing rights. This is unique.
>
> (Milevska 2015)

The universal basic income debate could very well be extended with the results of the pilot studies, which show what effect the contribution of even the smallest amounts of extra income can have on the lives of the poor as well as the hope and revival that such an intervention generates in the downward spiral of households in need. The provision of the universal basic income is by no means an alternative to overcome the structural discrepancies caused by the global economy. The universal basic income and the global wealth tax proposed by Piketty are solutions that will slightly improve the material dispositions of the economically marginalized masses for the continuity of the system. The practical feasibility of universalizing redistribution mechanisms remains a mystery. One can hardly be optimistic about a universal basic income in a time when individuals can simply change their citizenship in order not to pay wealth taxes or when immigration becomes a big challenge to existing redistribution mechanisms. The polarization of income levels and the wealth gap between the world's richest and poorest people is another practical limitation. Providing a respectable standard of living at 125 percent of the poverty line is an illusion for countries where the minimum wage is at 25 percent of the poverty line. The humanizing impact of the universal basic income cannot be disregarded; however, the efficiency of this ethical responsibility is hardly enough to reconstruct the social solidarity that has been completely shattered by unequal exchange. Proponents of such a short-term intervention omit the depth of the inequality problem for the sake of the security of the system instead of having to come to terms with an uncertain future.

This section has addressed three major debates regarding the challenges of work-centered social and economic organization. First, it looked at technological unemployment as the impact of technology-intensive production schemes on work and employment. Second, it examined industrial upgrading as a way of improving the skill composition and wage intervals of the workforce in a given setting. Third, it discussed the idea of a universal basic income and how it is a way to humanize the capitalist world economy and fulfill an ethical responsibility for those excluded from work opportunities. These challenges, however, only give a partial explanation of the changing place of work in social and economic organization. Neither technology nor industrial upgrading is a sufficient basis for explaining the changing world of work. In quantitative terms, continuous job creation and the commodification of certain services provide grounds for new work to be done. In qualitative terms, technology, innovation, and sectoral change may render some types of work obsolete while making others more prevalent. Universal basic income may address poverty and inequality, but it may further complicate the picture if it responds to the changing context of work.

This is why this book focuses on the externalization of work from the global economy. The formal mechanisms of the global economy are based on corporate power as its organizational axis, which operates within a legal institutional context erected upon the WTO, IMF, WB and other global entities. There is a significant portion of work that falls outside of the realm of this formal, solid construct of business: "If intra-firm trade is the result of firm internalization strategies, then the observed rise in non-arm's-length subcontracting should be explained by *externalization*" (Milberg 2004: 8). This externalization is not the same as the Marxist notion of the externalization of the social components of labor, or alienation; instead, it refers to the systematic exclusion and marginalization of the production process from economic organization. The concentration and centralization of capital that is personified in the multinational corporation primarily handle two major tasks: management and finance. Production takes place in the unseen depths of the system, in sweatshops and in small local businesses that basically have no name. There are companies that purely rely on freelancers, without having a single employee on their payroll (Pagliery 2013). Online platforms such as Task Rabbit, Freelancer or Elance (now UpWork) bring together employers and freelance workers. They are sites where work can get done without the formal employment pattern, work contract, social security, or social benefits. The following was found on the old Elance website: "Find freelancers at the world's most-trusted online workplace. Elance is where businesses go to find, hire, collaborate with and pay leading freelancers from more than 180 countries. With a community of over 3 million freelancers and 1 million businesses, on Elance it's easy to hire a top freelancer."[2] Another similar yet unsuccessful effort at creating an online platform of work exchange was Coffee and Power, which was established by the Philip Rosedale. By creating a virtual labor market that operates with the conventional labor market dynamics of supply and demand, Rosedale wanted Coffee and Power to replace "old-style" management with collective management. A major novelty was the changing notion of a company. Workers did not have to be tied down to a company any longer; instead, with workers' detachment, future companies would now be "smaller and more nimble" (Diamandis 2013).

There are several ways in which work is being externalized from the formal institutional structures of the capitalist world economy. Subcontracting and outsourcing are primary examples that are tangentially linked to formal mechanisms of production. The informal economy is another way production is externalized. In addition, informal employment in the formal economy is third way in which work loses its visibility, security and value. Finally, the creation of a virtual labor market over the Internet with the functional use of online platforms is a further sign of labor detachment. The unrecognized territories of economic activity pose unknown challenges to workers around the world. The lack of a legal framework or regulatory mechanisms is one such challenge. Wages are determined by the forces of supply and demand without the possibility of a minimum wage agreement, collective bargaining, or any kind of labor standards that can be monitored. Especially in the case of online freelance hiring, one can hardly ensure that the posted profile of the hiring party or the freelancer is accurate.

The externalization of work from the formal and regulated corporate framework also translates into a detachment of economic objectives from social objectives, fundamentally challenging the concept of "economy." There seems to have emerged an epistemological need to bring society back into the science of economics beyond the social confrontations caused by class. If social factors are merely reduced to externalities, and increasingly negative ones, the whole *raison d'être* of the economy as a system and economics as a scientific discipline becomes ambiguous.

As unemployment and underemployment become structural components of the global economy, the system is facing a trade-off between the economic benefits of rising productivity and the social risks of falling demand. Corporations rely less on labor and fragment work to the extent that its social returns are minimized. The breakdown of the complementary relationship between production and consumption, and capital and labor, elements of the class society on which the capitalist economy is erected, is addressed as a historical moment of uncertainty by many (Hobsbawm 1994; Arrighi 2009; Hopkins and Wallerstein 1996). Others, however, have policy suggestions that seek to reverse the adverse effects of the contemporary global economy.

As more is being done by machines through automation and computerization, the work available for human operation is changing in both qualitative and quantitative terms. There is less physical work to be done, and given the skill-based polarization of tasks, the returns on the decreasing amount of tasks are distributed in a most uneven manner. At one end of the spectrum, there are the super-salary managerial elite, the superstars of the business world, and at the other end there is the wretched of the labor market, who survive on scraps. There are a number of policy alternatives and organizational responses to this rather skewed distribution of work and its returns. Gorz calls for a shift in the way payments are determined: "The distribution of means of payment must correspond to the volume of wealth socially produced and not to the volume of work performed" (Gorz 1999: 90). The meaning of work as the central organizing axis of social life and the ultimate goal of individual progress has to change. There are several propositions to support this kind of a shift: the idea of work-sharing, voluntarism in exchange for social income, cooperative circles or local exchange-trading systems. All of these are viable alternatives that are already in the making, even if they are being founded in an unstructured, sporadic manner. They will be analyzed in greater detail in the next chapter. For now, it is necessary to take a step back to update the classical labor theory of value and to re-establish the boundaries of work and non-work and the reciprocal relationship between work and wealth, which is expressed in the form of labor value:

> On one level, this revaluation literature calls into question the usefulness of traditional notions of "productivity," which focus on physical outputs when measuring the relative contribution of jobs that require mental or emotional labor. Without a tangible product, the effort involved in service work often seems invisible. Moreover, even where "effort, skill, and responsibility" can be calculated, however imprecisely, ideology shapes the quantities measured. "Productivity" and "value" are deeply subjective, despite the quantitative apparatus involved.
>
> (Cobble and Merrill 2009: 169)

There are two critical interventions that are crucial for the revalorization of work. First, the concept of value at a higher level of abstraction has to be defined. This rather abstract definition will help analyze the contextual or historical transformations in production. According to Marx, "what exclusively determines the magnitude of the value of any article is therefore the amount of labour socially necessary, or the labour time socially necessary for its production" (Marx 1990 [1867]: 129). The first precondition of value creation is the input of labor, or labor-time. From there on, Marx distinguishes between use-value, the value of any commodity produced with respect to its utility, and exchange-value, the value a commodity carries in the market, that is, in the process of exchange. The former value is a qualitative measure with respect to labor, and the latter is a quantitative measure with respect to the medium of exchange. More important than use-value and exchange-value at this moment is the social component and the social context of value. Quoting from the very classical references of Marx, "finally, nothing can be a value without being an object of utility. If the thing is useless, so is the labour contained in it; the labour does not count as labour, and therefore creates no value" (Marx 1990 [1867]: 131). It is at this moment, without further ado, that the question of utility for the currently externalized workers has to be asked: Is the work of domestic workers of utility? Of textile workers? Of freelancers? At the other end of the spectrum, what is the social utility of the services produced by stock market brokers? Of managers of various sorts? Are the productive capacities of the two poles of the labor force so skewed that the exchange-value of their labor is justifiably unequal? The contemporary economic setting suffers from the social construction of value, irrespective of the utility of the goods and services produced. First, the value of goods and services, whether commodified or not, have to be re-established. Anyone can survive without the goods and services produced in the financial markets, but no one can survive without food, without cleaning, and without a well-functioning infrastructure. Second, the relationship between value, utility and labor has to be re-established. The excessive, intensified focus on skill formation, education and training creates an illusion of value which is stripped of its utility.

Second, a brief reference to the way in which work has been transformed, devalued and then revalued will underline the importance of the revalorization of labor in the production process. Technological transformations, sectoral shifts, and changes in geographical composition, whether in the form of expansion, contraction or relocation, are structural factors behind the historical transformation of value. Demographic factors such as population increase, wars, and the composition of the existing labor force also play into the valorization process. The Industrial Revolution rendered agrarian labor obsolete and confined female labor to the household as the primary provider of domestic services. Then came the two World Wars, and particularly World War II, which brought women to the center of industrial production. The shift in the value of women's labor before and during the wars is noteworthy, for it significantly contributed to the making of second-wave feminism. The expansion of the production process on a global scale and the relative integration of global labor markets led to another shift in the way labor was valorized. The availability of cheap labor in less developed countries did not decrease the utility of goods produced per se, but it decreased the value of the labor embedded in these goods. Such examples could very well be extended. The central idea is that value in general and labor value in particular are socially constructed with respect to the structural and relational dynamics that surround them. The process of revalorization is crucial to overcoming the structural limitations of the global economy.

Crisis and labor

This section will present the immediate difficulties experienced in the world of work due to increasing inequality, corporate responses to global economic crisis, and the changing atmosphere of work in a crisis-ridden economy. Part of this discussion regarding the precariousness of employment under globalization has been touched upon in Chapter 1. The global economic crisis, however, has worsened the work environment in a number of other ways. Globalization has generated a global division of labor that is more interlinked and more interdependent than ever before. The process of technological transfer, the movement of outdated technologies to less developed parts of the world with abundant cheap labor, is not a new phenomenon that is particularly related to globalization. Mandel refers to this kind of capital mobility and the transformations in the global division of labor in late capitalism (Mandel 1972). What is more peculiar with globalization is the emergence of a production network, where the production process is so meticulously divided into smaller components that interdependency becomes inevitable. Production networks, whether conceptualized as commodity chains or value chains, are operated by a managerial sector for optimum profitability in the capitalist system.

The global division of labor is such that advanced capitalist countries of the North specialize in the knowledge economy, developing tangible and intangible values, managerial and business-related services, and design-oriented production. The labor-abundant countries of the South specialize in various productive sectors that require limited capital input and skill formation. The mobility of capital and the relative immobility of labor on a global scale maintain this global division of labor. This book deals with is the impact of the global economic crisis on the global division of labor. One of these impacts is the fact that multinational corporations will have to reconsider their financial expansion on a global scale given the increasing fragility of the financial system. Another is that individuals in general and workers in particular will face further pressure in terms of declining employment opportunities, the depreciation of wages, and further difficulties in maintaining their standard of living.

One way to look at the impact of the global economic crisis on the global division of labor is through foreign direct investments. Table 4.1 shows FDI inflows by countries' income level for the last nine years. A number of observations are worth reiterating. First, there is a sharp decline in FDI inflows on

Table 4.1 FDI inflows by income level (billions of US$)

Income level	*2005*	*2006*	*2007*	*2008*	*2009*	*2010*	*2011*	*2012*	*2013*
High-income	1,040	1,346	1,851	1,545	854	988	1,145	886	927
Low- and middle-income	301	387	576	641	417	541	705	665	736
Low-income	4.6	5.2	9.6	11	9.4	13.7	19	24	25
Lower-middle-income	50	71	99	124	94	94	112	103	104
Middle-income	296	382	566	629	407	528	686	641	712
Upper-middle-income	247	311	467	505	314	433	573	538	607
World	1,340	1,730	2,430	2,190	1,270	1,530	1,850	1,550	1,664

World Development Indicators, World Bank

a world scale from 2008 to 2009. Although there seems to be a gradual picking up in the next five years, it seems to be way below the 2007 peak. Second, high-income countries seem to be suffering the most from this decline in percentage value. This is mostly due to the greater concentration of FDI in high-income countries. Third, despite the low impact of the 2008 crisis in terms of FDI inflows, low levels of investment in lower-income countries suggests that their productive capacity was already marginal. Even if the crisis did not affect them financially, it affected them indirectly with respect to power relations in the global market vis-à-vis the motives and policies of corporate capital.

Table 4.2 shows FDI inflows by region, which exposes the geographical distribution of capital and, to a certain degree, the extent of integration with the global economy. In 2008, Europe and Central Asia, the European Union, and North America occupy the top three ranks in FDI inflows by region, respectively, whereas the Middle East and North Africa, South Asia, and Sub-Saharan Africa occupy the bottom three ranks in the same category. The nature of this geographical distribution is by no means a surprise. The polarization of financial value, however, is more intriguing. To understand the immediate impact of the 2008 crisis on the regional distribution of FDI inflows, it may be more appropriate to explain the change from 2008 to 2009. In percentage value, FDI inflows decrease by 78% in Central Europe and the Baltics, which is the highest rate of decline, followed by the European Union with 58% and North America with 55%. The geographical impact of the

Table 4.2 FDI inflows by region (billions of US$)

Region	*2005*	*2006*	*2007*	*2008*	*2009*	*2010*	*2011*	*2012*	*2013*
Central Europe & the Baltics	53	79	150	138	30	14	44	35	10
East Asia and Pacific (all income levels)	193	296	411	407	325	513	616	572	626
Europe and Central Asia (all income levels)	813	862	1,249	1,021	498	450	613	408	383
European Union	751	708	1,050	853	361	323	462	262	278
Latin America and Caribbean (all income levels)	87	93	152	163	109	140	190	197	218
Middle East and North Africa (all income levels)	52	87	92	109	86	75	55	59	57
North America	164	354	461	395	178	288	293	247	303
South Asia	11	26	32	51	40	31	40	28	32
Sub-Saharan Africa (all income levels)	20	16	30	39	37	32	43	40	44
World	1,340	1,730	2,430	2,190	1,270	1,530	1,850	1,550	1,664

World Development Indicators, World Bank

global economic crisis is in fact consistent with its developmental impact, as less developed countries of the South were marginalized not only economically but also in terms of the power relations they were subject to in the global economy.

Globalization transformed work in a structural manner. The dispersion of work on a global scale was made possible by these structural transformations. The flexibilization of work has been discussed in Chapter 1. At least as important, however, has been the informalization and casualization of labor. The former refers to an increasing number of people being employed without security and benefits, unrecorded and without papers. The latter refers to the temporal and contractual irregularities that workers face in a labor market that is constantly in flux. Seasonal or piecemeal jobs and other employment forms that are shaped by demand fluctuations in the global market are examples of casual employment. The functioning of the system without any costly interruptions such as strikes and other forms of labor militancy has been guaranteed by an attack on unionism. This attack was carried out by the coordinated efforts of a number of actors. In a global economy driven by the investment motivation of MNCs, labor's bargaining power is crushed under the weight of international competition. The declining power of the state vis-à-vis capital and supranational regulation further reduces the chances for labor struggles to succeed on political grounds. Last but not least, international organizations that administer the global economy refrain from enforcing labor standards, leaving workers to get by under fully insecure labor conditions.

The global economic crisis further deteriorated the lives of workers. While employment has become a non-standard achievement due to extreme competition in the labor market, unemployment has been on the rise and underemployment has become the norm (Beck 2000). The blurred boundaries between work and non-work have further obscured the work-life balance, challenging the traditional family structure in a way that relationships of social solidarity become insufficient to cover for the changing employment patterns and family relations. More and more people have been pushed into diminishing living standards, if not into poverty due to the weakening of formal social safety nets. Furthermore, occupational categories have become much more volatile due to deskilling, high turnover rates and lack of lifetime full employment. Jobs are now being continually reproduced according to the shifts in the production process and the reconfiguration of tasks, something which is best exemplified with on-the-job training.

The material well-being of workers has reached an all-time low in the wake of the global economic crisis. A number of factors are worth reiterating here. The decline of real wages together with steady employment opportunities is one threat to workers who aim to maintain a certain standard of living. Beyond the lack of job security and income security, the weakness of social security and alternative social safety nets has increased the vulnerability of workers and their dependents. Lack of material well-being creates a vicious circle, as it generates further deprivation in terms of human development instruments. However, as Piketty states, the poor can only "catch up with the rich to the extent that they achieve the same level of technological know-how, skill, and education, not by becoming the property of the wealthy" (Piketty 2014: 71). Finally, governments aim to manage global economic crisis through budget cuts and monetary policy that is more inflationist and pro-capital.

The experiences of immigrant workers deserve particular attention within this setting. In addition to the aforementioned difficulties facing workers, immigrant labor faces racism, discrimination and xenophobia in all geographies irrespective of these geographies' level of development. The fierce competition in the labor market makes immigrant workers the primary target when it comes to assigning blame for rising unemployment. Hence, immigration adds another layer of difficulty to the problems of unemployment, deteriorating working conditions, and poverty.

A new labor solidarity

What does the solidarity economy introduce for work and employment relations? Only some forms will have a direct impact on work and employment, given the diversity of forms, relations and organizations in the solidarity economy. Working in units that prioritize social goals over economic ones, both for the sake of workers and for the sake of the enterprise, will imply significant shifts in the experiences and the perceptions of workers. Borzaga and Depedri's research on the non-profit sector in Italy suggests that although workers receive smaller wages in the non-profit sector as compared to the market economy, the alternative incentives, both intrinsic and extrinsic, provide sustained motivation to remain in the non-profit sector (Borzaga and Depedri 2009). The potential of the non-profit sector to generate employment opportunities suggests that public policy should be supportive of this sector for a number of reasons and in a number of ways. First, the social economy may serve as a bridge to overcome the social rupture created by the market economy. Second, the deficiencies in redistribution and in welfare provision may be treated by the social economy. And third, the social economy may help revive productive capacities otherwise left idle. What may be regarded as unproductive or not profitable by the market economy may in fact be of use in the non-profit sector. There are many ways in which the state may cater to the social economy, and these include tax incentives, legal provisions, simplified bureaucratic procedures, funding mechanisms, and land allocations.

Overall, the solidarity economy refers to economic arrangements that operate outside of the realm of the market and the state. The extent to which economic activity can be externalized from the market and the state depends on various political, economic and sociocultural factors. These factors will be indicative of the potential for the solidarity economy to become ingrained in society. In advanced capitalist countries, for example, where the commodification of goods and services has been entrenched for a long period of time and where it has received the long-standing supported of political institutions such as the welfare state, solidarity arrangements may turn out to be superficial in nature. In less developed countries, however, where part of the economic activity remains outside of the realm of the market, either in the form of pre-capitalist farming or the informal economy, there is greater room for the flourishing of alternative economic arrangements. In terms of political indicators, one has to distinguish between institutional structure and political culture. Although institutional structures formally may be indicative of participation, representative democracy, or basic freedoms, the latter shows how close actors are to the exercise their political rights. While patrimonialism is an important limitation against the exercise of political rights in the Middle East, militarism and a long-standing tradition of grassroots movements in Latin America push people beyond the conventional thresholds of political activism. This is by no means a reductionist argument for cultural relativism; rather, it is an argument about stressing the importance of the historical process by which political traditions are constructed. Different political cultures may generate different instruments to be mobilized toward solidarity and may establish different solidarity models, networks and relations. As the solidarity economy is defined as a set of economic relations that fall outside of the realm of existing institutional arrangements, it is based more on the immediate social organization, political culture and economic activity that operate at the local level. The solidarity economy is spatially fixed and socially constrained by the economic relations and practices prevalent at this locus of existence. If the solidarity economy is defined as something locally specific, then, inevitably, there will be significant diversity in the principles that it can be based on.

Globalization transformed the labor movement as much as it did labor itself. Neoliberal economic policies prioritized the sustained success of the market over the sustenance of workers and their social well-being; neoliberal economic goals affected the labor movement worldwide, and this can best be exemplified by the decline in union density, the weakening of bargaining power, and the overall retreat of labor. New international labor studies (Munck 2009) and social movement unionism studies (Waterman 1993), however, have been important academic outlets for providing a structural analysis of the rather sporadic attempts to bring labor back into the struggle. Community unionism stood out as an important alternative and as an agent of countermovement against globalization that emerged at the grassroots level and made its way to higher levels of organization through networking and alliances with other social movements (Fine 2006; Black 2005).

There are three major points about new labor internationalism that may cater to the making of a solidarity economy. First, non-union forms of organization have become more important in the labor movement. This is especially true in contexts where labor law limits and compartmentalizes unionization. There are various ways in which governments seek to control the labor movement for the sake of ensuring continuous investment. As a result, democratic outlets and the public sphere (civil society) have become much more fluid and the conventional forms of labor organization and struggle are virtually obsolete.

Cobble's critique of "the factory paradigm of labor organizing" is highly explanatory in this regard. The factory paradigm "presumes that workers who most closely resemble the archetypal male proletariat toiling away on the mass production assembly line are the most likely to organize" (Cobble 2010: 282). The primary underlying assumption of the factory paradigm is that it takes into account only workers in factories in the formal labor market, who are mostly male. Informal, unpaid, reproductive labor is excluded from this kind of a conceptualization because it is seen as unfit for collective mobilization and a challenge to the core of unionized laborers in the formal economy. A second problem has to do with the factory as the locus of organization. Collective mobilization based on the factory context will clearly exclude masses of workers employed in sweatshops, in service jobs and in more contingent settings, given the fragmentation of the production process, flexible specialization, and the geographical dispersion of production. Third, the factory paradigm focuses on labor issues *per se*, the most important instrument of struggle being collective bargaining and the most important demands being better wages and benefits, and decent working conditions. The problems workers face today are beyond the workplace. They have community issues, and social problems related to race, gender, and immigration. As a response to these limitations of the factory paradigm, Cobble argues that "intimate unionism," the formation of small-scale and local organizations that embrace the immediate interests of contemporary workers that fall outside of the factory realm of production, has been of increasing importance and efficiency since the 1980s. These unions attract members from service sectors and workers employed on a non-standard basis and address issues beyond work and labor relations. For Cobble, "what intimate unionism demonstrates is that monetary or 'standard of living' issues are a good place to begin in representing workers but not the place to end. Workers' psychological and relational needs must be addressed along with their economic needs" (Cobble 2010: 292).

The second point about new labor internationalism, related to the first one, is that the labor movement is gradually moving away from the political arena to that of civil society. The conventional forms of organization in unions and labor parties give way to worker centers and worker associations. The traditional alliances between unions and labor parties are replaced by alliances between various social movements such as those based on gender rights, human rights, environmental rights and labor rights. Membership and participation in these movements is not limited to work status or formal, legal categories, but instead extend to more marginal segments of society, such as illegal immigrants, informal workers, contract laborers and freelancers. These movements emerge at the grassroots level and are generally conceptualized as embodying community unionism. The advantage of community unionism is its ability to incorporate issues that are immediately related to community members, whether they pertain to labor or various other social concerns. Smith introduces three major challenges to the study of contemporary work and employment relations in her case study on temporary workers employed in a computer technology firm. Smith underlines the importance of collective action and social movements as a response to the weakening stance of the workforce vis-à-vis their employers in an environment increasingly characterized by the decentralization of the production process, the fragmentation of the workforce, and the increasing variety of employment contracts (Smith 1998: 429). The deepening of this fragmentation, in her view, will lead to further inequalities among the American workforce, and perhaps cause a greater stimulus toward labor organization.

The sphere of civil society turns out to be the most efficient outlet for interest-seeking and social organization in circumstances where the labor movement is significantly jeopardized due to the state's alliance with capital. The growth of community-based social movements in post-apartheid South Africa is one good example of how communities of marginalized segments of society united against various aspects of neoliberalism such as privatization, poverty, and unemployment. The historical backdrop for this development was supplied by the African National Congress (ANC) and Congress of South African Trade Unions (COSATU), which served as a learning phase and provided experience for community leaders. The actions of community-based movements, however, go beyond institutionalized struggles through formal channels. It is difficult to talk of a highly structured and expansive struggle, but South Africa still seems to be a noteworthy example of community mobilization (Clarke 2008: 196). One can also trace the making of a new set of "local" communities in relation to the globalization process. Portes, in his discussion of the rise of transnational communities, explains how migration is less about the desire of the immigrants to move to a land of opportunity, and more about the needs of global capital in the developed world. Waves of global migration lead to the building of transnational communities of immigrants in the vicinity of global cities like New York and Los Angeles, members of which are employed in low-skill, low-income jobs on an informal, casual basis. For Portes, transnational communities are a product of the globalization process, hence their struggles against neoliberal globalization in these new "local" settings become much denser: "Exchange under conditions of uncertainty creates stronger bonds among participants than that which takes place with full information and impartially enforced rules" (Portes 2000: 257). There is a strong current of mobilization among immigrant communities, not only to find solutions to economic and labor-related issues, but to political, social and cultural issues as well. The work of Yasemin Nuhoglu-Soysal on postnational citizenship and the mobilization of immigrants is also noteworthy in showing the political, social and cultural dimensions of immigrant mobilization (Nuhoglu-Soysal 1994).

The third point about new labor internationalism is its embrace of unconventional forms of resistance, such as occupation, encampment, and workers forums. These tactics become more efficient under circumstances where union density has declined and strikes have become obsolete. Hale refers to "bogus unions" that are established to serve the employers rather than the workers, in which case workers resort to civil society organizations that operate under the rubric of human rights or religion (Hale 2004). Such difficulties are more common in less developed parts of the world, especially in labor-intensive industries that mostly operate in export-processing zones. Workers are now starting to organize under different interests and engage in new forms of resistance and labor resurgence.

Munck evaluates the contemporary forms of labor internationalism within the context of global social movements and undertakes a comparative analysis of workers, peasants and environmentalists as cases of "local transnationalisms." Munck underlines the need to transcend the binary opposition of the global and the local, and states: "Indeed, we need to go further and deconstruct the traditional notions of spatial levels of social activity in the complex and hybrid nature of actually existing social contestation movements" (Munck 2007: 94). The traditional understanding of labor solidarity ranging from "Workers of the whole world, unite!" to various forms of international working class solidarity has to give way to newer forms of solidarity, new alliances with other movements, and even forms of action that may not necessarily seek international mobility. One can hardly expect a universal, linear model of labor organization and struggle, given the multitude of labor solidarity experiences around the world. Munck emphasizes three major points in discussing local transnationalism. First, the move away from the traditional global-local dichotomy may in fact benefit new labor internationalism, as the local level of organization may be both instrumental and effective against global actors (mainly MNCs). Second, rank-and-file internationalism may not be effective always and everywhere (Munck 2007: 97). This is especially true in the case of less developed countries, where unionization is oppressed by governments seeking to attract foreign investors. Last, alliances with other movements, such as with global justice movements in the case of Latin America, may be an outlet to unite labor interests at the regional level. The concept of local transnationalism suggests that probabilities in the future of labor are diverse and are based on multiple levels of organization, possible alliances with other actors, and the multiplicity of strategies and forms of action. Rather than focusing on the reductionist dichotomy of the global and the local, Munck underlines the importance and the inevitability of transcending conventional wisdom by constructing another form of knowledge when he says that "the coloniality of power is being confronted by rival knowledges, and false universalisms are being rightfully contested" (Munck 2008: 235).

Overall, the labor movement is in a state of transition in terms of its organization, its strategies, and its objectives. This transition will be progressive as long as it responds to the immediate needs of workers and relates to the shop floor where workers mobilize and to the community which is affected by workplace dynamics. The fragmentation of the production process and the spread of non-standard forms of employment suggest that the labor movement is facing new challenges that need to be approached with new strategies. This novelty comes from within the labor force, within the workplace, and is not imposed from above by outside agents. This motivation from within will be the most important catalyst for the emergence of a new labor solidarity.

Notes

1 The five tiers concluded by the authors are: the first-tier NIEs such as South Korea and Taiwan which show some industrial maturity; rapid industrializers such as Malaysia, Thailand and China; labor-intensive manufacturers such as Mexico and the Philippines; low-value-added manufacturers such as Argentina and Brazil; and natural-resources-dependent economies such as Chile, Venezuela and Saudi Arabia (Akyuz et al. 2004: 54).

2 www.elance.com, but see now https://www.upwork.com/.

5 Solidarity under focus

This chapter will present four major case studies that exemplify solidarity economies. The concept of solidarity embraces those activities, organizations and networks that fall outside of the realms of the state and the market. Major functions of solidarity are defined as production, redistribution, workplace democracy, and labor solidarity. The cases covered in this chapter serve these functions at least partially, if not totally. The cases are diverse in terms of their country of origin, the economic field they operate in, their target groups, their agendas, and their strategies. What unites them is their local origin, their responsiveness to the social and economic repercussions of neoliberal globalization, and the alternatives they present for those who seek to opt out of the global market and the neoliberal state. The research for this chapter mainly benefited from secondary sources and official data. For three of the cases, from India, the US and Turkey, in-depth interviews have been conducted to expose the processes of mobilization, organization and outreach. The geographical diversity of the four cases has been a major methodological obstacle.

Mondragon

One of the most efficient and well-known examples of cooperative systems is Mondragon in Spain. As Mondragon is one of the oldest and the most institutional examples of a cooperative, it is possible to trace its development for a few decades in parallel with that of Spain and the world.[1] The Mondragon Corporation (Mondragon) has been at the center of scholarly attention throughout its historical evolution due to its success and expansion (Gutierrez Johnson and Whyte 1977; Thomas and Logan 1982; Whyte and Whyte 1988; Cheney 2002). While some scholars have focused on the sustained success of its cooperative model, others have scrutinized its rather diluted socialist basis: Mondragon operates in and benefits from the capitalist system (Hindmoor 1999). Mondragon serves as a benchmark for the components of the solidarity economy explained throughout this book. Mondragon is closest to what might be a prototypical facilitation of production, redistribution, democracy and labor organization when compared to the rest of the cases covered here.

Because of its particular relationship with the state and because its production is geared toward the world market, its functional facilitation disqualifies it as a non-state, non-market alternative.

A review of the historical milieu in which Mondragon came into being will reveal the unique circumstances that promoted the development of the cooperative movement. Mondragon was established by Jose Maria Arizmendiarrieta in the Basque region of Spain in 1956. Arizmendiarrieta was a young priest who came to Arrasate-Mondragon (as it is officially known) after the Spanish Civil War and undertook the task of revitalizing the small war-torn town. In the 1950s, most of his efforts were geared toward resolving the immediate problems faced by the town on the local level and resolving social problems that lingered in the aftermath of the war. Initial projects consisted of organizing a soccer team, to promote a sense of community, and addressing the healthcare and education needs of the locals. The first cooperative of Mondragon Corporation was established by five workers under the leadership of Arizmendiarrieta that came to be known as ULGOR, a name composed of the initial letters of the workers' surnames. This was the basis of what is now known as Fagor Electronics, the primary industrial cooperative of Mondragon, which produces a wide array of industrial goods, including commercial cooking, laundry, cooling and refrigerating equipment. The development of this alternative economic system accelerated in 1959 with the establishment of several other industrial cooperatives.

There were two major developments that took place during the same year. The first was the establishment of a cooperative credit union, *Caja Laboral Popular*. The credit union represented significant progress in two respects. As a financial institution, it provided fiscal support to the emerging cooperatives. It also helped meet the financial needs of cooperative members, the most important of which was housing. *Caja Laboral Popular* provided relative financial autonomy for the evolving Mondragon structure on a social basis as well as a macroeconomic one. The second development was the establishment of *servicios de provisión social* ("social welfare services"). The provision of social services within the cooperative system indicated that the cooperative was in fact expanding from a production function to a redistribution function. If the cooperative production system could be seen as an alternative to the capitalist mode of production and to market dependency, then the cooperative redistribution function could be taken as an alternative to the welfare regime of the state. There were various types of welfare states in postwar Europe. Outside of Esping-Andersen's classical tripartite welfare state typology (Esping-Andersen 1990), Southern European welfare states were known to rely on a combination of traditional welfare provision schemes and formal welfare systems (Rhodes 1996). What has been appropriately conceptualized as the "southern syndrome" by Rhodes refers to the lack of balance between insurance, redistribution and social safety nets; the generosity of the system for certain groups or for certain periods; and the inefficient promotion of employment and/or provision of healthcare (Rhodes 1996: 14). In return, the weakness of southern welfare states is generally compensated for by family and/or traditional solidarity mechanisms. It is within this kind of context that the establishment of *servicios de provisión social* by Mondragon becomes a significant alternative to institutional welfare provision. Mondragon established "Lagun Aro, a voluntary mutual benefit organization" in 1958 in spite of the decision of the Ministry of Labor to exclude cooperative members from the social security system. As Mondragon secured sustained production, members' potential to accrue long-term savings and investment in their future social safety nets increased. This internalization of a welfare function by the cooperative system helped provide a solution for the deficiencies and inefficiencies of the Spanish welfare system. This expansion was responsive to the needs and demands of the cooperative's members. The enlargement of the solidarity network from a production function to a redistribution function was very much a result of the local social dynamics.

In addition to its industrial and financial operations, the Mondragon system also managed to initiate the development of an extended education network in the surrounding region (i.e. northwestern Spain). The vocational training provided at *Escuela Profesional* was geared toward creating a skilled workforce as well as toward providing an education to the local population, which was otherwise marginalized from Spanish society. Female students took chemistry and other science classes, among other subjects. Arizmendiarrieta's views on women's education was quite progressive for the time: "It is a big mistake that women do not enter vocational training on a general basis, nor take part in retraining and in-service training processes opening the way for professions which are rejected today as unsuitable" (Mondragon 2014).

The history of the Mondragon Corporation can best be understood when situated in a discussion of Catalonia and Spain. Catalonia has historically been a distinct part of Spain. Its inhabitants' revolutionary spirit, their demand for autonomy, and their commitment to Catalan culture have helped shape the history of the region. This unique political culture often clashed with the Spanish state. Catalonia gained autonomy during the Second Spanish Republic, but during and after the Spanish Civil War the central government targeted the political consciousness and the social and cultural components of Catalan society. Catalonia regained its political and cultural autonomy once more in post-Franco Spain, and the demands for independence continue to occupy the agenda of Catalan politics to this day. The Catalan parliamentary elections of 2015 resulted in a landslide victory for the separatists and compelled the Spanish government to compromise on the various political, economic and cultural demands made by the Catalans (Toyer 2015). As one of the most industrious regions of Spain from the nineteenth century onward, it has also harbored a strong labor movement. Smith's historical overview of the Catalan labor movement in the late nineteenth and the early twentieth century exposes the roots of the militant labor movement in Catalonia and more specifically the roots of the region's anarchist-syndicalist movement (Smith 2007). Smith's historical overview of the labor movement in Catalonia informs the reader about both the labor movement and the larger political culture of the time in Catalonia. It also helps unravel the political and economic rivalries and alliances that existed beyond the borders of Catalonia in the rest of Spain.

As Mondragon is one of the oldest and the most institutional examples of a cooperative, it is possible to trace its development – over the course of a few decades – in parallel with the development of the Spanish state both domestically and abroad. Nationally, the ending of the Franco regime in Spain in 1978 and the granting of relative autonomy to Catalonia have contributed to Mondragon's further expansion in industry and other fields of operation. Internationally, European Economic Community (EEC) and global transformations in the capitalist world economy created a new conjuncture for Mondragon. Beginning in the 1980s, the cooperative was faced with two major challenges: the first was about dealing with a greater number of workers in several different cooperatives operating in numerous industries; and the second was about the need for innovation to participate and compete in the market, that is, to attract sustained demand for continuous production. In the 1990s, Mondragon adopted an inter-cooperative solidarity system on the basis of the following principles (Mondragon 2014):

- Movement of staff between cooperatives.
- Pooling of profits.
- Fair distribution of profits.
- Initial provision of capital.
- Fair remuneration of management.
- Data feedback to Mondragon.
- No internal competition.

These principles indicated Mondragon's commitment to cooperative principles. However, the global expansion of the Mondragon Corporation, very much responsive to neoliberal globalization, was geared toward meeting the requirements of the new global market rather than toward the globalization of the cooperative experience. Mondragon promoted internationalization toward new markets and adopted the use of subsidiaries as deemed necessary. Extended investment in research and development activities resulted in innovative management and technology strategies. A commitment to good managerial practices, to the employment of local labor and to the people-oriented operation of work helped form a balance between the market-oriented goals and the socioeconomic basis of the organization.

The economic success of the Mondragon Corporation can easily be attributed to its strong commitment to the cooperative model. Local traditions of political autonomy and labor militancy provided fertile ground for cooperatives to flourish. The expansion of the cooperative model from industrial production to retail, finance, and education is a deliberate progression targeting the emerging needs of both workers and locals. The expansion of the Mondragon network from Catalonia to all around the world, with 122 production plants and 9 corporate offices, does not necessarily entail the abandoning of cooperative principles; instead, it is more of a response to globalization and challenging market conditions. The implementation of the cooperative model in industry as opposed to agriculture requires access to a broader segment of the market, since the products have to meet demand, wherever that may be.

Mondragon started out as a local cooperative in manufacturing and gradually transformed itself into an international corporate giant without losing its essential roots in cooperative organization. It operates in four major economic areas, with industry and retail as its principal sectors, and finance and education as its auxiliary sectors. According to its 2013 Annual Report, Mondragon incorporates 103 cooperatives and 122 production plants, with 10 support entities and 13 international service companies, and it employs approximately 74,000 workers (Mondragon 2013).

Mondragon is more than a typical cooperative; it is a complex organization whose size has increased for more than half a century. Despite its size, expansion and global operations, the principles of open admission, democratic organization, participatory management, labor sovereignty, and payment solidarity locates Mondragon within an overarching cooperative framework. This framework is further supported by the principles of universality, education, inter-cooperation, and social transformation.

Solidarity economies have been conceptualized as non-state, non-market alternatives that are organized according to the resources and the social and economic needs of local populations. Mondragon provides an alternative to the statist schemes of production and redistribution. This is best exemplified with the credit unions, welfare agents and schools of the Mondragon network. The unique political relationship between Catalonia and the Spanish government provides an appropriate political setting for the flourishing of a non-state solidarity network. However, the extent to which Mondragon can be considered a non-market alternative is rather unclear. Mondragon operates according to cooperative principles locally; however, its international plants – which are strategically deployed in several different countries – operate according to the dictates of conventional capitalist employment relations, which have been further degenerated by globalizing pressures. Mondragon represents an alternative within the capitalist world economy with respect to the rules of the global market – as opposed to an alternative to the capitalist mode of operation. None of the models discussed in this chapter qualify as an ideal type; rather, they are solidarity alternatives that are responsive to local factors and that are viable within the local social and economic frameworks in which they find themselves.

Self-Employed Women's Association

Similar to Mondragon, the historical backdrop of the Self-Employed Women's Association (SEWA) in India goes back several decades. It has also attracted a great deal of scholarly interest (Prugl 1999; Standing 2009). The brief description of SEWA on its official website manages to capture all of its principal characteristics:[2]

> SEWA is a trade union registered in 1972. It is an organisation of poor, self-employed women workers. These are women who earn a living through their own labour or small businesses. They do not obtain regular salaried employment with welfare benefits like workers in the organised sector. They are the unprotected labour force of our country. Constituting 93% of the labour force, these are workers of the unorganised sector. Of the female labour force in India, more than 94% are in the unorganised sector. However their work is not counted and hence remains invisible.

SEWA has been operating for more than four decades and currently represents over two million workers. There are several unconventional aspects of SEWA that need to be emphasized. First, it was initiated and established through a grassroots movement that developed an agenda primarily focused on local issues. SEWA's success as a grassroots movement was based on its ability to incorporate gender, labor, and community interests in its organization, and its ability to generate non-market, non-state resolutions on issues of poverty, gender inequality, harassment, illiteracy, informality at work, and more. According to Namrata Bali:[3]

> Almost a majority of our membership, young and old, comes from the rural areas and their Hindu and Muslim ethnic groups and different trade groups. In a 42 to 43 year-old organization you have granddaughters, daughters, daughters-in-law and mothers, and so it is very diversified. How we unify them is that we call each other as work sisters. Whatever you are, from whichever background you are, you come into the organization with your work – that is what is connecting you, that is what is relating you. For this, we do a lot of training and education. It is like every morning you come you are chanting all the prayers; no matter which religion you are, you are chanting all the prayers, especially those made by Mahatma Ghandi for secularism. So these are little things like eating together, sitting together, and praying together, which are normally not done in India, and in very conservative societies. People would not do that; they would not sit with everybody and eat, but here we all eat, sit, dance, and celebrate. If there is a crisis, we come together. That is the essence of our unity.

Second, SEWA was able to grasp segments of the labor force that would traditionally have been excluded from the union-type organization, given the irregular aspects of work and labor in India, such as the informality, gender dimension, and sectoral diversity of economic activity there. Workers in informal employment are the hardest to organize all around the world. Their labor has no visibility or value, and the mainstream labor organizations, whether labor unions or labor parties, have little to offer the marginal segments of the labor market. SEWA became a revolutionary example on the world stage by organizing predominantly informally employed women workers. SEWA uses very simple yet effective instruments to reach their constituents. This instrumental choice is partly due to informality and partly due to the lack of infrastructure in rural India:

> Normally how we organize is that because SEWA has been there now for some time people know what we do. But when it is a new area, women who are committed as leaders go to the new area to identify what the needs are in that particular area. No matter what there is – lack of jobs, insecurity, no work security, fear of contractors – your entry point can be anything. Maybe in that neighborhood, the whole issue is about water: they don't have water every day; there are no taps; or maybe they don't have toilets over there or people have been sick over there. They want a medical camp, and they want a doctor, so one needs to identify what the issue is. And we do this sometimes by using a lot of multimedia: we use radio programs.

The success of SEWA's outreach is partly due to its long history and partly due to the efficient combination of traditional and modern means of communication to reach out to constituents. SEWA does not depend solely on modern media (TV, radio, newspaper), the Internet (email, website), or social media (Facebook, Twitter) in order to generate publicity. Traditional and even folkloric means of communication and outreach had become important in areas that lacked modern communications infrastructure:

> Sometimes we broadcast on multiple issues. There is always a dedicated phone line, so you could always get a phone call with a problem or an issue and then you can go to a given area. Similarly, we have a van which is fitted with a television, a dvd player, and a megaphone, and has pamphlets and of course has a person. So this van goes to these areas, and they show films and documentaries and sing! If there is no electricity, then you use your own voice and additional communication methods by singing and dancing or just narrating stories for children and the elderly, but when you do that you have to be involved with the people.

The building of a trustful, long-term relationship with people takes effort and time. There may be many who come and go, and participate for some time but then leave, who cannot maintain the same level of commitment and motivation along the way. The building of a sizable community of members is like a snowball effect, once a strong tie is established with a few locals, they work as delegates to attract others to participate. Identifying local delegates has a lot to do with knowing the local structure, local social relations and the local problems that await resolutions:

> Once you start getting involved, but this takes some time…so before the organizing, these are the methods which help you build a rapport with the people. You go every day to that area, and once you start doing that you begin to identify a few people who really want to do something in their life. Out of 25, 30 people there might be just two who might say "I want to do something like this," so you try to identify those and then we start investing in those two or three women with training and education because once you move out of there they will be the community leaders. And then you start the organizing. Now, once this whole process has started then you explain to them how important it is to be together, how vulnerable we are when we are alone, and how we can get a voice and be represented in front of an employer, a contractor, a traffic officer or police officer, or a municipality or the state.

SEWA's organizational model requires particular attention in the way it constructs workplace democracy for informal workers, whose workplace is rather ambiguous. SEWA itself has a trade union structure, in which representatives of different trades are elected every three years. These representatives are organized in a hierarchical manner; this hierarchy depends primarily on the members' direct involvement and input. Informal employment, the lack of a formal workplace, and the absence of a practical basis for worker mobilization are significant limitations when it comes to the facilitation of workplace democracy and the articulation of workers' interests. SEWA overcomes these practical limitations by adopting alternative media to reach its constituents:

> SEWA trade union, which is the mother organization, has a trade union structure. So from the general membership you have your leaders, and then they form their trade committees. So no matter whether you are urban or rural you have your own committees. Like the number of trades I said, each trade has its own little group, like a tree organization. Every trade committee again there are members elected or represented by their members, and they form the trade council members. From the trade council members, there is the executive committee. So the number of general memberships can always increase or decrease. The trade committees are according to the number of trades. They can be area-specific, and they can be urban or rural: due to reasons of practicality, you can have your meetings in whichever area you are located in. But when we have elections every three years, for every group of 200 women in a trade, one leader is elected. So then the classification becomes kind of mixed. It can be from urban or rural areas. Then it becomes a group of mixed council members. Then from those members who are elected as trade council members we have elections for the executive committee, which can comprise up to 25 people. Plus there are seats reserved for four more people who can be non-working class but who can be with the organization if they want to make a time commitment and if they want to

do something. If this is the case, they can be with the women's movement for years.

Representation in the SEWA structure is socially diverse. SEWA as a work organization structures its representative bodies with respect to work areas rather than with respect to other social categories. The trades that poor, informally working women occupy are auxiliary segments of the textile industry, the food industry, the agricultural industry, and other low-skilled or semi-skilled, low-income-generating economic sectors. The trade with the maximum membership holds greater representation and leadership positions. Therefore, the key to the successful resolution of workers' problems depends on the number of members and extended organization:

> These elections are again according to the numbers in each trade, so it's all a numbers game actually. The maximum number you have in a trade, that person is elected as the president. At present, the president of SEWA is an agricultural worker because they have the maximum majority membership. The next one becomes the vice-president. The vice-presidents in SEWA right now are vendors and hawkers and home-based workers. Then you have the election for the general secretary. The position for the general secretary has to be thought of in a different way because it can be filled by someone who is working class or non-working class because it's more of an administrative kind of job and, given the reality that many women are not that formally literate, they have their knowledge but they are not equipped to do this kind of administrative work. The general secretary has two secretaries who assist her. Because it is a democratic organization and the elections happen every three years, those who ultimately come to the executive committee are a mix of urban and rural workers and a mix of Hindus and Muslims, so it is mainly the trades themselves that determine the majority.

Over the course of the four decades that it has been registered as a trade union, SEWA has expanded the scope of its operations to cover other areas at the request of its constituents. This organizational expansion has also been responsive to the needs and demands of SEWA members. SEWA has three sister organizations (agents) that provide financial services to its members: SEWA Bank, SEWA Insurance and Mahila Housing SEWA Trust (MHT). Many informally employed women have difficulty accessing mainstream financial institutions due to poverty and a lack of assets. Women have difficulty accessing business and housing loans because they are regarded as credit risks. SEWA's financial institutions provide services to poor, informally working women who are otherwise excluded from formal financial mechanisms.

In addition to its agents offering financial services, SEWA also has agents that offer healthcare and education services. Shri Gujarat Mahila Lok Swasthya Sewa Sahakari Mandali Ltd., the health agent, provides one-day camps where doctors provide basic diagnostic services and write prescriptions. The main objective is to provide access to healthcare and low-cost medication, if not in all medical branches, at least in major branches that covering women and children (e.g. family medicine, pediatrics). SEWA Academy and SEWA Manager Ni School provide education to members in a variety of fields. The topics covered are geared toward the social and economic development of informally employed women and their households. The education members receive teaches them the necessary skills they will need to manage their businesses and to further develop their market networks. This type of adult education is structured differently from the formal Indian education curriculum, and it also uses different kinds of media. SEWA Academy uses the online education model, with courses structured as modules. Online education is provided for groups of women and is not individually tailored because computing infrastructure is not available in every household:

> Using the mobile phone, using the Internet, everybody does not own a computer or the infrastructure for that. But at least they can learn how to use it, and wherever possible we can give them access: this is what SEWA Academy is doing. Another thing we adopted with mobile phones and Internet access is online training. We must understand that among the poor everybody does not own a laptop or a computer, so we have group-based online education. There is a big screen connected to a single computer, and you mobilize 20–25 people there. You have your participatory training online as a group on a particular subject. It's facilitated by a trainer. It is not a purely online experience, where a person can go online and sit and do it herself. It is a group sitting together in a classroom with a trainer who explains and reads the material out to them. It helps them to read also. Sometimes it's just images and films being shown on the computer.

The constituents of SEWA are informally working women. They work in the food and textile industries as well as in beedi production and incense-rolling. They consist of an auxiliary segment of the labor process in the textile industry, as they engage in home-based production for subcontractors. They prepare breads and spices for vendors and restaurants in the food industry. There is a very interesting extension of production from the textile mills to the home-based workers. The waste material from the textile mills is collected and sorted according to its size. The larger pieces are used for the production of sheets or clothing, while smaller pieces are made into quilts and patchwork. The whole network extends from the textile mill to wholesale and retail markets and then on to informal segments of the economy, which include the garbage collectors, porters, cart pullers, head loaders, vendors and sellers. Overall, the labor of informally working women remains invisible in many respects. Informality is an important barrier when it comes to defining work and the employment relations that frame it. There is an effort to work with contractors to keep the employment relations informal and unregulated, so as to ensure sustained employment for women because SEWA members are tangentially linked to the market. The long-term continuity of employment is prioritized over the provision of a minimum wage:

> Initially we are not great friends, but over the years we have built up a reputation. In a country like ours, we don't have so many policies, and when you start talking about policy and law, especially about minimum wage, the contractors don't like it. They start threatening you so, the women who work have strategized among themselves and have told the organization that they don't want minimum wage. "We want steady employment. We want a steady income coming into our families." When we negotiate and bargain or demand, of course we know what the scale is. We know what the minimum wage is, but we would negotiate it in a way that we have regular employment every day. That should be enough for us to get food for our families. When you start negotiating in that way and when there is a structure, there is a tripartite board where employers are represented and the Labor Department is also sometimes represented. Together, they sit and discuss. Women are very smart: they know how to negotiate very well. They say it's always better to at least get the half bread if you can't get the full bread. That's how they negotiate.

The way SEWA and its constituents relate to the market is unique in many ways. As informally employed women, SEWA's members fall outside of the formal employment relations of the market economy. As agricultural workers, beedi producers, incense rollers, or hawkers and vendors, they once again fall out of the main economic sectors and remain only marginally linked to the market economy. They operate in and for the domestic market as workers and producers; therefore, they remain outside of the global market and the larger capitalist world economy. The domestic market they participate in merely functions as a domain of exchange stripped of the competitive pressures and exploitative employment relations of global corporations. SEWA's operations, whether in cooperatives or in sister organizations that provide services to producers, make the organization a non-market alternative falling outside of the realm of the global market and its actors.

SEWA is a civil society organization, and its operations fall outside the realm of the state. It does not form alliances with political parties, it does not have political objectives and does not seek to acquire political power. It does form relations with the government both at the federal level and the state level in order to seek the interests of its members and make certain demands on its members' behalf. SEWA is not a mainstream organization in its operations, yet it uses mainstream channels to reach its ultimate goals:

> SEWA is 42 years old, and we are very political in the sense of our actions, but we are not associated with any party. Be it whichever government, be it the congress or be it the BJP or any other party, we have never

> been associated with or represented by any political party until today. I think that is our strength because we believe in our own strength and we believe in women building their own structures. But that does not mean that we do not want to be with the mainstream. We want to utilize government programs, and we want to see that they are implemented and programmed and that they reach the people whom they have to reach.

The advantage of a disengaging model of organization is its independence from formal political relations and alliances. These organizations have the autonomy to prioritize local objectives over national ones, social objectives over economic ones. Disengaging does not necessarily imply the total rejection of formal actors and the severing of all ties with them; rather, it means keeping these relations at a pragmatic distance:

> Whatever way we do it, we are focused on our members. If our members say "We need this," we do it no matter what model is working at the federal level or at the state level. But at the same time, our members are also very clear that if any political party does not believe in the values that they believe in, they [the members] will not follow it. For example, if we believe in certain values of communal harmony or secularism, it has to be there. If a government says the model is going to be different for different communities, we do not follow it. If it's good for our members and if the members want it, we will adopt it, no matter what government is in power and no matter what the model is.

SEWA, as a cooperative model, does not come in a standard form with a prescribed agenda that can be applied in a universal manner. SEWA can be regarded more as a set of principles than as a formal structure of institutions. The resolutions it seeks are immediate and responsive to existing issues; they are not part of a developmental agenda that could be adopted in a different setting. It seems more appropriate to think of the SEWA model as an abstraction that could be modified with respect to locally prevalent social and economic conditions, and the problems that local vulnerable groups experience:

> The SEWA model can be tailor-made in any place. We never propagated that it has to be the same model everywhere. But it is a model that can be tailor-made in your own constituency in your own state. In your own country, it can be adapted because the geographic conditions and the political conditions are always different. In our own country, we have so many states and each state has a different model. But the focus is to organize the informal, organize the women, and try to find out those democratic structures which give a voice to the women so that they are represented at the state level. At the same time, women do not stay as just the producers; they are managers and owners of their own organizations. These are very cross-cutting values, and that's how we structure SEWA:

> whoever wants to pick up this structure becomes a part of the SEWA movement. There are so many organizations in India and South Asia and Southeast Asia and in other countries westward as well that are picking up either microcredit or microfinance or livelihood issues the way we have done it. They may not take up the full structure, but they pick up whatever is useful for them. We are a little bit unique in this sense because SEWA is a very holistic organization; it is highly integrated. It does so many things which are in parallel with the government. But we are not the government; we know that.

Reaching out to poor, informally employed women who are also geographically dispersed is very difficult. SEWA's use of technology in this respect provides it with several advantages. First, the use of technology enables greater information dissemination. The broadcasting of a weekly radio program and the availability of a hotline for listeners during the broadcast was helpful in bringing forth issues not previously raised and reaching areas that were initially outside the reach of SEWA's operations. This outreach was further enhanced by the use of mobile phones and the Internet. Second, SEWA provides employment opportunities for women through its video cooperative. These women use the video equipment themselves and contribute to SEWA Academy's data collection and archiving efforts. The video cooperative also travels to remote rural areas in order to provide education and vocational know-how to women. The mobilization of more traditional and marginal segments of society does not necessarily entail the use of more traditional methods of mobilization; instead, it generates greater motivation to find more innovative ways of reaching out. The direct participation of women in the collection of data and the dissemination of information is the driving force behind this newly generated motivation:

> The same way we use the radio, we also use television. We have a video cooperative which is run by women themselves, in which women make films and documentaries for educational purposes. To sustain themselves, they make documentaries for our side organizations. We are using video and television. Just like radio, they go and replay it in the neighborhoods. Instantly, you get the feedback.

The strategies of outreach are further diversified with local events, celebrations and other festivities. These strategies serve several purposes. First, they generate public awareness of and recognition for SEWA. There is a sense of acquaintance and affinity as a result of direct engagement. Second, it also generates membership, if not directly and immediately, at least in the long run. Third, these strategies work as a learning process through the delivery of messages and the playing of games:

> The other strategies are the old traditional tools like singing, dancing, using musical instruments (puppets are very commonly used) because in

> areas where there is no electricity and no power, where you cannot use technology, these are your tools that will help you organize your engagement. In our communities, everybody loves it. These tools are a very important part of organizing, and SEWA Academy keeps bringing out new kinds of games and simulations, puppets, and songs. We use the folk songs a lot. In fact, we are archiving the folk songs right now. But we fuse our message songs with the folk songs. Similarly, there are special dances and festivals, and we celebrate them together with the communities. That's another way of doing it.

The strategic use of mobile phones among members is an interesting example where technological instruments could be used for alternative purposes. Mobile phones are used for information dissemination as much as for personal communication. This is especially important for those in the informal economy, as formal information channels are not targeted toward these economic activities:

> The more recent ones in technology have been mobile phones. Now the mobile phone is one of the most common things; you do not see a radio or a transistor at home, but you have a cell phone which is used as a radio as well. It's a tool for informing. Initially, women have been traveling such a long distance to get information, but now with the mobile phone they can get information about the price of produce they are making in the market; they know when the meeting is going to be and which village it is going to be in. It saves them time. They can make certain bookings online. In fact, it has become more important for women to learn how to use a mobile phone and have a mobile phone because even for your basics like having a gas connection or booking a cooking gas connection for your kitchen you need a mobile phone. It's all done online. For children who want to pursue further studies, you keep on encouraging members to put their girls, put their children in high schools – but then you have to deal with the fact that admissions are done online. The whole structure now is changing. In this world of globalized technology, if we don't give our people the opportunity to learn about devices like the mobile phone, the digital divide will become very big.

Working-class frameworks or labor relations analyses from the West cannot fully grasp the unique nature of working-class formation in India. Any expectation that the labor movement in India will be similar or reciprocal to historical examples elsewhere in the world would be unrealistic. SEWA is a social movement that is very much unique to the social and labor-related setting it comes from, and is not in any way representative of a typical labor movement. Looking at the spread of the SEWA model, Standing states that "it is a part of the associational revolution taking place in response to globalization and the withering of the labourist model" (Standing 2009: 292).

New Labor

The first two cases of alternative employment relations predate neoliberal globalization. They build upon existing structures and innovate under the emerging conditions of neoliberal globalization. They are transformed with respect to how they deal with external factors, cultivate internal resources and meet local needs. Alternative modes of organization do not have such an extended historical background and an institutionalized set of relations. New Labor is a labor organization that organizes immigrant workers in New Jersey, United States.

Worker centers have become an expanding category of labor organizations that partially takes over the responsibility of organizing and representing workers' interests (Fine 2006). New Labor was established in 2000 to organize immigrant workers in New Jersey in the US and defined itself as "an alternative model of worker organization that combines new and existing strategies to improve working conditions."[4] The challenge with new organizations begins at the moment of recruitment and involves building a structured and sustained relationship with constituents. The novelty affects the process of recruitment, as well as the process of convincing members to firmly commit to preset objectives. The organization has to clearly explain its mission in order to achieve this:[5]

> The most important thing is building relationships of trust. As a relationship-based organization, people refer to us to set up homes for their families; you need that because people have been hurt sometimes. The other thing is going out and showing and proving what is possible by coming together to win. That means tangible things like getting legislation passed that helps people in need, setting up ordinances, earning paid sick days, but also pursuing collective action, direct action, because the ones that are affected are the ones striking the blow. We go to employers' places of business or houses and protest until people get paid what they are owed.

In the case of labor organization, this challenge is further exacerbated by the coexistence of worker centers and traditional forms of labor organizing under unions. The weakening of the labor movement is not only an academic statement but it's also an experience workers face every day. Worker centers can be distinguished from unions in terms of organization, recruitment as well as the agendas they establish and the strategies they employ in order to forward their agendas:

> The other point is how you define organizing. Are we talking about a traditional union setting, of "organizing," or are we talking about coming together to improve conditions with a common goal and a common perceived benefit? We do the latter, but we help with the former

> too. We are a worker center, and we are not a union – although we do work with unions and one can say that we form our own kind of union.

New Labor is a local labor organization that focuses on certain industries and economic sectors that its constituents work in. It has the ability to mobilize in the immediate setting, whether it is the workplace or the community. The advantage of local organization is its proximity to its subjects: a large-scale bureaucratic representative body usually operates at a greater remove from its members. The local level organization becomes an important source of empowerment:

> We have 3,000 dues-paying members in mostly low-wage industries, so they run in all kinds of industries. Many are contractors in the residential construction sector. The other things are supply chains and warehouses. There is pressure from them: sometimes it is felt locally, but it will get worse if we go after them, since we get pushback. So we don't normally feel pressure from them. They don't like what we do, but we are out there and they know who we are. So we are like the police: sometimes bad companies will change their behavior because of us – and that's a good thing.

One major difficulty that local organizations face is local recruitment and the subsequent building of trust. In many cases, these organizations are not well publicized, and with limited recognition their potential for struggle and representation is downgraded. This makes recruitment all the more vital for success. It also creates a need to develop positive public relations. These organizations often lack the resources to invest in publicity; instead, they focus on elementary social relations:

> A lot of it is just by word of mouth more than anything else, and people come in after hearing about the education we provide, after confronting problems in the workplace, or after deciding to look for something better. These are the main ways people come in. We do have a street team to get out fliers and information in order to make some contacts, but the best way to make contacts is through people bringing in their friends and family. Sometimes, we focus on a particular street or a particular area and go door-to-door, at the micro level, where we have our established leaders create a physical presence and help develop in locals an affinity for labor. Then we also have people here [at the office]; we have English classes and sometimes people come for that, but then they see what else is going on, and then get involved in other things and play that process. We are always organizing and talking to people, meeting them to figure out what their root stories are, why they are the way they are, and what motivates them. We can then move them along in that process. We are building leadership and confidence at the same time.

With more than 3,000 active members, the organization operates according to five major principles: collaboration, opportunity creation, mutual respect, empowerment and equality. These principles are pursued within the workplace, and the struggles of immigrant workers are represented in the community through political channels. These principles frame the agenda of New Labor, which covers a diverse set of issues, including wage theft, race and gender discrimination, worker safety and workers' legal status.

The most important challenge that worker centers face is with employers. When it comes to low-skill, low-income workers, the task of transforming power dynamics in the workplace and establishing health and safety standards is accompanied by the equally challenging task of transforming the way employers think about workers and worker centers. Worker centers aim to establish elementary principles of deliberation that are inclusive and democratic irrespective of class and social status in the absence of tripartite arbitration, collective bargaining mechanisms and formal means of communication. Worker centers emphasize the shared dispositions of workers and companies, and the fact that strong workers also make strong companies:

> They don't necessarily like us because we call them out, right? So we tried to partner with some because they want to do the right thing, and it's still a work in progress. If they perceive us not necessarily as a threat but kind of like a representative group making sure that our voice is heard…it's a power shift because work is not always about a relationship of equals, it's hierarchical. We tried to create situations in which everyone's at the same table; that changes everything no matter what. There is always a power relationship; you never get out of that – the boss and the worker – but to form a health and safety committee, that's what you want to do. It is a joint initiative, so you'd not only have management, professionals, but also janitors, workers as well: everyone is at the same table working to solve problems involving health and safety. What the problems are and how to come to solutions that help workers flourish actually makes the company more productive in the long run, so that is what is sought. But sometimes it's perceived by employers as "wanting what we have."

New Labor is a worker center that represents the interests of local workers. Issues regarding the employment of immigrant workers, the discrimination they may face, and the legal problems they might come across as undocumented workers are part of New Labor's agenda because most of their constituents are immigrant workers. New Labor could be regarded more as a class-based movement than an immigrant-based civilian initiative. Immigration intensifies the problems workers face, yet workers in the labor market are exploited irrespective of their residential status. The focus on immigrant labor was not deliberately chosen; rather, it gradually developed over time:

> Since 2003, we have mobilized marches here locally and we've gone to DC with 19 busses full of people. Yet they don't want to pass immigration reform and that's the bottom line: there are always groups that are against it. So we support stuff, but even with what's out there with DAPA and DACA[6] and with what Obama has on hold, the situation is not that good: Obama's proposal is just for a certain amount of people. It's temporary. It's not a path to citizenship at all, so it's piecemeal. In that sense, it's very hard to have a full focus on that really, with what the reality is. There are crazy people out there that are even against the smallest changes. Even if there were to be immigration reform, that wouldn't really change the dynamic of the worker-employer relationship at all. You might want to speak up more if you have that freedom to, but if you don't allow workers to be citizens of this country, every worker is screwed. People might say that people with papers may have more opportunities and more rights, but there have been situations where this is not the case at all. Everyone's all in the same boat. We are more focused on the local, trying to fight for citizenship status and to overcome fear.

Discrimination is another issue many worker centers have to grapple with beyond exploitation, especially when the majority of their constituents are low-skill, low-wage immigrant workers. Discrimination on the basis of race, ethnicity or gender is not unique to the experiences of New Labor members, but it is a common occurrence in labor markets worldwide. The intersectional basis of exploitation and discrimination results in alliances between labor organizations and immigrant organizations, which operate together in a network of organizations promoting the fair treatment of marginal groups:

> We are part of the New Jersey Alliance for Immigrant Justice. We are on the executive board, so that's a group of worker center unions and faith-based groups that look to pass pro-immigrant policies in New Jersey. It has a pro-immigrant platform. It is currently passing a driver's license bill so that everyone, documented or not, will be eligible to have one. This is something that we also pushed for at the state level: we wanted anti-detainee policy advice and to get our members municipal IDs. Our focus, though, is more on the workplace. The way companies work is problematic: they pit workers against one another, and within an industry it is one nationality against another – it's the Hondurans against the Mexicans – and they benefit from worker animosity. But in general it's also Latinos against African-Americans. The companies say: "We want Latinos because the Blacks and the Whites don't work fast enough," and that creates animosity between groups. It's the old strategy of divide and conquer. Then there is also age discrimination: companies don't want older people because they can't work as fast. Gender discrimination is pretty much universal: women get paid less than men do. But even here agents will talk about "jobs for men" and

> "jobs for women," which are illegal because job descriptions can't specify one gender over the other.

Employers use different groups against each other to control the labor market by way of unfair competition; they also use the threat of deportation against the workers. The threat is no more than a bluff in many cases to intimidate workers and take advantage of their lack of knowledge about legal procedure. New Labor's approach to taking this power relationship out of the private realm and making it public is reminiscent of the motto "the personal is political," which seeks to publicly confront injustices that occur in the private realm in order to demonstrate that exploitative power relations are structural:

> There is also action if you have deportation. Companies will say "if they speak up, we'll call immigration," and they will say "you don't have papers." It's really a bunch of nonsense because, first of all, if they hire people knowing they don't have papers they are committing a crime too. They would get in trouble if they were to call immigration. Second of all, even if they do call immigration, it's highly unlikely that immigration is going to show up because they are more focused on large corporations and major political issues like border security. They want to make a big splash. They will not bother with a warehouse with twenty workers in New Brunswick. Third, putting up with constant immigration raids would create a panic around the country. The economy is based on legal and illegal immigrant labor: if there is panic and no one shows up for work, then the entire economy will be negatively affected in a big way. They [ICE – Immigration and Customs Enforcement] might be mean, but they are not stupid either. They are not just going to show up because someone calls them up and says: "This person over here is illegal." We always go over that with people, and again it's more about confronting this problem as a group, taking the exploitative use of power out of the private sphere and making it public. It's never just your problem, it's everyone's problem.

New Labor seeks policy changes and represents workers' interests at the local, state and federal levels. Its strategies and objectives are less political and more social when compared to those of unions and labor parties. The way New Labor sees politics as more of a means than an end is representative of the contemporary transformations that are taking place in employment relations. The local level provides a more immediate setting for political struggles compared to the traditional tripartite models of arbitration. Local governments and local businesses can be immediately mobilized toward addressing issues that are locally pertinent not only to workers but also to businesses and the local economy at large. The shift from state-level organization to local-level organization, accompanied by a parallel localization in agendas, strategies and political relations, enables the possibility of obtaining immediate resolutions – as opposed to lengthy bureaucratic procedures with regard to interest representation and policy change:

> Politics for us is an organizing tool, but it is not always necessarily an end. Because why make laws if you can't enforce them? So it's more about having rules starting from the ground up, building a base to be able to develop power. This is more important to us. This is where we have placed our focus – as opposed to trying to create policy. Policies are tools that help us improve conditions. Wage theft ordinances, for example, say that you have to pay people. There are prescribed legal procedures, but the employers don't always end up paying you. If you go to a court of law and the Department of Labor makes a decision in your favor, the employers still may not end up paying you, despite the fact that the local town can revoke their business license. So we use legal procedures as a threat. For example we used this tactic to recover like $10,000 from three different restaurants. Employers can either take the long legal road, or pay right away and avoid the hassle. And some businesses have chosen to pay right away.

The local focus in political orientation does not necessarily imply micro-level organization. The local provides an opportunity to deconstruct the vertical integration and operation of labor organizations toward a horizontally integrated, comprehensive organization that may embrace social transformations regarding workers and the employment relations they form. The new labor movement seeks alliances with other movements fighting for social justice on other issues and expands horizontally to incorporate a greater number of constituents – as opposed to the traditional labor movement, which formed alliances with labor parties that were ultimately seeking political power. This is not overriding the old school labor movement, but providing an alternative to it in a time when traditional labor organizations face significant limitations in achieving political power or even effecting the smallest changes in employment relations:

> When New Labor started, we were a low-wage class of workers, so that's how we started. But it did not mean that we would end up where we wanted to go. In doing so, we become more Latino-based. The initial step is forming an organization, but the next step is to show how injustice has happened. It's all part of the big picture, that is, the system itself. So we have participated in some of the police brutality protest marches; we went on the climate change march in New York City; and we have been involved with other labor and social groups and have thereby expanded our scope. In terms of labor, we've done some work with labor unions in terms of how we gain access to workers and how we organize them. We are now doing work with the steel workers around issues of health and safety. We are providing them with training. We are also helping them

> organize their union on a local basis. Our worker center is part of the Interfaith Worker Justice Network, the National Day Laborer Organizing Network, and the National Domestic Workers Alliance. And there are other organizations like ours that are involved in these networks as well.

New Labor as a developing worker center vividly exposes the changing dynamics of workplace democracy and organized labor. It has been evolving as a strong grassroots movement that mobilizes local workers on the basis of their local issues in relation to employers and political agents that are also local. Their approach incorporates several different tasks, which range from educating and training workers to drafting legal documents and disseminating information on labor-related issues. They are not a part of mainstream structures, either institutionally or functionally, yet they do cooperate with mainstream organizations. Their expansion strategy is not vertical or hierarchical; rather, it is more horizontal and network-based. New Labor's primary motivation for expansion is based on the needs and interests of its members. It is not based on political interests or a desire to gradually increase political influence. New Labor seeks to use politics as a channel to transform employment relations in a progressive manner by politicizing issues that may otherwise be regarded as private.

Compared to Mondragon and SEWA, New Labor does not have a productive angle. It indirectly improves redistribution mechanisms by seeking worker justice, providing education (hence contributing to skill formation), fighting against wage theft, and ensuring income for the lowest strata of the working class. As a community organization, New Labor also mobilizes its constituents to focus on their shared dispositions and shared problems in employment relations. Workplace affinity generates a sense of camaraderie in other social contexts.

Pankobirlik

The success of the cooperative model depends on the implementation of cooperative principles and the degree to which they can be implemented. The local political climate and economic structure determine the extent to which these principles can be implemented. The prevalence of a resistance culture and of traditional solidarity makes it easier to implement cooperative principles, and cooperative movements will survive temporarily in the absence of contributing factors (i.e. resistance culture and traditional mechanisms of solidarity, a strong basis for social organization, a history of social movements and autonomy in productive capacity, and democracy). The case of the Turkish cooperative movement is an exception to the rule. While all its principles and agents are present, its presence is only nominal and not functional. This section will focus on the largest agrarian cooperative alliance in the country in order to expose the impact of external factors on the evolution of a cooperative. Pankobirlik, the cooperative alliance of beet producers, was established to pursue rural development through intensive farming.

The Turkish economy had predominantly agrarian structure during the 1950s. Within the limitations of capitalist entrepreneurship and economic factors that promoted capitalist farming, cooperativism became an alternative developmental venue promoted by the state. Cooperativism in the Turkish case was not a grassroots movement based on local interest mobilization, but a top-down imposition of cooperative principles that was due to structural macroeconomic limitations. The massive number of farmers integrated across the country did allow for the sustained production, trading and processing of sugar beets, and farmers benefited from the relative security of the domestic market in a period characterized by statism and the protection of national industry.

The cooperative organization of beet farmers dates back to 1951. The 1950s was a period characterized by statist cooperativism rather than by grassroots movements. Cooperatives were regarded not as ends in and of themselves but as means to an end, a way to help the state achieve its development goals. The cooperative systems served many purposes during this period. The organization and motivation of beet farmers and the establishment of an industrial base through sugar factories would help usher in industrialization, increase employment and cater to the domestic market. The whole process would contribute to capital accumulation in a context where the national bourgeoisie was in the making (Keyder 1987).

The first sugar factory with cooperative input was established in 1952 in partnership with the state. Beet farmers became partners in the establishment of eleven sugar factories between 1953 and 1956. This marked the beginning of an expansion in cooperative alliances. However, this expansion inevitably brought the subordination of cooperative objectives to statist ones in a time when markets were heavily structured and regulated by the government. In 1972, Pankobirlik was established as an umbrella organization and it incorporated nineteen beet cooperatives across the country under the guidance of the national entity Turkish Sugar Factories, Inc. The 1970s represented a unique historical milieu for the world economy as well as for Turkey. As the highly protectionist national economies liberalized, the political and economic turmoil of the same period in Turkey forced the country to follow suit and align itself with the rest of the world. Production and redistribution were the primary functions of beet cooperatives up until this point. These cooperatives, however, provided a limited solidarity alternative due to the lack of democratic decision-making and therefore a lack of representation of farmers' and workers' interests.

An overview of the sugar industry at this point should provide some insight into the operation of the cooperative system in Turkey. First, the state is an active participant in the sugar industry together with private corporations, the cooperatives themselves and cooperative factories. The sugar market is far from one of perfect competition, and it is highly regulated. The most important instrument for market regulation is the quota system, which determines the supply of sugar that is marketed by private corporations in the domestic market. The quota also regulates the amount of sugar beet cultivated annually. Quota A refers to the amount of sugar produced and marketed for the domestic market annually. Quota B refers to a certain ratio of Quota A that has to be secured and kept for states of emergency (such as wars or natural disasters). Quota C refers to sugar and sugar by-products that fall outside of Quota A and Quota B, and which can therefore be exported. The expansion of Quota C does not necessarily indicate a growth in export margins. Global competition in the sugar market, especially after the extended use of corn syrup and other sugar substitutes, diminishes the export chances of those producing excess product for Quota C. The strict regulation of the domestic market and the fierce competition in international markets limit the ability of beet cooperatives to generate economic development by way of local production. The cooperative under the quota system becomes an agent of administration rather than one of solidarity. The farmers, faced with these pressures, either submit to these dynamics or move to other crops. Some farmers serve as intermediaries, as they trade quota shares or produce with other farmers. Overall, farmers have limited input in the way their produce is processed[7]:

> When Pankobirlik was first established, it potentially targeted beet farmers, but today there is greater diversity in membership. Farmers do not have to be members to cultivate beets and to sell them to the sugar factory; however, it is most probable that they are. They are probably members if they are not trading elsewhere, which is again, highly unlikely. There are farmers who serve as intermediaries; they do not use their own quota to produce beets, but they buy beets from other farmers and sell to the sugar factory and make money for whatever they are producing and the beets they are trading. This is not something we approve as the coop administration; we deal with producers rather than merchants.

The relative security and protection of the sugar industry and beet producers under state capitalism was replaced by pressures of deregulation, privatization and increasing competition due to trade liberalization after 1980. This was a period when the development goals of the Turkish economy were heavily undermined by the objectives of liberalization and opening up to the world economy (Onis 1999). Macroeconomic transformation affected the sugar industry, which also experienced privatization and liberalization. Konya sugar factory, established in 1954 with the contributions of cooperative farmers, was privatized in line with the neoliberal rubric dominating the Turkish economy during this period.[8] Privatization in the sugar industry had several consequences for beet farmers. First, the whole production process, in terms of the amount of land to be cultivated, targeted the amount of produce; the pricing of the produce was left to the patronage of the market. This had serious consequences for the function of the cooperatives. The functions of the market had priority over the interest of the farmers:

> The history of beet cooperatives goes back to 1950s, and they have a long history. They were established by farmers themselves and developed on the basis of membership dues, later to become the Beet Cooperatives Alliance [Pankobirlik]. Our primary goal is to provide the farmers with the most affordable agricultural input. In terms of fertilizers, animal feed and other products, we hold a price-determining position in the market. We provide the farmers with the best long-term payment plans and pre-payment options, or we deduct their debt from the amount they receive for their produce.

Second, the extent of financialization due to privatization meant that the shares of beet cooperatives in the sugar factories diminished significantly. This affected the economic returns as well as the involvement of farmers in the decision-making process:

> Legally, the membership dues farmers pay are incomparable to the capital holdings of sugar corporations. The corporation today has billions of dollars in holdings. Cooperative members receive dividends in proportion to their contribution to the cooperative. However, this does not entitle them to any profits from the corporation.

The farmers are left in an ambiguous position vis-à-vis corporate capital and vis-à-vis the state, as only part of the industry is privatized and the state is still a relevant actor in the industry both economically and legally. Third, privatization in certain locations resulted in the emergence of regional disparities in beet farming. The farmers in Konya were relatively protected by the private sector due to their proximity to private corporations and the intensity of their production, whereas the producers in western Turkey faced difficulties, as they had to maintain their market relations through the state. As a result, the market segmentation emerging from this partial privatization generated uncontrollable external factors that worked against most of the farmers (Unal 2008). Privatization was followed by the establishment of Torku Corporation, which became a major actor in the food industry, diversifying its product range into meat and dairy. Its expansion strategies were very much geared toward changing global dynamics, and because of its focus on local production and the integration of agrarian production with an industrial base, it held a significant market share both domestically and regionally. While agrarian and industrial production was well integrated and strategically expanded, redistribution was not part of Torku Corporation's innovative and revivalist agenda.

The impact of this structural shift on the sugar industry and beet farmers was immense. The decline of state subsidies toward farmers was a major economic hit that led to significant decline in economic returns. Second, faced with the competition of imported sugar products and the globalization of the food industry, local farmers received another economic backlash. Third, technological improvements and the widespread use of corn syrup as a replacement for beet sugar had a negative impact on beet farmers. The beet farmers in the cooperative system, already under heavy pressure from the quota system and a weakening competitive edge in the global market, held limited bargaining power, made minimal contribution to the decision-making process, and had limited economic returns for their highly regulated production:

> Beets are supposed to be subject to crop rotation, so every four years the farmer has to change the crop for sustained product levels. The process is audited by the Turkish Sugar Company owned by the state. However, farmers are less inclined to wait for four years and usually change the crop earlier. Sunflowers and corn are becoming more common crops. The beet farmer has no alternative but to sell the crops to the sugar factory. Beets are not tradable otherwise, but they guarantee that they will receive their pay from the factory. They are not faced with a no-pay problem in the market. The import of corn syrup may have indirectly caused a decline in beet farming. The main reason for transition from beets to other products has to do with low sugar content. Alpullu was the first sugar factory in the country, yet beet farming in its hinterland is almost non-existent. Most people switched to livestock imports due to state subsidies.

The beet cooperatives are subject to the unique structure of the sugar industry in Turkey. It is very difficult to abstract the operation of beet cooperatives from the state-regulated and partially privatized sugar industry. The heavy emphasis on industrial farming in the sugar industry overrides the cooperative motivation toward rural development and local mobilization. Still, there are successful agrarian cooperatives in Turkey that take off from local initiatives and that are independent from statist interventions and market impositions. Dairy producers start up their own cooperatives to market their products collectively. It starts off in a single village and over time a few other villages in the vicinity are collectively organized. Membership in these cooperatives ranges from 100 to 2,000, and, depending on their marketing potential, they start processing under their own brands. Tire-Sut, a dairy cooperative with 2,000 members, markets its products under its own brand name. Or-Koop, similarly started off with seven members in 1979 with the intention of selling their produce at fair prices. Currently, the cooperative sells a great deal of raw milk to large-scale industry while gradually building its processing capacity locally. Similar collective efforts are concentrating on other products. Community-supported production schemes become popular apart from cooperatives. The motivation in this model is economic and ecological: emphasis is placed on organic produce. Community-supported production schemes also link cities to the countryside, as rural products are periodically marketed to metropolitan areas. Successful examples underline the importance of grassroots mobilization, democratic decision-making and the immediate circumstances that are favorable for solidarity.

Delaney's ethnographic account of cooperation in a Turkish village does a good job of explaining detachment between traditional modes of cooperation that maintain the village and the social relations embedded in it and the more formal cooperative models that are social and economic in organization and outcome. The traditional mode of cooperation, *imece*, refers to informal social and economic cooperation toward solving problems, addressing emergency situations, and helping the needy. Delaney's examples include the building of a bridge over a creek or helping an elderly couple repair their damaged and aging house. Another example is the cooperation between villagers in harvest time or in any other stage of cultivation. As for formal cooperatives, Delaney states that most had collapsed and many were officially closed with the 1980 military coup:[9]

> At first I was told that part of the failure of these activities had to do with the lack of trust between participants; a generalized fear that some clever person would divert the funds into his own use. But this suspicion is a fairly endemic aspect of Turkish village life and, in any case, had clearly been transcended for certain periods of time. Others explained that during the preceding years of political upheaval co-operative behavior had come to be labeled "communist" and thus tainted.
>
> (Delaney 1993: 153)

Had the cooperative movement incorporated traditional cooperative relations in a comprehensive manner, the course of history for Turkish cooperatives would have been different. The cooperative tradition in its crudest form has always been delinked from modern economic alternatives. Part of this could be explained on the basis of traditional political clashes, namely, the resistance of the village life to new modes of organization, while another part could be explained on the basis of the external dynamics and the impacts of the top-down policy approach that hinder the potential for grassroots mobilization.

A comparative analysis of the Turkish cooperative example may reveal greater theoretical insight. First, it is not the institutional, organizational or legal framework of cooperatives *per se* that is important; instead, the function of cooperatives embedded in a set of social relations makes a historical difference. In the case of Mondragon, cooperatives were an outlet in a geographically and politically contingent area. They became the sole proprietor of development. The primary objective was local development based on the needs of the local population. In the Turkish case, cooperatives were initiated by the state and filled up an economic gap in the weakness of the state as an economic actor and in the absence of capitalist enterprise. Social relations became a derivative of cooperative economics as opposed to cooperatives becoming social institutions. The local in the Turkish context was subordinated to the national.

Second, solidarity economies are theoretically constructed to represent a non-state, non-market alternative. The choice of opting out of the conventional statist or market-based paradigm is an essential component for the success of a cooperative, yet the extensity of opting out may differ on the basis of various economic, demographic, and geographical factors. Compared to Mondragon and SEWA, the extent to which Pankobirlik may opt out of the conventional statist and market-based paradigms is rather limited. The history of beet cooperatives is more rooted in the state than in the local. The organizational responses emerging in the 1970s were more market-oriented than local. The current institutional entanglement of cooperatives, factories, the state and the new generation of entrepreneurs in Turkey is an example of crony capitalism rather than local development or a solidarity economy. The beet farmers had no input in the development and decision-making processes of beet cooperatives, which are in fact the most extensive cooperative organizations in the country.

Last, how does the institutional restructuring in the sugar industry compare to global processes? In principle, cooperatives are based on voluntary membership, and they are democratically governed: the decision to reinvest, to expand and to expand into particular areas depends on local factors and the interests of members. Mondragon's expansion and innovation strategies are very much responsive to the changing market dynamics of the globalized economy. SEWA's use of education and technology to generate greater know-how and local development is more representative of local dynamics. In the case of Pankobirlik, despite its sizable membership, local interests are heavily undermined by those of the state and the market. Their responses do include innovative practices, branding, product diversification and an expansion of market share in Torku Corporation, yet the trickledown effect does not reach local producers. In the case of smaller, local cooperatives that solely depend on local initiatives, the economic returns are much more limited, yet the autonomy to determine the structure and progress of cooperation is much greater. It is possible to conclude that the cooperative model can only truly be considered operational if principles of openness, democratic participation and reciprocity are fully incorporated into collective action and the decision-making process.

Notes

1 Mondragon started on a local basis with the primary intention of using local means to meet local needs; however, it evolved into a network of cooperatives over time without losing the commitment to cooperative principles, adapting to social transformations and economic transitions.
2 http://www.sewa.org
3 The quotes in this section come from an interview with Namrata Bali, the Director of SEWA Academy, SEWA's educational wing. The full interview, which was conducted by the author of this book, was published in Turkish in the Turkish journal *Birikim* in September 2015.
4 New Jersey is one of the smallest states in the US; however, because of its population density and high levels of industrialization it is a major site of labor struggles. The quotes came from an interview conducted at New Labor (http://newlabor.org/).
5 A thirty-minute semi-structured interview was conducted with a New Labor representative in order to get a general idea about the structure and scope of the organization.

6 DAPA refers to Deferred Action for Parents of Americans and Lawful Permanent Residents, an immigration policy in the US that lawfully grants deferred action to immigrants who have children as American citizens or legal permanent residents. DACA, which refers to Deferred Action for Childhood Arrivals, applies to undocumented immigrants younger than 16 years of age who entered the country before June 2007. It allows them to qualify for a two-year work permit and deportation exemption. Neither of the programs provides full legal status or the granting of citizenship.

7 A semi-structured phone interview was conducted with a Pankobirlik representative from the central office regarding the changing role and share of cooperatives in the sugar industry. The interview was conducted on January 26, 2016, and lasted about thirty minutes. Additional data was obtained from official resources and press releases for the organization.

8 Two points about Konya are important for a complete understanding of its transformation. Konya, as Turkey's largest city by size, is known for its strong agricultural sector. It makes up a significant percentage of sugar beet and wheat production in the country. Politically, Konya is also known as the birthplace of various Islamist politicians as well as the Turkish branch of political Islam itself. The privatization of the sugar factory and the establishment of Torku Corporation coincide with the rule of the moderate Islamist government of the AKP, which suggests the existence of a typical patron-client relationship and the existence of cronyism.

9 A note of clarification is necessary on the 1980 military coup. The 1980 military coup in Turkey was directly linked to the liberalization program in Turkey, which was initiated earlier in the same year with a stand-by agreement with the IMF. The coup attacked the leftist movement in general, and put a ban on leftist parties, politicians, and labor unions. The cleansing of the left and the oppression of opposition movements secured the transition of the Turkish economy from an import substitution economy to a free market economy.

6 Solidarity economies

A conceptual exercise

The problems and limitations generated by neoliberal globalization received a wide array of responses from different social segments all over the world. The structural problems of the global economy have been addressed by these social segments in a diverse yet unstructured manner. These responses include practical transformations, organizational innovations, strategic reconfigurations – whether in the form of increasing diversity or new sorts of alliances – and changes in the mode of thinking regarding social and economic organization. The task of this chapter is to review the defining elements of solidarity economies that emerge as a response to neoliberal globalization and to use a comparative analysis to construct a framework of action and evaluation that may lead to further avenues of inquiry. It will also focus on the practical transformations and the material basis of solidarity economies and the ways in which we can think about these challenges analytically.

Local responses to global pressures

The primary definitive element of solidarity economies is that they are local. They emerge out of the unified interests of local populations; they make use of the locally available resources and processes. They may come in the form of alternative production relations, redistribution mechanisms, or organizing principles. The local responses are not universal in form or in structure; rather, they depend on the prevalent political culture of mobilization, social dynamics, demographics, and locally available economic resources and relations. This parallels the unequal impact of neoliberal globalization. The local focus does not necessarily imply the refusal of global networks and the neglect of improved means of communication and transportation. Most of these local solidarity networks benefit from information dissemination through information technology, which helps reconnect distant networks with one another. It also facilitates a learning process wherein networks share know-how, success stories and possible limitations that they have encountered along the way.

Solidarity economies have been analyzed on the basis of four major functions. The first two functions of production and redistribution refer to the material basis of solidarity in terms of making strategic use of material resources and sharing the returns of production in a more efficient and sustainable manner. The latter two functions of solidarity economies are workplace democracy and the reorganization of labor. The weakness of democratic systems comes from their representative structure and the fact that they are bound by the intuitive alliance between the political and the economic elite. The labor movement has historically been a political movement in the way it has sought to attain political power or in the way it has sought to expand labor's status through fighting for political, civil and social rights associated with citizenship. Yet the weakening of the nation-state during neoliberal globalization diminished the clout that the labor movement had achieved through democratic means. It is under these circumstances that workplace democracy carries the rights-based arguments and struggles to the workplace and to the local context. Instead of seeking structural transformations vis-à-vis the nation-state or supranational entities, the struggles are more local and the solutions are less structural (and yet still viable). Similar to the contemporary limitations of democratic practices, organized labor movements, particularly labor unions, have shown limited adaptability to recent global transformations. The rise of identity politics has been a challenge that they have found difficult to grapple with. The national level of organization in which they find themselves in provided limited grounds to fight against the increasing pressures of the global market and globally mobile capital. Workers sought alternative organizational models in the wake of the weakness of unions' adaptive strategies to voice their opinion and represent their interests. Worker centers and other non-governmental organizations emerged to fulfill these functions and serve as fora for deliberation.

The local is a functional and an organizational alternative. The four functions of solidarity economies, namely production, redistribution, democratic practice and labor struggle, can all be organized at the local level in order to overcome the efficiency problem that mainstream organizations are now facing. The global level of organization leads to the formation of new alliances and generates greater publicity, yet it is a far cry from making the necessary policy changes toward structural transformation. The ILO, the ITUC and the G20 are examples of entities whose work on social and economic issues has gained a significant amount of publicity, but whose ability to affecting policy change is rather limited. The greatest problem that the global level of organization suffers from is its detachment from the grassroots level. By the time an issue has been carried from the grassroots to the national, regional or global level, it has been significantly transformed, generalized and/or trivialized. The extremity of an issue becomes a benchmark of global representation. There are successful global organizations that are less mainstream and that are more representative of grassroots movements, most notably the WSF, yet they lack the financial and organizational means to extend their outreach.

The national level of organization is problematic for other reasons. The division of sovereignty between supranational institutions and the nation-state limits the latter's ability to manoeuvre, making the national-level demands of workers irrelevant. The local level of organization as opposed to the global or the national levels proves to be more efficient in responding to immediate issues, giving room to local groups in interest representation and issue resolution. The relative independence and autonomy of local agents vis-à-vis a globally restrained state or mainstream global institutions increase efficiency in the use of available resources and in the addressing of local problems in a sound manner.

The local focus is a functional, an organizational and a political alternative. Capitalism's consolidation of the market in the form of its global outreach has its antithesis in the local. The increasing demands for autonomy represent a significant political divergence in a world of mainstream political structures. These demands are not merely political in terms of self-determination or self-governance; they are also economic in terms of managing and redistributing the returns of local resources. The demands of the Zapatistas in Mexico or the Kurds in Turkey, Iraq, and Syria, as well as the Catalan demands for separation from Spain are all demands for autonomy against the nation-state, the supranational organizations it shares its sovereignty with, and other hegemonic agents that externalize local demands from their agendas. The demands and the strategies of these autonomy movements may differ, but they are quite similar in abstract terms, standing in stark contrast to the globally integrated capitalist world economy and its political extensions.

The local as an alternative does not come without limitations. First, the local does not come out as a replacement for the global but as an alternative that will coexist with it. There are only certain products and economic functions that could be realized on the local level. The full mobilization of local resources and the local economy will decrease dependency on the global market, yet it will not bring about full freedom from the market. The mobilization of local resources requires continuous commitment and the internalization of the principles of solidarity; however, the local level of organization always carries the risk of traditional hierarchies penetrating into economic relations and overriding the solidarity objective. These hierarchies could be ethnic, religious or otherwise, and force themselves into the evolving structures of solidarity economies. Failures in solidarity economies are as common as success stories. Instead of glorifying an illusion, alternatives need to be evaluated in a holistic and down-to-earth manner.

Non-state, non-market alternatives to the global economy

Karl Polanyi proposed the idea of *substantivism* to counter the malfunctions and social consequences of the market ideology. According to him, the economy essentially holds two meanings. The first is the neoclassical meaning that focuses on the concept of *homo economicus*, the rational individual that maximizes utility. The second meaning focuses on humans building a life within the limits of their social and environmental surroundings. Polanyi follows upon the latter meaning and discusses the possibility of sustaining production and redistribution in a non-market society. The four principles of the non-market society, in his view, are reciprocity, redistribution, symmetry and centricity (Polanyi 1967: 46). Reciprocity refers to reciprocal exchanges between social groups and/or their members, as opposed to the utility maximization of the rational human being in the market. Redistribution, in a self-explanatory manner, refers to the redistribution of accumulated goods and services to members of the society. Symmetry and centricity are two principles that ensure the sustenance of non-market economic relations. In symmetry, Polanyi argues that partners may ensure continued exchange without a formal record. As for centricity, Polanyi sees it as referring to the collection of goods and services in a centralized manner so as to thereafter be redistributed to the members of the social group. Polanyi's references to this substantivist model of economic relations embedded in social relations is very much in line with the local level of social organization and challenges the top-down determination of the global market.

Solidarity economies stand in contrast to mainstream institutional configurations of political economy. They coexist with and relate to the state and its agents, or the market and its constituents. The locally organized solidarity economy does not aim at a revolutionary overthrow of the bourgeoisie, a dictatorial overtake as a means to transition to a utopian society. Solidarity economies are very much grounded in existing social and economic circumstances and aim to expand their maneuvering space independent of the market and the state. The solidarity economy challenges the market ideology, which is so readily accepted and applied by the state, and the market logic that is continuously imposed upon and indoctrinated into the individual. The idea is of an organizational pluralism that may enable alternative models to flourish on the basis of solidarity, cooperation, inclusion and participation.

Unger's critique of the left and the proposal of a new alternative is an important benchmark in thinking about the possibility of solidarity economies. Unger considers the viability of organizational pluralism by questioning existing institutional structures, and the political and economic relations embedded in the market-dominant environment:

> It means to reject the contrast between market orientation and governmental direction as the axis organizing our ideological contests, and to replace it with a contrast among ways of organizing economic, political, and social pluralism. It means to root a bias to greater equality and inclusion in the organized logic of economic growth and technological innovation rather than making it rest on retrospective redistribution through tax and transfer.
>
> (Unger 2009: 21)

It is within this kind of a pluralist view that solidarity economies become a viable alternative. Solidarity economies in themselves show diversity in terms of organization, function and outreach. It is the principles of solidarity, mutuality, and unity that frame these diverse configurations under the same category. By stating that "free trade is a means, not an end," Unger argues that countries have the liberty to opt out of "general trading rules" or, more generally, out of globally dispersed market relations (Unger 2009: 137). Solidarity economies provide a venue for opting out, at least for a portion of society willing to do so, if not for an entire nation.

Overcoming divergence of work and industrial relations sociology

The disciplinary foundations of labor studies diversified toward the second half of the twentieth century. In the words of Kalleberg, "ensuing decades brought greater specialisation in the sociological study of work, but the study of work also became increasingly fragmented in the 1960s and 1970s, both within sociology and between sociology and other social science disciplines" (Kalleberg 2009). Harry Braverman's work on labor in the twentieth century became a milestone in the construction of labor studies as a field (Braverman 1974). In *Labor and Monopoly Capital*, Braverman locates the archetypes of capital, division of labor, and workers within a twentieth-century setting, which becomes significantly transformed due to the advent of scientific management and various technological advancements. The globalization of the division of labor and the market proved *Labor and Monopoly Capital* to be an illuminating inquiry. As Braverman was writing on American labor, Ernest Mandel was taking the Marxist analysis of labor relations one step further in *Late Capitalism* (Mandel 1972). Mandel's structural analysis of late capitalism contributed to the periodization of history of capitalism and the waves of economic development. From a labor perspective, his detailed elaboration of the concentration and centralization of capital in different geographies during various phases of capitalism has informed scholars' understanding of the global division of labor and the industrial restructuring that followed. The concentration of capital in a certain location suggests a transformation in the industrial composition of employment there and elsewhere (Mandel 1972). Both Braverman and Mandel came from the world of labor itself. They were theorists and activists at the same time, which further intensified their knowledge of and experience with labor. A decade after Braverman's work, Piore and Sabel's *The Second Industrial Divide* made a critical intervention in labor studies by exposing the limits of mass production and the transition to a new dominant mode of production in the capitalist world economy as a way of overcoming the crisis of the 1970s (Piore and Sabel 1986). Flexible specialization, which was seen as the light at the end of the tunnel at that time, turned out to be nothing more than a mirage.

During this period of theoretical expansion, labor studies as a field was enriched by in-depth historical studies that provided extended insight into industrial transformations and labor relations. E. P. Thompson's *The Making of the English Working Class* provided a deep historical account of the immediate circumstances of work during the early industrialization period in

England (Thompson 1966). Thompson became a well-cited reference for scholars in terms of his conceptualization of the proletarianization process. The changing social and material conditions of the working class were elaborated vividly. Thompson's depictions of the structural transformation in the production process with respect to the temporal and spatial organization of work and with respect to the separation of the spheres of work and non-work have been enduring contributions to labor studies. In addition to Thompson's book, Hobsbawm's *Industry and Empire* and *Workers: Worlds of Labor* later provided further historical analysis on the changing world of work after the Industrial Revolution (Hobsbawm 1968; Hobsbawm 1985). Hobsbawm's work was more historical and less theoretical than Thompson's; however, his Marxist perspective and his focus on the social components and consequences of historical materialism made his analysis of significant value for labor scholars.

The task for the contemporary scholar of work and labor is to further the quest for meaning in an age of uncertainty, where the boundaries of conventional dichotomies are blurred and conceptual categories become more permeable. Munck, commenting on the new international labor studies (NILS) that came out in the late 1970s and early 1980s, argues that "NILS brought to the fore a critical concern with the 'labouring poor' as a broader category than that of a classical proletariat. Likewise the hidden forms of workers' struggles were highlighted, as were broader 'sociological' approaches to class formation and proletarianization. There was also keen attention to and feminist-inspired debates on the domestic mode of production" (Munck 2009). There is an immense amount of literature that came into being as a result of concerns for previously untouched aspects of labor, and it has used different methodologies and fields of inquiry. The growing size of the literature diminishes the chances that newer generations of scholars will be able to make theoretical contributions, since heavy reliance on empiricism and micro-level analysis contributes to the literature in a more quantitative manner. In an article written in 1993, Abbott makes one of the most extensive studies on the evolution of labor studies by reviewing institutional structures, the many topics covered in labor studies, methodological approaches, different levels of inquiry, and the historical progress by which all of these aspects have been transformed and reformulated. Abbott reviews articles published in numerous databases, and he critically underlines that the focus on quantitative research without a matching interest in theory weakens the contribution of contemporary studies: "In the meantime, lack of theory covering multiple levels in both space and time makes most pieces of quantitative research on work mutually irreconcilable and hence meaningless. It remains true that for all our modern insights, there is only one truly general theory of work, that of Marx" (Abbott 1993). The comment on Marx's contribution is not without a criticism on its assumptions about work and the weakness of its policy suggestions.

Munck addresses the divide between industrial relations and labor studies in a critical manner. The former is representative of the ILO discourse on social partnerships, human relations and labor relations, and is characterized by its limited analytical capacity to incorporate other variables into an equation on labor and the global economy. Munck openly criticizes the tripartite or bipartite conceptualization of labor in industrial relations in terms of its inability to grasp the global transformations that labor is subject to. At the other end of the spectrum is the labor studies approach, which can be characterized by its exclusive commitment to Marx. The traditional mode of thinking about the working class ignores changing class dynamics and the diverse experiences and dispositions of the workers within the global division of labor:

> The break with class essentialism and the adoption of a broader, more "culturalist" and gendered approach to labor is certainly overdue. As is an understanding of globalization not as monolith but as a complex, contingent and hybrid set of shifting social relations. The world is changing rapidly and our theoretical lenses need to be adjusted accordingly to take account of the fluid and complex setting of labor and social movement activities.
>
> (Munck 2004: 257)

Hence, we have come to a point where the terminology of labor studies has to be redefined with respect to emerging dynamics (Standing 2009). This process of revitalization should take place on multiple levels, where the individual experience provides insight into the immediate consequences of the contemporary conduct of capitalism (Sennett 2000) and collective experience suggests alternative routes out of capitalism (Santos 2007; Waterman 2004). The current global economic crisis once again exposes the internal contradictions of the capitalist economy on a more structural level of inquiry (Panitch et al. 2010; Calhoun and Derluguian 2011).

The brief historical account of labor studies that has been provided so far has by no means been holistic and comprehensive enough to detail the immense amount of progress made since the beginning of the industrial era. The diversity of issues undertaken in scientific research through a multiplicity of research methodologies in different disciplinary settings cannot be encompassed in a simple and humble overview. The mere purpose of the historical periodization presented here is to contextualize the current study within the larger domain of labor studies both temporally and spatially.

Relinking empirical studies and theoretical analysis

Empirical studies on employment relations, the organization of production, and solidarity economies take off from a certain theoretical moment and then carry their practical observations to a certain level of abstraction by way of analysis. The specific theoretical milieu and the methodological capacity of the research determine the level of abstraction that the observations (i.e. the findings) will be elevated to. This process of analysis needs to be complemented, however, by a synthesis in order for it to make a holistic theoretical contribution to the field. The moment of research initially comes across two roads that diverge, one toward an empirical emphasis on fieldwork, data collection, and evaluation, and the other, while presumably considered less meticulous, toward a non-empirical emphasis on theoretical inquiry.[1]

The whole process of scientific inquiry is further complicated by the multi-disciplinary nature of the study of work, labor and employment. One major divergence, which has been talked about on several occasions in this book, is between labor studies and industrial relations. While this division could be an internal compartmentalization, it is further complicated by the tangents followed by the fields of labor economics, human resources management, and industrial psychology. The multiplicity of disciplines, perspectives and methodologies is a challenge to the newer generations of scholars seeking to establish themselves within the universe of scholarly inquiry.

Beyond the practical and organizational concerns over the research process, the geographical diversity of empirical research is an important challenge to the heavy reliance of the field on empiricism. Global inequality and the North-South divide affect academic structures and the availability of resources. The way inequality is present in academia itself is particularly important in the study of work and labor relations. The transformations in the global division of labor, the movement of manufacturing and (later) service industries to less developed parts of the world, suggest that the object of inquiry in the study of work and labor relations is predominantly located in the South, in less developed parts of the world. This is not to undermine the transformations in work and labor relations in the North, but to expose the reproduction of existing inequalities by explaining why the research tendencies are so geographically determined. Employment relations, lack of labor standards and unregulated working conditions in the South generate deeper social problems, health and safety problems, and economic inequality. The emphasis of empirical analysis, however, is more on the North because of the abundance of resources in the North; because of the sizable grant market, and because of a relative abundance of capital, both economic and academic. In many of the Northern countries, the workers in the lowest strata of the labor market who are subject to the harshest conditions are immigrants – legal or illegal – from the South.

Knowledge has become the currency of neoliberal globalization. Inventions and innovations in electronics, transportation, communication, and information dissemination have made knowledge ever more central and diffuse in people's daily activities. Beyond its logistical contributions, knowledge has become the primary and the most valuable commodity in the global economy. The commodification of knowledge, whether in the form of hardware (smartphones, laptops and tablets) or in the form of software (smartphone and computer "apps" used for personal and business-related activities), leads to the emergence of sizable niches in the market with considerable economic returns. The growth of the knowledge economy and the accompanying technological progress has generated a digital divide between the advanced capitalist countries and the rest of the world. The exceptional technological leaps of India or

Taiwan have not translated into corresponding leaps in human development large enough to overcome economic inequality gaps.

The commodification of knowledge has led to a detrimental transformation in academia as the primary agent of knowledge production. The conversion of the university into an academic enterprise has resulted in the automated mass production of standard academic knowledge, the quality of which is highly debated, together with a distinct set of academic superstars that make up a minuscule fragment of academic society. In a world of competitive publishing, the unstoppable assembly lines of academic journals have released millions of articles, which have become the currency of academic capitalism. Ever since academic merit has come to be measured on the basis of this currency, the richness and the originality of academic thought has been forsaken for the richness of the academic resume, which, once again, has come to be measured on the basis of the academic articles contained therein. Although the impact of capitalism on academic structures and processes has affected different disciplines in different ways, in the natural sciences, the social sciences and the humanities it has created a major shift in the way knowledge is pursued, produced and used. The work of Rhoades and Slaughter in representing the neoliberal transformation of the university is noteworthy in this regard:

> Universities are not just servants of or suppliers to the marketplace. They are active players in the marketplace. [...] Universities, public and private alike, have gone way "beyond the ivory tower," participating in privatization, deregulation, and commercialization to a greater degree than any public institutions other than the federal laboratories.
>
> (Rhoades and Slaughter 1997: 13)

How is this discussion of academic capitalism relevant to the study of solidarity economies and the search for alternative theory and practice? The fast pace of academic research has led to an overemphasis on empirical analysis and a trivialization of theoretical analysis. Innumerable academic journals annually publish thousands of academic articles on various topics in several different languages. In many cases, the authors lack the time and the ability to review the existing literature. The transformation of the university into a capitalist enterprise and the commodification of academic knowledge within this neoliberal academic setting threaten the authenticity of academic knowledge, subordinate the research process to the grant market, and weaken the potential contributions of theoretical analyses.

Research construction in general and research construction with regard to labor relations in particular require a careful examination of the inherent peculiarities of the object of inquiry and the external dynamics that directly impact the research process. The inherent peculiarities refer to the relationship between the subject and the object of inquiry, the geographical scope of research and the extent by which the conceptual framework matches with the object of inquiry. The external factors can be expressed as the relationship of the researcher to the domain of knowledge production. The researcher needs relative autonomy in the construction of the research in order to avoid possible lapses or biases. Most importantly, the major objective of every empirical inquiry has to be the theoretical contribution that would serve as a guideline for future researchers. The sense of academic community will flourish through productive collaboration, but it will become stale with empirical repetition.

Note

1 The critique of empirical analysis is not a postpositivist or postempiricist critique of the methodology or the relationship between the researcher and the research itself. Rather, the critique emerges out of the question of how to incorporate the most vivid and most geographically diverse set of inquiries into the process of theorizing. The former could be found more in Bryant (1996) and the latter more in Abbott (2005).

Conclusion

This book has sought out possible alternative paths for the current transformations taking place in employment relations. One source of inspiration for this objective was born out of what has generally been called the Great Recession, which in fact refers to another cyclical crisis in the long history of the capitalist world economy. The ongoing global economic crisis reiterates the fact that capitalism every so often falls into crisis irrespective of its potential to renew itself along with its components, which include the market, the division of labor, a dominant mode of production, and the commodification process. A second source of inspiration has been the weakness of the state in handling the current crisis. This weakness can be attributed to the changing nature of the alliance between capital and the state with increasing mobility of capital and a reluctance to pay dues to the state to support its conduct and control the dangerous classes. It could also be attributed to the changing perception of the nation, national identity and alternative identity markers that individuals adhere to in an ever more globalized world. Hence, the economic clout and the political functions of the state are being heavily undermined.

It is in this setting that the failures of mainstream institutional mechanisms and relations have resulted in global inequality, persistent underdevelopment and the weakening of social safety nets. Individuals have been left with no choice but to resort to alternative paths of economic relations. This book has attempted to expose these alternatives, which may not challenge existing structures but may provide room for those excluded, those who do not have access to the globally organized streams of capital. The search for alternatives is a difficult process, but one that is surely worth undertaking. The objective of scholarly inquiry is not necessarily to provide solutions but to expose possible alternative patterns that may lead to solutions. Solidarity economies are presented as the alternative patterns which enable their participants to opt out of mainstream, institutionalized economic relations.

Solidarity economies are defined as non-state, non-market alternatives to existing employment relations. This definition requires a note of clarification. Solidarity economies are not replacements for the existing structures of the market and the state; they do not form alliances; they do not rely on the resources of the state or the market; and they do not operate on the principles of economic optimums. Instead, they are social forms that emerge from the local and that depend on local resources and locally available labor. They are geared toward catering to the immediate needs of the local population. Communities become predominant units of mobilization and operation in solidarity economies. The local, irrespective of its size and its constituents, becomes the core of economic relations, both in terms of production and consumption. The size and scope of solidarity economies may be extended with product diversification, local development, and investment in new areas to the extent that the market reliance of local populations are significantly reduced.

This book has focused on four major components of solidarity economies. The first two of these components, production and redistribution, represent the material basis of solidarity economies. Uplifting productive capacities at the local level, reorganizing production relations so that they become free from market optimality, and prioritizing solidarity over profitability have been debated in discussions of social capitalism, sustainable development, and other alternative economic paradigms. Production alternatives represent the non-market dimension of solidarity economies. In terms of redistribution, local solidarity mechanisms, whether in the form of simple truck and barter, time banks, local safety networks for those in need, or income polarization through wage policy, are a necessary complement to solidaristic production systems. Redistributive alternatives represent the non-state dimension of solidarity economies. But more importantly, it is the complementary relationship between productive and redistributive alternatives that makes solidarity economies emerge as viable alternatives to existing economic relations. Reorganizing economic relations solely on the basis of production or redistribution, however, will only partially improve existing inequalities generated by mainstream economic relations.

The last two components of solidarity economies are workplace democracy and alternative labor solidarity. Workplace democracy defines the principles that democratize relations of production in the alternative workplace. The agenda in a democratic struggle incorporates the rights of the workers, labor standards, and fair wages, and the struggles of working-class families and working-class communities that are united under the roof of solidarity economies. While workplace democracy is more comprehensive in its agenda and more representative in terms of its constituents, the labor movement is currently undergoing significant transformations with the emergence of alternative organizations and the diversification of interests being pursued. Labor parties and unions have ceased to be the sole representative bodies in the labor movement. The disintegration of tripartite structures and the weakening of class-based struggles have necessitated this kind of a transformation. Just as production and redistribution are the material basis of solidarity economies, so too workplace democracy and alternative labor solidarity provide an organizational framework for solidarity economies. This framework helps construct a comprehensive agenda to expand the venues of participation and to mobilize an ever-increasing and diverse set of constituents.

Solidarity economies do not come in a single form despite the efforts in this book to construct a comprehensive organizational framework. Solidarity economies vary in terms of function and outreach, and in the way they mobilize locally available resources. The local basis of solidarity economies is another important source of variation. Solidarity economies emerge out of certain social needs that the state or the market mechanisms are unresponsive to. They flourish because of the immediate circumstances of their constituents, and they are unified by the principle of non-state, non-market, alternative operation.

The current state of the global economy provides limited insight into the future of the global market, corporate capital and the public economies forced into austerity. The end of the tunnel is dimly lit. The potential of the capitalist world economy to renew itself is taken for granted, yet this potential for renewal may be effective only temporarily due to the inherent contradiction of the system in generating growth and inequality at the same time. The revolutionary overthrow of this system in the form of mass mobilization toward structural transformation does not seem to have any traction in contemporary social mobilizations and social movements. The disillusionment caused by the Soviet experience, even when considering the ways in which it diverged from the classical Marxist socialist vision, continue to have an impact on leftist movements and their outreach. The questioning of the state apparatus, the weakening sovereignty, and the inefficiency of representative democracy has increased the political clout of leftist parties in general and labor parties in particular. Solidarity economies stand out as viable alternatives amid the weakness of alternative venues of mobilization that may interlink the economic interests and aspirations of grassroots movements with their political mobilization. The current state of solidarity economies may be sporadic and diversified, yet the future may see the flourishing of more extended networks that may penetrate as yet unreached segments of society. The penetration of the global economic crisis, both geographically and socially, will increase the likelihood that solidarity economies will flourish. Solidarity economies may become a more common mode of organization given the lack of mainstream institutional interventions.

Amid the bleakness of future scenarios for the progress of the capitalist system, inquiry into alternative economic systems will remain relevant for a long time to come. Further research may focus on the possible adoption of solidaristic principles in newer sectors of the economy. Additionally, it can also focus on the diversification of redistributive tasks in solidarity economies, from fair wage distribution and alternative social safety nets to solidaristic care networks or community-supported systems. At a higher level of abstraction, the capacity of workplace democracy to provide an alternative venue of interest representation may serve to be a comparative angle on the way in which democracy has been operationalized in scholarship.

The labor theory of value and the relations of production maintain their centrality in explaining the contradictory essence of the capitalist mode of production. This essence is further complicated by the historical transformations in the organization of production, the institutional frameworks circumscribing the production process, the changing nature of work, and the rise and fall of certain occupational categories and of employment relations more generally. The need to rethink the concepts pertaining to the world of work and employment relations will continue to exist. The framework of solidarity economies as presented in this book has partially fulfilled this need. Future transformations, whether radical or moderate, will necessitate further deliberation.

Epilogue

The classics have provided us a universe, in which concepts and relations pertaining to production, work and labor have been organized and reorganized across time and space. It is in this universe that the meaning of material existence, its value and conditions of exchange have been structured. The transition from the traditional mode of production to a modern one through the Industrial Revolution generated massive transformations in the organization of production and in the social organization surrounding it. This tremendous social change was interpreted in many different ways, which has generated a body of literature that would capture the attention of generations of labor studies scholars. Adam Smith's seminal *Wealth of Nations* begins with the discussion of the division of labor, which takes up the first three chapters, and which includes the well-known example of the pin factory. Here, Adam Smith introduces his readers to the world of economics with a basic discussion of the division of labor, which "so far as it can be introduced, occasions, in every art, a proportionable increase of the productive powers of labour" (Smith 1776: 12). He then goes to explain that

> each individual becomes more expert in his own peculiar branch, more work is done upon the whole, and the quantity of science is considerably increased by it. It is the great multiplication of the productions of all the different arts, in consequence of the division of labour, which occasions, in a well-governed society, that universal opulence which extends itself to the lowest ranks of the people.
>
> (Smith 1776: 16)

About thirty years after the publication of Smith's work, David Ricardo introduced his labor theory of value with a very basic description: "The value of a commodity, or the quantity of any other commodity for which it will exchange, depends on the relative quantity of labour which is necessary for its production, and not on the greater or less compensation which is paid for that labour" (Ricardo 1817: 1). Similar to Smith, Ricardo aims to establish a deeper and universal understanding of the way the economy operates, although he does it with a more capitalist tone, which was very much in line with his personal career as a broker. It wasn't the division of labor, but the operation of the market, production, trade and monetary exchange that acquired greater emphasis in his writing. Elaborating on the value of labor, he focused on the value of labor in the market – that is, embedded in marketed goods – and the reverse ratio it stands in vis-à-vis profits: "There can be no rise in the value of labour without a fall of profits. If the corn is to be divided between the farmer and the labourer, the larger the proportion that is given to the latter, the less will remain for the former" (Ricardo 1817: 58).

Around the same time that Ricardo was writing, across the English Channel in Paris Saint Simon was establishing the preliminary drafts of a class-based analysis. In his "Letters from an Inhabitant of Geneva," he distinguishes three classes:

> The first, to which you [an imaginary correspondent] and I have the honour to belong, marches beneath the banner of human progress: it consists of the scientists, the artists, and of all men of liberal ideas. On the banner of the second class is inscribed "No innovation." All the property-owners who do not qualify for the first class belong to the second. The third class, which rallies to the word "equality," comprises the rest of humanity.
>
> (Saint Simon 1964 [1803)

In his later work, "On Social Organization," Saint Simon made policy proposals regarding the status of the proletariat. These included promoting the interest of the proletariat so as to maintain the public order, easing the inheritance of landed property, and giving workers the highest political importance (Saint Simon 1964 [1825). His work, which ranged from industry, class structure, to social organization and the role of the state in the adoption of appropriate policies toward the working class, is filtered through a Newtonian lens and carried the tenets of universalism one step further (Saint Simon 1964 [1808).

It would by no means be unfair to state that Marx alone has made the greatest contribution to labor studies in both qualitative and quantitative terms. The multilayered analysis of the capitalist mode of production took labor theory one step further by exposing the immediate class formation that took place during the production process as well as its social consequences which were capital accumulation, on the one hand, and pauperization, on the other. Marx was able to show the dialectical continuity of class conflict elaborated through historical materialism. At least as important, however, has been the reformulation of the labor theory of value. The concept of alienation has become an alternative venue of inquiry that continues to attract researchers on a wide array of issues. It is the concept of alienation that explicitly displays the social and material consequences of production: "Through alienated labour, then, man creates not only his relationship to the object and act of production as to alien and hostile men; he creates too the relationship in which other men stand to his production and his product and the relationship in which he stands to these other men" (Marx in McLellan 1977: 84). The contemporary operation of the global market, with the global division of labor, constant promotion of consumerism and global inequality as a consequence of the former two processes, is a perfect example of the continuing validity of alienation.

Together with Marx, Emile Durkheim and Max Weber, as the founders of sociology, paid attention to the transformations in the means of production and the changing division of labor in society. However, neither in Durkheim nor in Weber was there an overarching focus on the political economy of capital and labor, or the production process and the division of labor, as was the case in Marx. Weber's contribution to class analysis and his emphasis on the role of cultural factors in economic organization and class relations should by no means be underestimated; however, the depth of Weber's analysis is sacrificed in favour of its breadth.

The limits of this universalist approach have less to do with theory and more to do with methodology. The inadvertent efforts of early authors to establish a positivist meta-narrative aiming to explain economic conduct beyond time and space created a myopic view of the non-linear, multilayered historicities of different geographies. The analytical efforts to explain a universal domain underestimated the importance of divergent paths of historical progress, especially in the periphery. Twentieth-century literature on labor has been more diverse in focus and more advanced in methodology thanks to technological innovations and, to a certain extent, its ability to overcome the theoretical rigidities of the universalism.

It was the moderns in the twentieth century who contributed to the regeneration of the practices and the relationships that exist all throughout the world. However, the historical continuities *per se* provide an insufficient basis for commitment to classical universalisms. The historical and geographic discontinuities compel readers to redefine the core concepts of political economy and the connections between them. The moderns carried the analytical capacity of the classics one step further. Theoretical diversity increased as methodological considerations toward non-linear, multilayered, comparative research in multiple settings flourished. Starting with a discussion of the failure of nineteenth-century civilization, Karl Polanyi makes three critical interventions in the study of the market and labor. First, Polanyi refuses the reductionist view of these entities as economic inputs by defining land, labor and money as fictitious commodities. Second, Polanyi's concept of the double movement explains the strain between the free market on the one hand and society's response to protect itself from the unintended consequences of the free market on the other. Third, by making references to pre-modern societies Polanyi seeks an alternative social order without the market. The current global crisis has rendered the work of Polanyi and his idea of a countermovement much more relevant.

Writing around the same time with Polanyi, John Maynard Keynes in his *magnum opus, The General Theory of Employment, Interest and Money,* diverted attention away from labor as such and the labor theory of value and refocused it on the concept of employment. While refusing the assumption that full employment is the ultimate end result of competitive markets, he underlined the inevitability of market regulation to avoid underemployment and decreasing investments. Keynes' contribution to labor studies has been practical as a consequence of the Keynesian consensus that led to the establishment of the Bretton Woods system following World War II. It was the institutional regulation of the market and the monetary policies of the Bretton Woods system that gave the postwar economic order its character, which in turn led to an economic boom promoting higher rates of employment and better labor conditions . The success of the Keynesian consensus, however, turned out to be only conjunctural, as were the beneficial circumstances for labor at that time.

It is within this historical context that this book has sought to engage in a quest for certainty and meaning in modern work experiences and labor relations. Contemporary economic relations are much more diverse and complex than fifteenth-century capitalist world economy or eighteenth-century industrialization. One can hardly observe a single-handed production scheme that is spatially concentrated where there is a physical encounter between capital and labor and where production is mainly of a tangible commodity. The temporal dimension of production is enhanced by the time difference between remote corners of the world, where an American company subcontracts business to an Indian subsidiary and profits from the time compression. The time-space compression generated by high-tech globalization transformed production and consumption concomitantly (Harvey 1989: 284–285). Therefore, the universe that was initially established by the classic thinkers of political economy is in a constant state of flux, and as a result economic concepts, relations and meanings have changed. Further challenges posed by the historical transformations and cyclical downturn of the capitalist world economy necessitate an effort to establish new definitions and to analyze the changing dynamics of existing economic relations.

Bibliography

Abbott, Andrew. 1993. "The Sociology of Work and Occupations," *Annual Review of Sociology*19: 187–209.

Abbott, Andrew. 2005. "Linked Ecologies: States and Universities as Environments for Professions," *Sociological Theory* 23(3): 245–274.

Acemoglu, Daron. 2009. *Introduction to Modern Economic Growth*. Princeton: Princeton University Press.

Akyuz, Yilmaz, Richard Kozul-Wright, and Jorg Mayer. 2004. "Trade and Industrial Upgrading in Developing Countries," in William Milberg (ed.), *Labor and the Globalization of Production: Causes and Consequences of Industrial Upgrading*, 21–57. New York: Palgrave Macmillan.

Alvarez, Roberto, and Jose De Gregorio. 2014. "Understanding Differences in Growth Performance in Latin America and Developing Countries between the Asian and the Global Financial Crises," *IMF Economic Review* 62(4): 494–525.

Amin, Ash. 2009. "Locating the Social Economy," in Ash Amin (ed.), *The Social Economy: International Perspectives on Economic Solidarity*, 3–21. New York: Zed Books.

Appay, Beatrice. 2010. "'Precarization' and Flexibility in the Labour Process: A Question of Legitimacy and A Major Challenge for Democracy," in Carole Thornley, Steve Jefferys, and Beatrice Appay (eds.), *Globalization and Precarious Forms of Production and Employment: Challenges for Workers and Unions*, 23–39. Cheltenham, UK: Edward Elgar.

Arrighi, Giovanni. 1994. *The Long Twentieth Century: Money, Power and the Origins of Our Times*. London: Verso.

Arrighi, Giovanni. 2009. *Adam Smith in Beijing: Lineages of the 21st Century*. London: Verso.

Arrighi, Giovanni, Terence K. Hopkins, and Immanuel Wallerstein. 2012. *Anti-Systemic Movements*. London: Verso.

Bair, Jennifer. 2005. "Global Capitalism and Commodity Chains: Looking Back, Going Forward," *Competition and Change* 9(2): 153–180.

Barbieri, Paolo. 2009. "Flexible Employment and Inequality in Europe," *European Sociological Review* 25(6): 621–628.

Barrientos, Stephanie, and Sally Smith. 2007. "Do Workers Benefit from Ethical Trade? Assessing Codes of Labour Practice in Global Production Systems," *Third World Quarterly* 28(4): 713–729.

Beck, Ulrich. 2000. *The Brave New World of Work*. Cambridge: Polity Press.

Bennett, W. Lance. 2012. "The Personalization of Politics: Political Identity, Social Media, and Changing Patterns of Participation," *The Annals of the American Academy of Political and Social Science* 644(1): 20–39.

Bernhardt, Dan, and Vladimir Dvoracek. 2009. "Preservation of Trade Secrets and Multinational Wage Premia," *Economic Inquiry* 47(4): 726–738.

Bertocchi, Graziella, and Chiara Strozzi. 2010. "The Evolution of Citizenship: Economic and Institutional Determinants," *Journal of Law and Economics* 53(1): 95–136.

Bianchi, Suzanne M., and Vanessa R. Wight. 2010. "The Long Reach of the Job: Employment and Time for Family Life," in Kathleen Christensen and Barbara Schneider (eds.), *Workplace Flexibility: Realigning 20th Century Jobs for a 21st Century Workforce*, 17–42. Ithaca: Cornell University Press.

Black, Simon J. 2005. "Community Unionism: A Strategy for Organizing in the New Economy," *New Labor Forum* 14(3): 24–32.

Blanchflower, David G., and Andrew J. Oswald. 1987. "Profit-Sharing–Can It Work?" *Oxford Economic Papers* 39(1): 1–19.

Boatright, John R. 2004. "Employee Governance and the Ownership of the Firm," *Business Ethics Quarterly* 14(1): 1–21.

Bonoli, Giuliano. 2010. "The Political Economy of Active Labour Market Policy," *Politics and Society* 38(4): 435–457.

Bornstein, Avram. 2009. "N30 + 10: Global Civil Society, a Decade after the Battle of Seattle," *Dialectical Anthropology* 33: 97–108.

Borzaga, Carlo, and Sara Depedri. 2009. "Working for Social Enterprises: Does It Make a Difference?" in Ash Amin (ed.), *The Social Economy: International Perspectives on Economic Solidarity*. London: Zed Books.

Boyle, Brendan, and Anthony McDonnell. 2013. "Exploring the Impact of Institutional and Organizational Factors on the Reaction of MNCs to the Global Financial Crisis," *Asia Pacific Business Review* 19(2): 247–265.

Bradley, Keith, and Alan Gelb. 1985. "Employee Buyouts of Troubled Companies," *Harvard Business Review*, September-October, 121–130.

Braverman, Harry. 1974. *Labor and Monopoly Capital*. New York: Monthly Review Press.

Brenner, Robert. 2002. *The Boom and the Bubble: The US in the World Economy*. London: Verso.

Brooks, Robin. 2003. "Population Aging and Global Capital Flows in a Parallel Universe," *IMF Staff Papers* 50(2): 200–221.

Bryant, Christopher. 1996. *Practical Sociology: Post-Empiricism and the Reconstruction of Theory and Application*. Cambridge: Polity Press.

Brynjolfsson, Erik, and Andrew McAfee. 2012. *Race Against the Machine: How the Digital Revolution Is Accelerating Innovation, Driving Productivity, and Irreversibly Transforming Employment and the Economy*. Lexington, MA: Digital Frontier Press.

Burgess, John, and Julia Connell. 2013. "Asia and the Pacific Region: Change and Workforce Adjustments Post-GFC," *Asia Pacific Business Review* 19(2): 162–170.

Burns, Rebecca. 2015. "'Uber Is a Rip-Off for its Drivers and the Public': Cab Drivers Protest Rideshares in Chicago," *In These Times*, February 19. http://inthesetimes.com/working/entry/17662/uber_ripoff. Accessed on March 22, 2015.

Calhoun, Craig. 2013. "Occupy Wall Street in Perspective," *British Journal of Sociology* 64(1): 26–38.

Calhoun, Craig, and Georgi Derluguian (eds.). 2011. *Aftermath: A New Global Economic Order?* New York: New York University Press.

Caprile, Maria, and Karsten Kruger. 2005. "Flexibilisation, Deregulation and Working Time: A Gendered Question: Evidence from Spain," in Bram Peper, Anneke van Doorne-Huiskes, and Laura den Dulk (eds.), *Flexible Working and Organisational Change: The Integration of Work and Personal Life*, 136–163. Cheltenham, UK: Edward Elgar.

Castells, Manuel. 1996. *The Rise of the Network Society*. Oxford: Blackwell.

Castells, Manuel. 1999. "Grassrooting the Space of Flows," *Urban Geography* 20(4): 294–302.

Castells, Manuel. 2000. "The Rise of the Fourth World," in David Held and Anthony McGrew (eds.), *The Global Transformations Reader: An Introduction to the Globalization Debate*, 348–354. Cambridge: Polity Press.

Castells, Manuel. 2012. *Networks of Outrage and Hope: Social Movements in the Internet Age*. Cambridge: Polity Press.

Cattaneo, Olivier, Gary Gereffi, and Cornelia Staritz. 2010. "Global Value Chains in a Postcrisis World: Resilience, Consolidation, and Shifting End Markets," in Olivier Cattaneo, Gary Gereffi, and Cornelia Staritz (eds.), *Global Value Chains in a Postcrisis World: A Development Perspective*, 3–20. Washington, D.C.: The World Bank.

Cheney, George. 2002. *Values at Work: Employee Participation Meets Market Pressure at Mondragon*. Ithaca: Cornell University Press.

Chuang, Ya-Chung. 2002. "Re-Theorizing Social Movements in a Changing Global Space," *Social Analysis* 46(2): 131–138.

Chung, Chris C., Jane W. Lu, and Paul W. Beamish. 2008. "Multinational Networks during Times of Economic Crisis versus Stability," *Management International Review* 48(3), 279–295.

Clark, John. 2011. "Civil Society in the Age of Crisis," *Journal of Civil Society* 7(3): 241–263.

Clarke, Marlea. 2008. "Challenging Labour Market Flexibilisation: Union and Community-Based Struggles in Post-Apartheid South Africa," in Marcus Taylor (ed.), *Global Economy Contested: Power and Conflict across the International Division of Labour*, 181–201. London: Routledge.

Cobble, Dorothy Sue. 2010. "More Intimate Unions," in Eileen Boris and Rhacel Salazar Parrenas (eds.), *Intimate Labors: Cultures, Technologies, and the Politics of Care*, 280–294. Stanford: Stanford Social Sciences.

Cobble, Dorothy Sue, and Michael Merrill. 2009. "The Promise of Service Worker Unionism," in Cameron Lynne Macdonald and Marek Korczynski (eds.), *Service Work: Critical Perspectives*, 153–174. London: Routledge.

Cockburn, Alexander, and Jeffrey St. Clair. 2000. *5 Days That Shook the World: Seattle and Beyond*. London: Verso.

Coffey, Dan, and Carole Thornley. 2010. "Legitimating Precarious Employment: Aspects of the Post-Fordism and Lean Production Debates," in Carole Thornley, Steve Jefferys, and Beatrice Appay (eds.), *Globalization and Precarious Forms of Production and Employment: Challenges for Workers and Unions*, 40–61. Cheltenham, UK: Edward Elgar.

Cohen, Lawrence B. 1976. "The Structure of Workers' Decisions," *Journal of Economic Issues* 10(2): 524–537.

Collom, Ed. 2001. "Social Inequality and the Politics of Production: Identifying Potential Supporters of Economic Democracy," *Sociological Forum* 16(3): 471–501.

Connell, Raewyn. 2007. *Southern Theory: The Global Dynamics of Knowledge in the Social Sciences*. Crows Nest, AU: Allen and Unwin.

Council of Europe. 2015. "The 12 Principles for Good Governance at Local Level, with Tools for Implementation." http://www.coe.int/t/dgap/localdemocracy/Strategy_Innovation/12principles_en.asp. Accessed on November 15, 2015.

Cox, Kevin R. 2004. "Globalization and the Politics of Local and Regional Development: The Question of Convergence," *Transactions of the Institute of British Geographers* 29(2): 179–194.

Crouch, Colin. 1998. "The Globalized Economy: An End to the Age of Industrial Citizenship?" in Ton Wilthagen (ed.), *Advanced Theory in Labour Law and Industrial Relations in a Global Context*, 151–164. Amsterdam: North-Holland.

Dadush, Uri, and Lauren Falcao. 2009. *Migrants and the Global Financial Crisis.* Washington, D.C.: Carnegie Endowment for International Peace.

Davis, Gerald F. 2013. "After the Corporation," *Politics and Society* 41(2): 283–308.

Deane, George. 2013. "Technological Unemployment: Panacea or Poison?" Institute for Ethics and Emerging Technologies Blog. http://ieet.org/index.php/IEET/more/deane20130305. Accessed on March 9, 2015.

Delaney, Carol. 1993. "Traditional Modes of Authority and Co-operation," in Paul Stirling (ed.), *Culture and Economy: Changes in Turkish Villages*, 140–155. Huntindgon, UK: The Eothen Press.

Della Porta, Donatella. 2007. *The Global Justice Movement: Cross-national and Transnational Perspectives.* Boulder, CO: Paradigm Publishers.

Della Porta, Donatella. 2005. "The Social Bases of the Global Justice Movement: Some Theoretical Reflections and Empirical Evidence from the First European Social Forum." Programme Paper 21. Geneva: United Nations Research Institute for Social Development (UNRISD).

"Democratic Governance." 2015. National Democratic Institute. https://www.ndi.org/governance. Accessed on October 27, 2015.

Diamandis, Peter. 2013. "Creating a Company without Employees: Philip Rosedale on Coffee and Power and the Future of Entrepreneurship." http://www.huffingtonpost.com/peter-diamandis/creating-a-company-withou_b_2838450.html. Accessed on March 16, 2015.

Drago, Robert, and Mark Wooden. 2010. "Work Hours Mismatch in the United States and Australia," in Kathleen Christensen and Barbara Schneider (eds.), *Workplace Flexibility: Realigning 20th Century Jobs for a 21st Century Workforce*, 262–275. Ithaca: Cornell University Press.

Dreze, Jean, and Amartya Sen. 2015. *An Uncertain Glory: India and its Contradictions.* Princeton: Princeton University Press.

Eberstadt, Nicholas. 2010. "The Demographic Future: What Population Growth – and Decline – Means for the Global Economy, "*Foreign Affairs* 89(6): 54–64.

Ernst, Dieter. 2000. "Global Production Networks and the Changing Geography of Innovation Systems: Implications for Developing Countries," *Economics of Innovation and New Technology* 11(6): 497–523.

Ernst, Dieter, and Linsu Kim. 2001. "Global Production Networks, Knowledge Diffusion, and Local Capability Formation: A Conceptual Framework," Paper presented at the Nelson and Winter Conference in Aalborg, Denmark, June 12–15, organized by the Danish Research Institute for Industrial Dynamics (DRUID).

Escaith, Hubert, Nannette Lindenberg, and Sebastien Miroudot. 2010. "Global Value Chains and the Crisis: Reshaping International Trade Elasticity?" in Olivier Cattaneo, Gary Gereffi, and Cornelia Staritz (eds.), *Global Value Chains in a Postcrisis World: A Development Perspective*, 73–124. Washington, D.C.: The World Bank.

Esping-Andersen, Gosta. 1990. *The Three Worlds of Welfare Capitalism*. Princeton: Princeton University Press.

Esping-Andersen, Gosta. 1996. *Welfare States in Transition: National Adaptations in Global Economies*. Thousand Oaks, CA: Sage.

Fanon, Frantz. 1963. *The Wretched of the Earth*. New York: Grove Press.

Fine, Janice. 2006. *Worker Centers: Organizing Communities at the Edge of the Dream*. Ithaca: Cornell University Press.

Fleisher, Lisa. 2014. "Thousands of European Cab Drivers Protest Uber, Taxi Apps," *Wall Street Journal*, June 11.

Frank, Andre Gunder. 1978. *Dependent Accumulation and Underdevelopment*. New York: Monthly Review Press.

Gajewska, Katarzyna. 2014. "Technological Unemployment but Still a Lot of Work: Towards Prosumerist Services of General Interest," *Journal of Evolution and Technology* 24(1): 104–112.

Gatta, Mary L. 2005. *Not Just Getting By: The New Era of Flexible Workforce Development*. Lanham, MD: Lexington Books.

Gereffi, Gary. 1994. "The Organization of Buyer-Driven Global Commodity Chains: How U.S. Retailers Shape Overseas Production Networks," in Gary Gereffi and Miguel Korzeniewicz (eds.), *Commodity Chains and Global Capitalism*, 95–122. Westport, CT: Praeger.

Gereffi, Gary, Miguel Korzeniewicz, and Roberto P. Korzeniewicz. 1994. "Introduction: Global Commodity Chains," in Gary Gereffi and Miguel Korzeniewicz (eds.), *Commodity Chains and Global Capitalism*, 1–14. Westport, CT: Praeger.

Ghosh, Bimal. 2010. *The Global Economic Crisis and Migration: Where Do We Go from Here?* Geneva: International Organization for Migration (IOM).

Gibson-Graham, J.K. 2006. *A Postcapitalist Politics*. Minneapolis: University of Minnesota Press.

Gorz, Andre. 1999. *Reclaiming Work: Beyond the Wage-based Society*. Cambridge: Polity Press.

Grewal, Rajdeep, and Patriya Tansuhaj. 2001. "Building Organizational Capabilities for Managing Economic Crisis: The Role of Market Orientation and Strategic Flexibility," *Journal of Marketing* 65(2): 67–80.

Guest, David E., and Riccardo Peccei. 2001. "Partnership at Work: Mutuality and the Balance of Advantage," *British Journal of Industrial Relations* 39(2): 207–236.

Gutierrez Johnson, Ana, and William Foote Whyte. 1977. "The Mondragon System of Worker Production Cooperatives," *Industrial and Labor Relations Review* 31(1): 18–30.

Hale, Angela. 2004. "Beyond the Barriers: New Forms of Labour Internationalism," *Development in Practice* 14(1/2): 158–162.

Hardy, Stephen, and Nick Adnett. 2006. "'Breaking the ICE': Workplace Democracy in a Modernized Social Europe," *International Journal of Human Resource Management* 17(6): 1021–1031.

Harrington, Alexandra R. 2012. "Corporate Social Responsibility, Globalization, the Multinational Corporation, and Labor: An Unlikely Alliance," *Albany Law Review* 75(1): 481–508.

Harris, Jerry. 2010. "The World Economic Crisis and Transnational Corporations," *Science and Society* 74(3): 394–409.

Harrison, Bennett. 1994. *Lean and Mean: The Changing Landscape of Corporate Power in the Age of Flexibility*. New York: Basic Books.

Harvey, David. 1989. *The Condition of Postmodernity: An Enquiry into the Origins of Cultural Change.* Oxford: Blackwell.

Harvey, David. 2007. "Neoliberalism as Creative Destruction," *The Annals of the American Academy of Political and Social Science* 610(1): 21–44.

Heckman, James J., and Burton S. Singer. 2008. *Longitudinal Analysis of Labor Market Data.* Cambridge: Cambridge University Press.

Held, David. 2010. "Reframing Global Governance: Apocalypse Soon or Reform!" in Garrett Brown and David Held (eds.), *The Cosmopolitan Reader*, 293–311. Cambridge: Polity Press.

Henderson, Jeffrey, Peter Dicken, Martin Hess, Neil Coe, and Henry Wai-Chung Yeung. 2002. "Global Production Networks and the Analysis of Economic Development," *Review of International Political Economy* 9(3): 436–464.

Hindmoor, Andrew. 1999. "Free Riding off Capitalism: Entrepreneurship and the Mondragon Experiment," *British Journal of Political Science* 29(1): 217–224.

Hobsbawm, Eric. 1968. *Industry and Empire.* London: Weidenfeld and Nicolson.

Hobsbawm, Eric. 1985. *Workers: Worlds of Labor.* New York: Pantheon.

Hobsbawm, Eric. 1994. *Age of Extremes: The Short Twentieth Century, 1914–1991.* London: Abacus.

Hopkins, Terence K., and Immanuel Wallerstein. 1986. "Commodity Chains in the Capitalist World-Economy Prior to 1800," *Review* 10(1): 157–170.

Hopkins, Terence K., and Immanuel Wallerstein. 1994. "Commodity Chains: Construct and Research," in Gary Gereffi and Miguel Korzeniewicz (eds.), *Commodity Chains and Global Capitalism*, 17–19. Westport, CT: Praeger.

Hopkins, Terence K., and Immanuel Wallerstein (eds.). 1996. *The Age of Transition: Trajectory of the World-System, 1945–2025.* London: Zed Books.

"How Does It Work?" 2015. *Ovolos.gr.* http://ovolos.gr/en/how-does-it-work.html. Accessed on November 15, 2015.

Hughes, James J. 2014. "Are Technological Unemployment and a Basic Income Guarantee Inevitable or Desirable?" *Journal of Evolution and Technology* 24(1): 1–4.

Ietto-Gillies, Grazia. 2010. "The Current Economic Crisis and International Business. Can We Say Anything Meaningful about Future Scenarios?" *Futures* 42(9): 910–919.

Iwao, Sumiko. 2010. "Government Policies Supporting Workplace Flexibility: The State of Play in Japan," in Kathleen Christensen and Barbara Schneider (eds.), *Workplace Flexibility: Realigning 20th Century Jobs for a 21st Century Workforce*, 317–336. Ithaca: Cornell University Press.

Jessop, Bob. 2007. "Dialogue of the Deaf: Reflections on the Poulantzas-Miliband Debate," in P. Wetherly, C. W. Barrow, and P. Burnham (eds.), *Class, Power and the State in Capitalist Society: Essays on Ralph Miliband*, 132–157. Basingstoke, UK: Palgrave.

Jessop, Bob. 2015. "Neoliberalism, Finance-Dominated Accumulation and Enduring Austerity: A Cultural Political Economy Perspective," in Kevin Farnsworth and Zoe Irving (eds.), *Social Policy in Times of Austerity: Global Economic Crisis and the New Politics of Welfare*, 87–112. Chicago: Policy Press.

Johnson, Kimberley. 2004. "Community Development Corporations, Participation, and Accountability: The Harlem Urban Development Corporation and the Bedford-Stuyvesant Restoration Corporation," *Annals of the American Academy of Political and Social Science* 594: 109–124.

Justino, Patricia. 2006. "The Impact of Collective Action on Economic Development: Empirical Evidence from Kerala, India," *World Development* 34(7): 1254–1270.

Kaldor, Mary. 2003. *Global Civil Society: An Answer to War*. Cambridge: Polity Press.
Kalleberg, Arne. 2009. "Rethinking the Sociology of Work, Workers and the Workplace," *Labour and Industry* 19(3): 29–48.
Keane, John. 2003. *Global Civil Society?* Cambridge: Cambridge University Press.
Keyder, Caglar. 1987. *State and Class in Turkey: A Study in Capitalist Development*. New York: Verso.
Kondratieff, Nikolai D. 2010 [1935]. *The Long Waves in Economic Life*. Whitefish, MT: Kessinger Publishing.
Korpi, Walter, and Joakim Palme. 2003. "New Politics and Class Politics in the Context of Austerity and Globalization: Welfare State Regress in 18 Countries, 1975–95," *American Political Science Review* 97(3): 425–446.
Korzeniewicz, Roberto P., and William Martin. 1994. "The Global Distribution of Commodity Chains," in Gary Gereffi and Miguel Korzeniewicz (eds.), *Commodity Chains and Global Capitalism*, 67–91. Westport, CT: Praeger.
Korzeniewicz, Roberto P., and Timothy P. Moran. 2009. *Unveiling Inequality: A World-Historical Perspective*. New York: Russell Sage Foundation.
Koser, Khalid. 2009. *The Impact of Financial Crises on International Migration: Lessons Learned*. Geneva: International Organization for Migration.
Lee, Ronald, and Andrew Mason. 2010. "Some Macroeconomic Aspects of Global Population Aging," *Demography* 47: S151–S172.
Lee, Seung-Hyun, and Mona Makhija. 2009. "Flexibility in Internationalization: Is It Valuable during an Economic Crisis?" *Strategic Management Journal* 30(5): 537–555.
Lyon, Sarah, and Mark Moberg (eds.). 2010. *Fair Trade and Social Justice: Global Ethnographies*. New York: New York University Press.
Mandel, Ernest. 1972. *Late Capitalism*. London: NLB.
Marchant, Gary E., Yvonne A. Stevens, and James M. Hennessy. 2014. "Technology, Unemployment and Policy Options: Navigating the Transition to a Better World," *Journal of Evolution and Technology* 24(1): 26–44.
Markey, Raymond. 2001. "Introduction: Global Patterns of Participation," in Raymond Markey, Paul Gollan, Ann Hodgkinson, Alain Chouraqui, and Ulke Veersma (eds.), *Models of Employee Participation in a Changing Global Environment*, 3–22. Aldershot, UK: Ashgate.
Marshall, T. H. 2009. "Citizenship and Social Class," in Jeff Manza and Michael Sauder (eds.), *Inequality and Society*, 148–154. New York: W. W. Norton.
Marx, Karl. 1990 [1867]. *Capital Volume I*. New York: Penguin Classics.
Mason, Ronald M. 1982. *Participatory and Workplace Democracy: A Theoretical Development in Critique of Liberalism*. Carbondale, IL: Southern Illinois University Press.
Massey, Douglas, Joaquin Arango, Graeme Hugo, Ali Kouaouci, Adela Pellegrino, and J. Edward Taylor. 1993. "Theories of International Migration: A Review and Appraisal," *Population and Development Review* 19(3): 431–466.
Matsui, Noriatsu, and Yukio Ikemoto. 2015. "Solidarity and Social Business: Theoretical Background," in Noriatsu Matsui and Yukio Ikemoto (eds.), *Solidarity Economy and Social Business: New Models for a New Society*, 1–11. Tokyo: Springer.
McCarthy, Dermot, and Donal Palcic. 2012. "The Impact of Large-Scale Employee Share Ownership Plans on Labour Productivity: The Case of Eircom," *International Journal of Human Resource Management* 23(17), 3710–3724.

McLellan, David (ed.). 1977. *Karl Marx: Selected Writings.* Oxford: Oxford University Press.

Melman, Seymour. 2001. *After Capitalism: From Managerialism to Workplace Democracy.* New York: Alfred A. Knopf.

Mew, Sue. 2012. "Contentious Politics: Financial Crisis, Political-Economic Conflict, and Collective Struggles – A Commentary," *Social Justice* 39(1): 99–114.

Mignolo, Walter. 2012. *Local Histories/Global Designs: Coloniality, Subaltern Knowledges, and Border Thinking*. Princeton: Princeton University Press.

Milberg, William. 2004. "Globalized Production: Structural Challenges for Developing Country Workers," in William Milberg (ed.), *Labor and the Globalization of Production: Causes and Consequences of Industrial Upgrading*, 1–18. Basingstoke, UK: Palgrave Macmillan.

Milberg, William, and Deborah Winkler. 2010. "Trade, Crisis, and Recovery: Restructuring Global Value Chains," in Olivier Cattaneo, Gary Gereffi, and Cornelia Staritz (eds.), *Global Value Chains in a Postcrisis World: A Development Perspective*, 23–72. Washington, D.C.: The World Bank.

Milevska, Tanja. 2015. "EU 'Has the Power' to Put in Place a Universal Basic Income," *Euractiv.com*, April 14. http://www.euractiv.com/sections/social-europe-jobs/eu-has-power-put-place-universal-basic-income-301526. Accessed on March 14, 2015.

Miller, Claire. 2015. "Is Owning Overrated? The Rental Economy Rises," *New York Times*, August 29.http://www.nytimes.com/2014/08/30/upshot/is-owning-overrated-the-rental-economy-rises.html?_r=0. Accessed on March 22, 2015.

Moen, Phyllis, and Qinlei Huang. 2010. "Customizing Careers by Opting Out or Shifting Jobs: Dual-Earners Seeking Life-Course 'Fit'," in Kathleen Christensen and Barbara Schneider (eds.), *Workplace Flexibility: Realigning 20th Century Jobs to 21st Century Workers*, 73–94. Ithaca: Cornell University Press.

Mondragon. *Annual Report*. 2013. http://www.mondragon-corporation.com. Accessed on March 27, 2015.

Mondragon. 2014. "Mondragon 1956-2014: A Review of The Key Milestones in the Co-Operative Group's History." http://www.mondragon-corporation.com/wp-content/themes/mondragon/docs/History-MONDRAGON-1956-2014.pdf. Accessed on April 11, 2016.

Monteagudo, Graciela. 2008. "The Clean Walls of a Recovered Factory: New Subjectivities in Argentina's Recovered Factories," *Urban Anthropology and Studies of Cultural Systems and World Economic Development* 37(2): 175–210.

Mosley, Layna. 2011. *Labor Rights and Multinational Production*. Cambridge: Cambridge University Press.

Munck, Ronaldo. 2000. *Marx@2000: Late Marxist Perspectives.* Basingstoke, UK: Palgrave Macmillan.

Munck, Ronaldo. 2002. *Globalisation and Labour: The New "Great Transformation."* London: Zed Books.

Munck, Ronaldo. 2004. "Globalization, Labor and the 'Polanyi Problem'," *Labor History* 45(3): 251–269.

Munck, Ronaldo. 2007. *Globalization and Contestation*. London: Routledge.

Munck, Ronaldo. 2008. "Globalisation, Contestation and Labour Internationalism: A Transformationalist Perspective," in Marcus Taylor (ed.), *Global Economy Contested: Power and Conflict across the International Division of Labour*, 220–238. London: Routledge.

Munck, Ronaldo. 2009. "Afterword: Beyond the 'New' International Labour Studies," *Third World Quarterly* 30(3): 617–625.

Nolan, Stephen, Eleonore Perrin Massebiaux, and Tomas Gorman. 2013. "Saving Jobs, Promoting Democracy: Worker Co-Operatives," *Irish Journal of Sociology* 21(2): 103–115.

Nuhoglu Soysal, Yasemin. 1994. *Limits of Citizenship: Migrants and Postnational Membership in Europe*. Chicago: University of Chicago Press.

Offer, Shira, and Barbara Schneider. 2010. "Multitasking among Working Families: A Strategy for Dealing with the Time Squeeze," in Kathleen Christensen and Barbara Schneider (eds.), *Workplace Flexibility: Realigning 20th Century Jobs for a 21st Century Workforce*, 43–56. Ithaca: Cornell University Press.

Olmsted, Barney, and Suzanne Smith. 1994. *Creating a Flexible Workplace: How to Select and Manage Alternative Work Options*. New York: AMACOM.

Onis, Ziya. 1999. *State and Market: The Political Economy of Turkey in Comparative Perspective*. London: Milet Publishing.

Oomen, T. K. 2009. "Development Policy and the Nature of Society: Understanding the Kerala Model," *Economic and Political Weekly* 44(13): 25, 27–31.

Ortiz, Isabel, and Matthew Cummins. 2011. "Global Inequality: Beyond the Bottom Billion – A Rapid Review of Income Distribution in 141 Countries." UNICEF Social and Economic Policy Working Paper. New York: United Nations International Children's Emergency Fund.

Pagliery, Jose. 2013. "Business Saves $270K. The Trick? No Employees," *CNN Money*, February 26.http://money.cnn.com/2013/02/26/smallbusiness/temp-workers/. Accessed on March 16, 2015.

Panitch, Leo. 2014. "Whose Crisis? Capital, Labour and the State Today," *Journal of Australian Political Economy* 74: 5–18.

Panitch, Leo, Greg Albo, and Vivek Chibber (eds.). 2010. *Socialist Register 2011: The Crisis This Time*. London: Merlin Press.

Panitch, Leo, and Sam Gindin. 2010. "Capitalist Crises and the Crisis This Time," in Leo Panitch, Greg Albo, and Vivek Chibber (eds.), *Socialist Register 2011: The Crisis This Time*, 1–20. London: Merlin Press.

Papavasiliou, Faidra. 2010. "Fair Money, Fair Trade: Tracing Alternative Consumption in a Local Currency Economy," in Sarah Lyon and Mark Moberg (eds.), *Fair Trade and Social Justice: Global Ethnographies*, 202–228. New York: New York University Press.

Parayil, Govindan. 1996. "The 'Kerala Model' of Development: Development and Sustainability in the Third World," *Third World Quarterly* 17(5): 941–957.

Pearce, John. 2009. "Social Economy: Engaging as a Third System?" in Ash Amin (ed.), *The Social Economy: International Perspectives on Economic Solidarity*, 3–21. London: Zed Books.

Peper, Bram, Anneke van Doorne-Huiskes, and Laura den Dulk (eds.). 2005. *Flexible Working and Organisational Change: The Integration of Work and Personal Life*. Cheltenham, UK: Edward Elgar.

Pianta, Mario, and Raffaele Marchetti. 2007. "The Global Justice Movements: The Transnational Dimension," in Donatella Della Porta, (ed.), *The Global Justice Movement: A Cross-National and Transnational Perspective*, 29–51. Boulder, CO: Paradigm Publishers.

Pierson, Paul. 1994. *Dismantling the Welfare State? Reagan, Thatcher, and the Politics of Retrenchment*. Cambridge: Cambridge University Press.

Pierson, Paul. 2002. "Coping with Permanent Austerity: Welfare State Restructuring in Affluent Democracies," *Revue Française de Sociologie* 43(2): 369–406.

Piketty, Thomas. 2014. *Capital in the 21st Century.* Cambridge: Belknap Press of Harvard University Press.

Piore, Michael, and Charles Sabel. 1986. *The Second Industrial Divide: Possibilities for Prosperity.* New York: Basic Books.

Polanyi, Karl. 1967. *The Great Transformation.* Boston: Beacon Press.

Portes, Alejandro. 2000. "Globalization from Below: The Rise of Transnational Communities," in Don Kalb, Marco van der Land, Richard Staring, Bart van Steenbergen, and Nico Wilterdink (eds.), 253–270. *The Ends of Globalization: Bringing Society Back In*, Boulder, CO: Rowman and Littlefield.

Prugl, Elisabeth. 1999. "What Is a Worker? Gender, Global Restructuring, and the ILO Convention on Homework," in Mary K. Meyer and Elisabeth Prugl (eds.), *Gender Politics in Global Governance*, 197–209. Lanham, MD: Rowman and Littlefield.

Pylas, Pan. 2015. "HSBC Cutting up to 25,000 Jobs, Aims for Cost Savings as It Turns Focus to Fast-Growing Asia," *Canadian Business*, June 9. http://www.canadianbusiness.com/business-news/hsbc-cutting-staff-by-10-per-cent-aims-for-cost-savings-up-to-5-billion-by-2017/. Accessed on March 25, 2015.

Quijano, Annibal. 2006. "Alternative Production Systems?" in Boaventura de Sousa Santos (ed.), *Another Production is Possible: Beyond the Capitalist Canon*, 417–445. London: Verso.

Radice, Hugo. 2010. "Confronting the Crisis: A Class Analysis," in Leo Panitch, Greg Albo, and Vivek Chibber (eds.), *Socialist Register 2011: The Crisis This Time*, 21–43. London: Merlin Press.

Rainnie, Al, Andrew Herod, and Susan McGrath-Champ. 2013. "Global Production Networks, Labour and Small Firms," *Capital and Class* 37(2): 177–195.

Rhoades, Gary, and Sheila Slaughter. 1997. "Academic Capitalism, Managed Professionals, and Supply-Side Higher Education," *Social Text* 51: 9–38.

Rhodes, Martin. 1996. "Southern European Welfare States: Identity, Problems and Prospects for Reform," *South European Society and Politics* 1(3): 1–22.

Ricardo, David. 1817. *On the Principles of Political Economy and Taxation.* London: John Murray.

Rifkin, Jeremy. 1995. *The End of Work: The Decline of the Global Labor Force and the Dawn of the Post-Market Era.* New York: Putnam.

Ritzer, George. 2000. *The McDonaldization of Society.* Thousand Oaks, CA: Pine Forge Press.

Ritzer, George. 2011. *Globalization: The Essentials.* Malden, MA: John Wiley and Sons.

Rohit. 2013. *It's not Over: Structural Drivers of the Global Economic Crisis.* Oxford: Oxford University Press.

Roman, Joseph. 2004. "The Trade Union Solution or the NGO Problem? The Fight for Global Labour Rights," *Development in Practice* 14(1/2): 100–109.

Rostow, Walt Whitman. 1960. *The Stages of Economic Growth: A Non-Communist Manifesto.* Cambridge: Cambridge University Press.

Rothschild, Joyce. 2000. "Creating a Just and Democratic Workplace: More Engagement, Less Hierarchy," *Contemporary Sociology* 29(1): 195–213.

Saad-Filho, Alfredo. 2010. "Crisis in Neoliberalism or Crisis of Neoliberalism?" in Leo Panitch, Greg Albo, and Vivek Chibber (eds.), *Socialist Register 2011: The Crisis This Time*, 242–259. London: Merlin Press.

Saint-Simon, Henri de. 1964 [1803]. "Letters from an Inhabitant of Geneva," in Henri de Saint-Simon, *Social Organization, the Science of Man and Other Writings*, 1–11. New York: Harper and Row.
Saint-Simon, Henri de. 1964 [1808]. "Introduction to the Scientific Studies of the 19th Century," in Henri de Saint-Simon, *Social Organization, the Science of Man and Other Writings*, 12–20. New York: Harper and Row.
Saint-Simon, Claude Henri. 1964 [1825]. "On Social Organization," in Henri de Saint-Simon, *Social Organization, the Science of Man and Other Writings*, 76–80. New York: Harper and Row.
Santos, Boaventura de Sousa (ed.). 2006. *The Rise of the Global Left: The World Social Forum and Beyond*. London: Zed Books.
Santos, Boaventura de Sousa (ed.). 2008. *Another Knowledge Is Possible: Beyond Northern Epistemologies*. London: Verso.
Santos, Boaventura de Sousa, and César A. Rodriguez-Garavito. 2006. "Introduction: Expanding the Economic Canon and Searching for Alternatives to Neoliberal Globalization," in Boaventura de Sousa Santos (ed.), *Another Production is Possible: Beyond the Capitalist Canon*, xvii–lxii. London: Verso.
Sass, Magdolna, and Andrea Szalavetz. 2014. "Crisis-Related Changes in the Specialization of Advanced Economies in Global Value Chains," *Competition and Change* 18(1): 54–69.
Schneider, Barbara. 2011. "The Human Face of Workplace Flexibility," *The Annals of the American Academy of Political and Social Science* 638 (1): 103–122.
Seidman, Gay. 2000. "Adjusting the Lens: What Do Globalization, Transnationalism, and the Anti-Apartheid Movement Mean for Social Movement Theory?" in John Guidry, Michael Kennedy, and Mayer Zald (eds.), *Globalizations and Social Movements: Culture, Power and the Transnational Public Sphere*, 339–357. Ann Arbor: University of Michigan Press.
Seidman, Gay. 2004. "Deflated Citizenship: Labor Rights in a Global Era," in Alison Brysk and Gershon Shafir (eds.), *People Out of Place: Globalization, Human Rights and the Citizenship Gap*, 109–129. London: Routledge.
Sen, Amartya. 1997. "From Income Inequality to Economic Inequality," *Southern Economic Journal* 64(2): 383–401.
Sen, Amartya. 2015. "The Economic Consequences of Austerity," *New Statesman*, June 5–11, 28–33.
Sen Gupta, Sukanya, Keith Whitfield, and Bob McNabb. 2007. "Employee Share Ownership and Performance: Golden Path or Golden Handcuffs?" *International Journal of Human Resource Management* 18(8): 1507–1538.
Sennett, Richard. 2000. *The Corrosion of Character*. New York: W. W. Norton.
Serlen, Rachel F. 2011. "Selling Shares in the Supermarket? Community Corporations in Community Development," *Journal of Affordable Housing and Community Development Law* 20(3/4): 331–370.
Shaikh, Anwar. 2010. "The First Great Depression of the 21st Century," in Leo Panitch, Greg Albo, and Vivek Chibber (eds.), *Socialist Register 2011: The Crisis This Time*, 44–63. London: Merlin Press.
Shen, Jie, and Brian D'Netto. 2012. "Impact of the 2007–09 Global Economic Crisis on Human Resource Management among Chinese Export-Oriented Enterprises," *Asia Pacific Business Review* 18(1): 45–64.
Silva, Eduardo. 1993. "Capitalist Coalitions, the State, and Neoliberal Economic Restructuring: Chile, 1973–88," *World Politics* 45(4): 526–559.

Slaughter, Sheila, and Gary Rhoades. 2004. *Academic Capitalism and the New Economy: Markets, State, and Higher Education.* Baltimore: Johns Hopkins University Press.

Smith, Adam. 1776. *Inquiry into the Nature and the Causes of the Wealth of Nations.* London: Printed for W. Strahan and T. Cadell.

Smith, Angel. 2007. *Anarchism, Revolution and Reaction: Catalan Labour and the Crisis of the Spanish State, 1898–1923.* New York: Berghahn Books.

Smith, Helena. 2013. "Euros Discarded as Impoverished Greeks Resort to Bartering," *Guardian*, January 2. http://www.theguardian.com/world/2013/jan/02/euro-greece-barter-poverty-crisis. Accessed on October 29, 2015.

Smith, Vicki. 1998. "The Fractured World of the Temporary Worker: Power, Participation, and Fragmentation in the Contemporary Workplace," *Social Problems* 45(4): 411–430.

Standing, Guy. 2009. *Work after Globalization: Building Occupational Citizenship.* Cheltenham, UK: Edward Elgar.

Stockhammer, Engelbert. 2012. "Rising Inequality as a Root Cause of the Present Crisis," Working Paper 282. Amherst, MA: Political Economy Research Institute.

Taylor, Marcus (ed.). 2008. *Global Economy Contested: Power and Conflict across the International Division of Labour.* London: Routledge.

"The Rise of the Sharing Economy." 2013. *Economist*, March 9. http://www.economist.com/news/leaders/21573104-internet-everything-hire-rise-sharing-economy. Accessed on March 22, 2015.

Therborn, Goran. 1987. "Welfare States and Capitalist Markets," *Acta Sociologica* 30(3/4): 237–254.

Thomas, Henk, and Chris Logan. 1982. *Mondragon: An Economic Analysis.* London: Allen and Unwin.

Thompson, E. P. 1966. *The Making of the English Working Class.* New York: Vintage Books.

Thornley, Carole, Steve Jefferys, and Beatrice Appay (eds.). 2010. *Globalization and Precarious Forms of Production and Employment: Challenges for Workers and Unions.* Cheltenham, UK: Edward Elgar.

Tilly, Charles, and Sidney Tarrow. 2007. *Contentious Politics.* Boulder, CO: Paradigm Publishers.

Toyer, Julian. 2015. "Victorious Catalan Separatists Claim Mandate to Break with Spain," *Reuters*, September 27. http://www.reuters.com/article/us-spain-catalonia-idUSKCN0RQ0RN20150927. Accessed on September 28, 2015.

Trewhitt, Lisa. 2000. "Employee Buyouts and Employee Involvement: A Case Study Investigation of Employee Attitudes," *Industrial Relations Journal* 31(5): 437–453.

Tsuboi, Hiromi. 2015. "Distributing Clean Water in Communities," in Noriatsu Matsui and Yukio Ikemoto (eds.), *Solidarity Economy and Social Business: New Models for a New Society*, 53–58. Tokyo: Springer.

Unal, Bayram. 2008. "Organizational Deviations in Turkish Sugar Industry during the Privatization Process," *Turkish Journal of Agricultural Economics* 14(1): 3–11.

UNCTAD. 2014. *World Investment Report 2014.* New York: United Nations Conference on Trade and Development.

"Local Governance." 2015. *United Nations Development Program.* http://www.undp.org/content/undp/en/home/ourwork/democraticgovernance/focus_areas/focus_local_governance.html. Accessed on October 27, 2015.

Unger, Roberto M. 2009. *The Left Alternative.* London: Verso.

Usami, Koichi (ed.), *Non-Standard Employment under Globalization: Flexible Work and Social Security in the Newly Industrializing Countries*, Palgrave Macmillan, 2010.

Valenzuela, Luis A. 2007. "Modelling Employment, Output and Labour Costs: A General to Specific Methodology," *Revista Chilena de Economía y Sociedad* 1(2): 34–40.

Varoufakis, Yanis. 2015. *Europe after the Minotaur: Greece and the Future of the Global Economy*. London: Zed Books.

Verma, Anil, and Gail Elman. 2007. "Labour Standards for a Fair Globalization for Workers of the World," *The Good Society* 16(2): 57–64.

Vieta, Marcelo. 2014. "Learning in Struggle: Argentina's New Worker Cooperatives as Transformative Learning Organizations," *Industrial Relations* 69(1): 186–218.

Wall, Ronald S., Martijn J. Burger, and G. A. (Bert) van der Knaap. 2011. "The Geography of Global Corporate Networks: The Poor, The Rich, and The Happy Few Countries," *Environment and Planning A* 43(4): 904–927.

Wallerstein, Immanuel. 1974. *The Modern World System*. New York: Academic Press.

Wallerstein, Immanuel, and Etienne Balibar. 1988. *Race, Nation, Class: Ambiguous Identities*. London: Verso.

Wan, William P., and Daphne W. Yiu. 2009. "From Crisis to Opportunity: Environmental Jolt, Corporate Acquisitions, and Firm Performance," *Strategic Management Journal* 30(7): 791–801.

Warhurst, Chris, Doris Ruth Eikhof, and Axel Haunschild (eds.), 2008. *Work Less, Live More? Critical Analysis of the Work-Life Boundary*. New York: Palgrave Macmillan.

Waterman, Peter. 1993. "Social-Movement Unionism: A New Union Model for a New World Order?" *Review* 16(3): 245–278.

Waterman, Peter. 2004. *Globalization, Social Movements and the New Internationalisms*. London: Routledge.

Weitzman, Martin L. 1984. *The Share Economy Conquering Stagflation*. Cambridge: Harvard University Press.

Weitzman, Martin L. 1985. "The Simple Macroeconomics of Profit Sharing," *American Economic Review* 75(5): 937–953.

Werner, Marion, Jennifer Bair, and Victor Ramiro Fernandez. 2014. "Linking Up to Development? Global Value Chains and the Making of a Post-Washington Consensus," *Development and Change* 45(6): 1219–1247.

Whyte, William Foote, and Kathleen King Whyte. 1988. *Making Mondragon: The Growth and Dynamics of the Worker Cooperative Complex*. Ithaca: Institute for Labor Relations Press.

Williams, Christopher, and Candace A. Martinez. 2012. "Government Effectiveness, the Global Financial Crisis, and Multinational Enterprise Internationalization," *Journal of International Marketing* 20(3): 65–78.

World Cooperative Monitor. 2014. *Exploring the Cooperative Economy*. http://ica.coop/sites/default/files/attachments/WCM2014_print.pdf. Accessed on May 1, 2015. European Research Institute on Cooperative and Social Housing.

Wright, Erik Olin. 2010. *Envisioning Real Utopias*. London: Verso.

Zhang, Chenchen, and Nathan Lillie. 2015. "Industrial Citizenship, Cosmopolitanism and European Integration," *European Journal of Social Theory* 18(1): 93–111.

Zhao, Xin, Xianling Jiang, and Zhaoyang Li. 2015. "The Impact of the Economic Crisis on the Financial Performance of Multinational Corporations," *International Review of Economics and Finance* 37: 55–68.

Index